YACHT CRAFTSMAN'S HANDBOOK

Garth Graves

International Marine Publishing
CAMDEN, MAINE

Published by International Marine Publishing

10 9 8 7 6 5 4 3 2 1

Library of Congress Cataloging-in-Publication Data

Graves, Garth.
    Yacht craftsman's handbook / Garth Graves.
        p.   cm.
    Includes bibliographical references and index.
    ISBN 0–87742-271-0
    1. Yachts and yachting—Furniture, equipment, etc.—Design and
construction.   2. Boats and boating—Equipment and supplies—Design
and construction.   I. Title.
    VM331.G647 1991
    623.8'223—dc20   91–24940
                                                                    CIP
                                                                    r91

TAB BOOKS offers software for sale. For information and a
catalog, please contact TAB Software Department, Blue Ridge
Summit, PA 17294-0850.

Questions regarding the content of this book should be
addressed to:

International Marine Publishing
P.O. Box 220
Camden, ME 04843

Typeset by A & B Typesetters, Bow, NH
Printed by Arcata Graphics, Fairfield, PA
Design by Patrice M. Rossi
Illustrated by the author
Edited by Hyman Rudoff, Pamela Salomon
Production by Janet Robbins

To my father,
who influenced this effort
in many ways.

———————————

Contents

Preface

After years of woodworking for the home, designing and building indoor and out-door furniture and amenities, I switched my priorities drastically when a mahogany sloop arrived in our family, and landbound projects gave way to bluewater competitors.

Many past projects became the subjects of how-to articles in boating and home-improvement publications, all submitted with the goal of promoting woodworking, as well as to encourage woodworkers to extend themselves into new areas of enjoyment and to develop greater confidence and skill. The ideas, descriptions, drawings, and methods are presented here with these goals in mind.

Yacht Craftsman's Handbook is a collection of woodworking projects for power and sailboats. The projects are designed for the novice and experienced woodworker alike. The variety is intended to encourage you to adopt and adapt the designs to meet your needs, your tastes, and your time.

There are no bills of materials or blueprints to follow. Rather, this book contains a selection of ideas on how to approach these projects, based on the design, physical space, and arrangement of your boat. You yourself are to develop the final blueprint that will complement your boat, agree with your boating habits, and meet your ambitions.

I hope that the hobbyist will select and tackle a project that is more complex than any he has tackled before, and that the shipwright will find here and there a useful variation on an old technique.

Please do improve on the approach, enhance the design, and, most importantly, enjoy your time in the shop developing and making the project—and your time on board using and admiring it.

My thanks to Jonathan Eaton, of International Marine Publishing, whose direction was on target, and to Hyman Rudoff, Ph.D., scholar, boatman, and woodworker, who edited the work, and to his sources, including David Wheatley.

1.

SOME INTRODUCTORY THOUGHTS

The project designs contained between these covers were chosen to help you enhance your boat and to show off your woodworking skills. With your own hands you will be able to make and install practical, attractive additions and thus upgrade your boat. The projects I have chosen range from a safe, handy stowage for binoculars and a rack for your navigational charts, to tables, cockpit grates, and bow planks. And lots of others in between.

There are as many approaches to designing and making boating projects as there are woodworkers. I hope you will mix and match, adopt the ideas, and adapt them to your own vessel, be it sail or power, while preserving its design and character.

Any one of these projects can be carried out in a home workshop. Whether your shop is fully equipped or contains only the bare necessities, you can tailor the project and its tasks to your own interests, skills, time, and equipment. For example, if dovetailing is called for, but you've never particularly liked dovetail joints, or are not equipped by skill or temperament to make them, you might substitute a joint—such as, perhaps, a box joint—producible with the tools you have on hand. If lathe-turning is an unfulfilled ambition, one of the woodturning projects might be your justification for equipping your workshop for a whole new facet of woodworking enjoyment.

A brief summary of chapter content is presented below. The projects are grouped by their function: soles, grates, racks, boxes, and so forth. You may find that your skills are such that everything appears easy, or you may be a true novice. Never mind, the levels of difficulty given below are only a guide.

Chapter	Project	Difficulty
2	Decorative Carvings	Easy to Moderate
3	Boxes	Easy to Moderate
4	Holders, Cases, and Supports	Moderate
5	Rails and Posts	Moderate
6	Soles and Grates	Moderate
7	Racks and Shelves	Moderate
8	Ventilating Panels	Moderate to Difficult
9	Ladders	Moderate to Difficult
10	Tables	Moderate to Difficult
11	Hatch Covers and Skylights	Difficult

Wood

Poems are made by fools like me,
But only God can make a tree.
—Joyce Kilmer

Trees are one of nature's more bountiful and beautiful resources. The world's forests have a regenerative character. By absorbing carbon dioxide and releasing oxygen, they renew the air we breathe, and with some help, they renew themselves too, year by year, as they are harvested. Forests also provide shelter and sustenance to the living things within. The symbioses in the forest are of the highest order. Trees are also a crop, satisfying our needs for wood, and should be treated as such. With proper management, areas can be logged and reforested, perpetuating the bounty now and, one hopes, forever, protecting our world's forests while providing the wood we use.

Wood is the world's first reinforced plastic, an insulating material, a structural material, a sculptor's inspiration. . . . We workers transform this unique structural and aesthetic material into objects of function and beauty. For our boats, of course. Creating these items can be a satisfying experience at any skill level—to the shipwright or the hobbyist.

Despite these accolades and the high level of respect it deserves, wood can be frustrating too. Frustration most likely occurs when you have selected the wrong wood for your project, or it's too wet, or cut in the wrong direction. Optimum growing conditions for woods vary. "Optimum" could be drought-like conditions, leading to a struggling, gnarled burl that someday will make a fine briar pipe, or abundant water supplying a Sitka spruce that grows fast, straight, and true, ready to be transformed into a fine spar.

Hardwoods and Softwoods

This classification is confusing. It does not necessarily indicate the hardness or softness of the wood, or its working qualities.

Hardwoods are families of broad-leaved trees, usually deciduous (losing leaves in winter). Softwood families consist primarily of evergreens, such as conifers and other trees with needle-like foliage that is kept through the winter, with a few exceptions such as bald cypress, tamarack, and larch.

I have recommended certain woods for certain projects and suggested some woods to avoid where there are inherent shortcomings for the intended use. The final selection is yours, although tradition provides a good guide to the selection of time-proven woods.

As a design objective for your new projects, try to pick woods that blend with surrounding woods, and shapes and forms that follow the existing style and scale as well.

Ease of use is an important attribute with respect to both the finished project and your sense of accomplishment. Douglas fir, for example, (sometimes sold as Oregon pine) is not a jewel in the rough, whereas alder and birch are more evenly textured and are easier to work. Major differences exist within single families of trees. The mahogany family, to name one, includes Philippine mahogany, which can be extremely porous compared with Honduras mahogany, which is considerably harder and has a more even texture and better color.

Special characteristics have made some woods highly prized; holly is very white, while teak, with its oil content, holds up extremely well to the weather. However, it won't glue well unless the surface of the joint is carefully wiped free of the natural oil with acetone, methyl ethyl ketone, or some other solvent just prior to gluing. White and red oak differ in that white is the denser wood; it can be steamed and bent nicely, whereas red oak tends to expose open capillaries that will later absorb moisture. Consult your local lumberman when in doubt about the suitability of woods.

The color of wood will change with time, especially in direct or even indirect sunlight. Light woods will darken and dark woods will lighten, so the high contrast of a new light-and-dark element such as a cabin sole will mellow with time.

Saw Milling

I admire the woodsmen and craftsmen who can spot a burl, a crotch, or a whole tree that will someday be theirs to work. With pioneer spirit (and permission if required) they fell the tree, cut it to rough length, and gang-saw it on site or wrestle it back to the mill for cutting and drying. One advantage of fetching your wood from an available tree (aside from the price being right) is that you must and do learn firsthand how to mill the log; that is, how to make the best cut for the intended project, and how to dry the wood properly.

My own pioneering spirit extends only to driving to the nearest lumberyard, or ordering by catalog from a hardwood specialist.

Grain, figure, and texture. *Grain* refers to the direction of the cells or fibers; *figure* is the pattern produced by the grain on exposed surfaces; *texture* arises from the size and concentration, or *packing*, of the cells.

Fibrous woods are highly figured. In woods where the concentration of cells is more compact, the wood is more homogeneous and may be worked with less regard to grain direction (Figure 1-1). Look at the cross section of a log. The center is the *heartwood*, the structural armature of the tree. Surrounding the heartwood is *sapwood*, distinguished by growth rings progressing concentrically outward, and representing the amount of growth that has accreted year by year. The latest growth is the outermost, the cambium layer where cells divide and multiply to provide the nutrition network and new growth. The protective outer layer is the bark.

The annual rings themselves comprise two layers: *springwood*, the inner part of the growth ring, and *summerwood*, which develops outward toward the end of the growing season. Springwood (or early wood) grows faster and usually is more fibrous than late or summerwood.

In addition to annual growth rings there are concentrated lines of cells (*rays*) radiating from the center; the tree uses these cells for storage.

Flat-sawn. The most common way of slicing a log (it's the least expensive and yields the most board feet of lumber per log) is called *plain sawing, flat sawing,* or *flat cutting.* The resulting boards—except for a few from the middle of a plain-sawn log—are *slash-* or *flat-grained.*

Figure 1-1. *The basic cuts in making and trimming boards.*

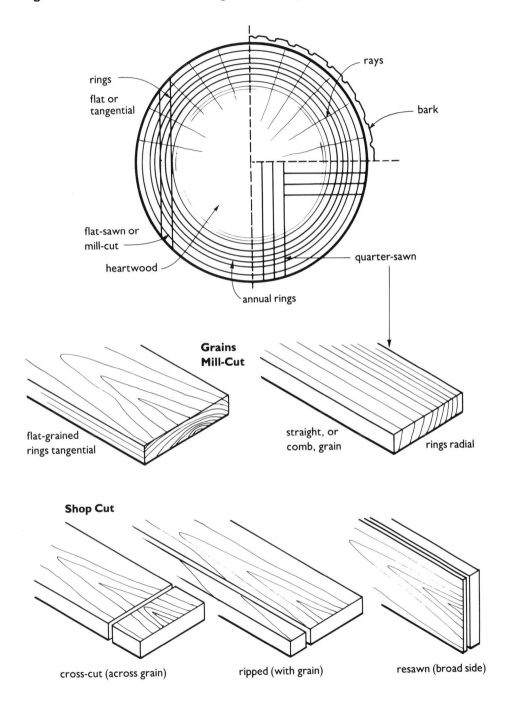

rings

flat or
tangential

rays

bark

flat-sawn or
mill-cut

heartwood

quarter-sawn

annual rings

**Grains
Mill-Cut**

flat-grained
rings tangential

straight, or
comb, grain

rings radial

Shop Cut

cross-cut (across grain)

ripped (with grain)

resawn (broad side)

The log is sliced in a series of parallel cuts starting at the bark edge and progressing toward the heartwood. The face of the board will be tangent to the arcs of the growth rings. Where the grain too is tangent to the growth rings, the surface is more highly figured—the cut exposes the rings and the fibrous springwood and denser summerwood.

Flat-grained boards tend to warp. When they are used for planking over frames, even on smaller projects such as hatch covers, rings should "open" into the frames. That is, the outer face of the board (the side nearest the bark, away from the heartwood) should be out, and the arcs of the rings concave inward. Fasteners will hold the center to the frame and counter the curling action. However, if you are edge-gluing boards to make a fairly wide expanse that will not be fastened to a frame member, alternate the surfaces of the boards, so that the rings will be oriented alternately up and then down. This will minimize overall warpage of the whole piece.

Quarter-sawn. Logs may be ripped along the centerline, then quartered as in Figure 1-1, then planked from the quarter's two flat sides. Planks made this way are said to be *quarter-sawn*. Here annual rings show up as a series of parallel lines of fibers exposed on the top and bottom faces of the boards. *Vertical grain, straight grain, comb grain, edge grain*, and *rift grain* are terms used to define a grain that is roughly perpendicular to the wide flat surface (less than 45° off). This cut is ideal for surfaces where foot traffic is likely, such as cabin soles and wooden grates (Figure 1-1).

Working wood that is too wet will invite shrinkage, while too dry will risk swelling. Lumber is nearly always dried before use. The lumber you buy may (rarely) be green or wet, air-dried, or kiln-dried. (There are some special uses for green lumber in construction of workboats, but it's not seen much nowadays in yachts.) In the final analysis, you will probably want dried wood.

Wood swells as it absorbs moisture in summer, taking in up to 30 percent of its dry weight, and shrinks in winter. Most of this water is "free water"; that is, moisture contained within the cell cavities, much as a tank holds liquid. The free water can be taken in or given off without any appreciable change in dimensions.

Any further drying will affect the dimensions, however—and the strength, too—since now the cell walls must give off moisture that is part of their chemical structure. The effects may range from excessive dimensional change when the wood is a little too dry, to loss of strength and integrity when it's much overdried. Avoid excessively dry wood.

Wood shrinks and swells in all directions. Longitudinal shrinkage is very slight, but across the grain the dimensional change may be as much as 10 percent, flat-cut boards experiencing the greatest change.

Plywood. Most plywood is made by peeling thin sheets of wood (called *veneers*) from thick poles, much like taking wrapping paper off a roll, but in this case using a long sharp knife and a very large lathe to cut and peel at the same time. The sheets include knots and other imperfections that may be met along the way. Such plywood is labeled *rotary-cut*. It's the most common, but the veneers may also be *ribbon-cut* or sliced.

Cores are made of either lumber or veneer. Grain directions in successive veneers run at 90° angles to one another to give dimensional stability. Chapter 3 (Boxes) contains a table of plywood characteristics, but we can summarize here: Use EXTerior or MARINE-grade plywood only for any item that will be subjected to moisture. You can tell what kind of plywood you have by the capital letters marked as shown here. Where an exterior-grade plywood may be used with confidence, it might be considered overdesign to employ MARINE plywood, unless the object under construction will be submerged.

Avoid using plywoods designated "X" (as in "ABX"), which indicates that although waterproof glue has been used (primarily for production economy), the product is not really suitable for marine applications. Use only the "EXT" or "MARINE" types.

Other reconstituted boards, such as chipboard and particle board, are not to my liking for boat projects. I'd suggest avoiding these materials, unless your boat is so large you can exchange your kitchen cabinets at home for the onboard galley cabinets.

Shop Cuts and Joints

Your preferences in sawing, planing, and surfacing logs, timbers, and planks will depend on your time, space, and the capacity of your power tools. Most home workshops are not equipped to handle timbers (5-inch stock) or even planks, but if you have a fairly large bandsaw and a thickness planer, you can mill the stock for the projects in this book from rough-sawn wood.

It is more likely that your workshop is equipped to handle "S2S" (surfaced-two-sides) stock up to 2 inches thick. The price you pay per board foot will be more than for rough lumber, but through careful selection, you'll have less waste and be able to pick just the right texture and figure for the project.

Your array of tools will also largely determine how you go about cutting pieces to length and milling to shape the parts. Figure 1-2 illustrates most of the more common ones.

Butt joints (Figure 1-2) require straight, true cuts. You can make them with a sharp cross-cut saw and a good eye and a steady hand. Straight and miter joints can be made true using a hand-, saber-, circular, or table saw with a miter box, guide, or tilting table or arbor. Box and finger joints require the additional process of cutting or dadoing interleaving "fingers." A table or radial-arm saw is recommended here.

Dovetailing is accomplished with the proper router bit, powered by a portable router or a drill press, and guided by a dovetailing jig. Rabbeted or lap joints are cut using a dado blade on the table or radial-arm saw, or by routing or planing the rabbet. Mortise-and-tenon joints start with the preparation of the hole (*mortise*) and then the "gazinta." The gazinta is the piece that gazinta the mating hole. The books call it a *tenon*.

7

SOME INTRODUCTORY THOUGHTS

Figure 1-2. *The most popular corner joints. The corner post is best for plywood construction, hiding raw edges.*

Corner Joints

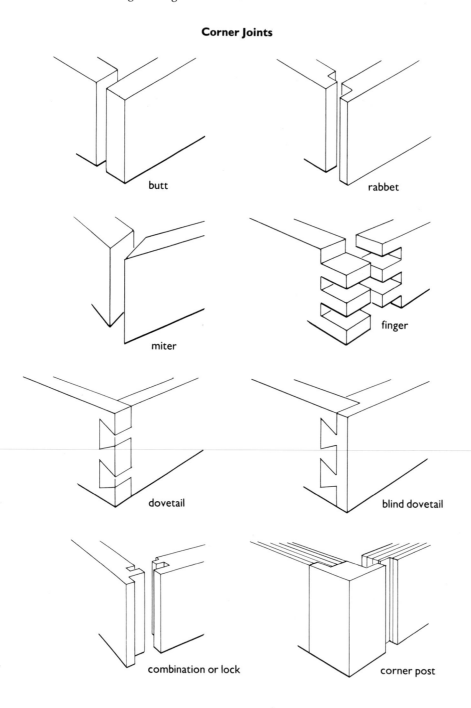

butt

rabbet

miter

finger

dovetail

blind dovetail

combination or lock

corner post

For reference, the bottom portion of Figure 1-1 illustrates the three basic cuts. A *cross cut* is made across the grain with a fine-toothed blade. To *rip* is to cut through the small dimension—the thickness—of a board in the direction of the grain; this is usually done with a coarser blade (i.e., fewer teeth per inch). To resaw is to cut in the grain direction through the greater dimension—the width—of the board. Any cut made with the grain is also referred to as a *rift* cut.

A ledge or step at the edge of a board is a *rabbet* (or rebated), cut to accept a mating piece. The same cut made away from the edge is either (1) a *dado* cut across the grain or (2) a *groove* cut in the direction of the grain. The term *let in,* refers to any boxed joint or housing where one piece fits into another.

Common corner joints (Figure 1-2) include butt, rabbet, miter, finger, dovetail, blind dovetail, and combination dado and rabbet. For plywood or other composite material, the joint may include a corner post to let in and hide the edges of the composite.

Operations producing decorative edges, let-in pieces, rabbets, and carved adornments—from filigrees to scallop shells—can be accomplished with a portable router, a mill router, or a high-speed drill press using router bits in the chuck. The router bit follows a design cut into thin template material using a saber-, scroll-, or jigsaw.

Boards can be joined edge to edge or end to end with the common joints shown in Figure 1-3. Small pieces, or nonstructural members could be butt-glued and fastened (not illustrated). For added strength, butting edges can be match-drilled for a *doweled* or *dowel-pinned* joint. A *lap* joint consists of two mating rabbeted edges to increase the gluing area. Tongue-and-groove joints can be flush with or beveled on the exposed seam to disguise slight irregularities. A glue-joint cutter in a shaper or router will cut a rabbet and groove in one operation. (One board is inverted for the mating profile.)

Spline joints are strengthened by inserting a properly oriented piece of wood, the spline, into matching, facing grooves in the two gluing edges. If the spline stops short of the exposed ends of the joints, it makes a *blind* spline joint. If not, the joint is *exposed.*

A more complex application of the spline is the *dovetail key,* in which the edges are grooved using a dovetail bit, and the mating dovetail spline is cut to a slight interference fit so that it forces the joint closed when driven in place.

Whatever joint is used, the edges must be straight and true for best adhesion and appearance. Where a tongue-and-groove is employed, allow some clearance in the groove for the glue, but not enough to prevent a good fit at the exposed surface.

Boards joined end to end are *scarfed.* When joining boards (for example in decking or planking), the inclined length of the scarf—which determines the gluing area—should be at least three times the width of the boards being joined. Joining boards on the vertical dimension as in fashioning a toerail also requires a long, low angle for the scarf. This joint can include a return notch to catch the upper board. Fasteners running through both pieces of the scarf will ensure that the two pieces are nicely faired to the contour of the sheer.

Figure 1-3. *Edge joints and scarf joints for gluing wide or long pieces.*

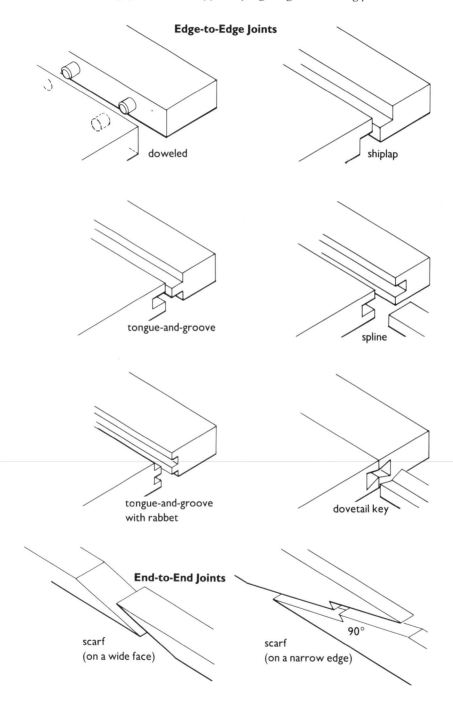

Edge-to-Edge Joints

doweled

shiplap

tongue-and-groove

spline

tongue-and-groove
with rabbet

dovetail key

End-to-End Joints

scarf
(on a wide face)

scarf
(on a narrow edge)

90°

TOOLS

The tools in your workshop reflect your woodworking interests.

If you are into duplicating hundreds of parts, you probably have a mill router. If you are into fluting or helixing turned posts, you may have special fixtures for your lathe or router. These are specialty tools acquired only as your ambitions dictate.

Hand tools guided by master craftsmen have performed all of these operations without the aid of the power tools we enjoy. Even with every power tool available, hand tools still play an important role in most projects. For example, a good set of wood chisels and gouges, wood rasps, files, a brace and bit, handsaws, back saws, bench planes, etc. will go where the power tools cannot. Besides, handwork adds that special "crafted" touch.

A good quantity and variety of clamps in various shapes and lengths is equally important to ensure success. Pipe and bar clamps will hold large components together during assembly. Woodworkers' gluing clamps (dual acme-threaded rod-type) adjust their hardwood jaws to almost any angle. You can't have too many C-clamps and spring clamps, which are used in so many gluing setups. When gluing round or square members, use the web or band clamp to surround and hold the parts, forcing all the mating surfaces together.

Measuring rules, straightedges, various squares (combination, adjustable, carpenter's) start us off right on the road to straight cuts. Adjustable bevel squares are handy for gauging and duplicating angles. All guides and measuring tools must be true and accurate, but even with the most precise scale, always "measure twice but cut once."

Sharpening

Trite but true: Sharp tools are safe tools. Prolong the life of every cutting edge by removing any buildup of pitch and tar with a solvent. Hand- and circular-saw blades can be resharpened in your shop, if you are set up for the task, or taken to the local sharpener. After a few trips to the sharpener, teeth may lose their consistent height and pitch. The worst blades should be tossed, the better ones set aside for rough or messy cutting, and only the best reserved for your precious work. Carbide-tipped cutters, be they blades, router bits, or drill bits, should be sharpened by a professional.

To keep your tools keen and sharp, have available a good supply of whetstones in varying abrasives, grits, and shapes, as well as a bench grinder equipped with assorted abrasive wheels. A honing wheel, consisting of a hard rubber disc impregnated with fine abrasive will hone to a good cutting edge. Specialty sharpeners are also available for most cutting blades. These are fancy bench grinders, sometimes water-cooled, and usually designed for specific cutters such as drill bits, chisels, or planing blades (Figure 1-4).

Depending on their intended purpose, twist-drill bits can have included angles ranging from 45° for wood to 59° for steel (more for some special jobs). Wood-boring bits

Figure 1-4. *Details of edge tools for drilling, boring, and turning. More common in a home workshop, twist drills will work in a variety of materials. Wood-boring twist drills have a pronounced point (45° included angle); metal-boring drill bits are flatter (59° included angle). These are used on acrylic, but if chipping occurs, grind to a zero rake. High-speed spade wood-boring bits can be ground easily to an odd diameter. After years of use, lathe-tool angles may change. Try these angles, grinding to the values given, whetting, and honing. Use a conical or gouge stone on the gouge.*

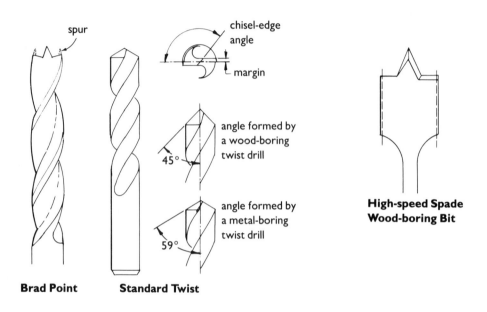

spur

chisel-edge angle

margin

angle formed by a wood-boring twist drill

45°

angle formed by a metal-boring twist drill

59°

High-speed Spade Wood-boring Bit

Brad Point   **Standard Twist**

Lathe Chisels

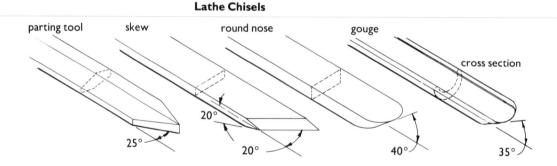

parting tool   skew   round nose   gouge

cross section

25°   20°   20°   40°   35°

sometimes have brad points; the variety with two sharp spurs makes clean accurate holes and tends to keep in line without being drawn aside by the grain of the wood.

Flat, high-speed wood-boring bits are not as kind to the wood being drilled but are easily ground to drill a custom diameter for that one-time need to press fit a wooden block around stanchion tubing of nonstandard diameter. Grind down and hone the sides of the next larger bit to make your "special." Be careful to take equal amounts from each side to maintain the symmetry of the bit.

Metal-cutting twist drills, usually the flatter 59° angle, may be used on wood and acrylics as well, although some alteration is suggested for drilling acrylics. This alteration consists of reducing the rake angle to zero, thus providing a scraping action to prevent chipping of the brittle material.

To do this, the cutting edge of a twist drill needs to be relieved slightly on the side of a grinding wheel. Just touch the bit to the wheel square to the two cutting flutes, barely flattening the cutting edges. Be careful not to alter the point angle. Test the rake by drilling in scrap acrylic before taking on the workpiece. Where the thickness of the sheet is greater than the hole diameter, slightly flatten the point angle of the bit.

For longer life from your drill bits and blades, invest in special holders to be used in conjunction with a bench grinder. One example would be a bit sharpener, which holds the drill bit at the proper angle and aligns it on center. Wide blades, such as those of planes, rotary jointer/planers, and even thickness planers should be professionally sharpened, or sharpened with the aid of special holders. Most blades, long or pointed, can be honed using a whetstone to keep a keen edge.

Wood chisels, designed to penetrate the surface of the work, are sharpened to a 30° angle. Lathe-turning chisels are designed to peel rather than to penetrate or powder, and therefore have a different angle.

Manufacturers' angles on a set of lathe chisels should be maintained. However, over years of repeated honing and occasional grinding, the original shapes may need to be renewed. Suggested angles are shown.

Dress abrasive wheels as required to present a flat, true surface to the blade being sharpened. Clean any deposits from the wheel with a dressing stick. Resurface and square the circumference with a grinding wheel dresser.

VARNISHING

Keeping brightwork bright is a constant battle. Brightwork at its finest is a joy to behold; when it starts to deteriorate, it's the pits.

Do something nice for the wood of your boat: Leave the heavy power sanders in their cases. Hand sanding with blocks is best, but sometimes power is required. The best and kindest power sanders are the high-speed orbital types such as those made by Rockwell and Makita. With a top-grade, no-fill paper, one of these little hummers will prepare new work and strip old work of failed varnish.

Speaking of stripping: Where a heavy buildup of varnish needs to be removed because it's excessively spider-webbed by the ultraviolet rays of the sun, a heat stripper and a scraper will make quick and clean work of removing the stuff. This beats chemical removers, especially if the areas are flat.

New Work

Most of the effort in quality varnishing lies in the preparation. The actual application of the varnish is quick and easy.

Beginning early in the project, be careful when applying glues to joints—this is critical to the ultimate finish. By applying a thinned coat of varnish or sanding sealer next to glue joints before applying the glue, you discourage penetration and staining by any errant glue—which is a nice bit of insurance during the gluing process.

Start your preparation by hand sanding lightly with the grain. Use progressively finer grits, down to 180- to 220-grit. Don't use too fine a grit; some tooth is necessary for adhesion. This process can be very discouraging as you rough up your fine woodwork to prepare for the varnish coats to follow.

A quality bench or dust brush can remove much of the sanding residue, and a tack rag will finish the job. Tack well, but be careful that a fresh tack rag doesn't leave more residue than it removes. Use a very light touch with a new rag, followed by a good wipe-down with clean rags containing a hint of mineral spirits to leave the surface completely free of dust and lint and ready for varnish.

On new work or wood that has been stripped for refinishing, thin the first varnish coat with mineral spirits or a commercial extender (I use Penetrol in all coats to promote penetration, spread, and flow). The initial varnish coat reduced with 10 to 20 percent of thinner will be absorbed into the porous grain. Use less Penetrol or other extenders in the following four to six varnish coats. The weather will determine how much you need to use.

It is best to varnish when the temperature is between 65° and 85° Fahrenheit and the humidity is fairly low. If you find you must varnish when it is on the cool side, you may want to thin the varnish a little more to aid flow. Likewise, if you must varnish when the temperature is high, some extender will slow the drying process so the brush can be removed at the end of each stroke.

I have found cross-brushing to be a good way to prevent *holidays* in the varnish. Even with this technique, these missed spots may mysteriously appear. Inspect your fresh varnish frequently, viewing the work from various angles to the light. If you find a holiday and its edges are dry by the time you have discovered it, you could feather varnish in the spot on an early coat, or just cover it over with the next coat if you do it soon.

It's best always to work with a wet edge. Over larger areas the brushing pattern should not continue too far in any one direction. It's best to brush in patterns of stripes, squares, or rectangles just large enough always to work to a wet edge.

Brushes

Your good varnish brushes (boar bristle, badger hair, or foam throw-away) should see only varnish. No foreign paints or other substances, except thinners and linseed oil, should violate the purity of these bristles.

One school of thought recommends keeping varnish brushes perpetually wet by suspending them in linseed oil. My own school taught that this can gum up the brush. My school cleans varnish brushes in a series of baths; two each of mineral spirits and lacquer thinner.

With time, particles suspended in a bath of used thinner will settle to the bottom, so don't worry about what to do with the bath. Allow time for the particles to settle thoroughly, pour off the clean thinner for reuse, and throw away the sediment. Be sure that everyone in the household knows your system so nobody starts to clean a brush from another project in the can containing layers of thinner and sediment awaiting pour-off.

ADHESIVES

Adhesion of most glues is best where gluing surfaces are free of all dust and foreign matter and the glue is thin enough to spread and "lock into" all the tiny irregularities of the surface.

End grain takes up the most glue. When gluing extremely porous woods, and especially on end grain, you may want to apply a thin coat of glue to cover the surface evenly, allow it to dry, and then recoat and clamp the assembly.

As mentioned earlier, you can protect exposed edges from errant glue by applying sanding sealer or thinned varnish to the area adjacent to the joint, but not on the surface of the joint itself. This precaution will aid in the cleanup of any glue spread, and prevent discoloration of the wood.

Interior projects that will be well sealed can be assembled using a non-waterproof glue, such as a carpenter's glue, which is a *thermoplastic* material—it can be softened with heat. It will also be affected by water, but this will take a long time.

For exterior projects use a water-resistant or waterproof glue or epoxy. Glues or cements of this type are *thermosetting*, which means that once cured, they cannot be softened by heat, and they are also much less affected by moisture than any thermoplastic or "natural" glue. Urac, for example, is a fairly resistant glue of this kind. It comes as a two-part powder system.

Resorcinol-formaldehyde, another two-part glue, comes as a powder hardener and a liquid. When cured it is very dark, but I have found it to be more water-resistant than the lighter-colored Urac.

The epoxy glues, also thermosets, are expensive by comparison but are good, strong adhesives impervious to most chemicals and to the elements. They will also adhere well to many dissimilar or nonporous surfaces.

HARDWARE

Most of us cringe when we price marine hardware. Although we suspect the cost is based on what the "affluent" boat owner will bear, there is a practical reason for the cost, and that is the quality.

Brass, chrome, bronze, and stainless steel must be of the highest quality to withstand the attack of water, wind, heat, and cold. The saltwater environment is especially harsh on many metals, and most especially on substandard alloys. Our suspicions of a piece of hardware often prove valid only when, having laid down the premium price for what is represented to us to be "marine-standard," we find out the hard way a year later that it wasn't.

Fasteners from reputable chandlers and marine suppliers should withstand the stresses of compression, tension, and fatigue to hold up well under use. With a little preventive maintenance, they should continue to shine over years of service.

If you favor traditional boats or traditional hardware, you can get custom bronze fittings, either cast or fabricated, from specialty outlets including The Bronze Star in San Diego and other sources such as WoodenBoat, H&M, etc. Such purveyors are affiliated with their foundries and fabricators, and offer quality workmanship and the most distinctive designs.

Contemporary hardware, fittings, and fasteners available from your local chandlery or marine supply catalog also provide the quality desired. Marine-quality brands are best, and will last long after the knock-off versions have turned color and self-destructed.

SAFETY

Whatever you make in your shop, make it strong and safe. Moreover, how you go about making it must be safe as well.

First, the products. A few projects in this collection could be structurally critical, including a cockpit grate that spans an open well or hold, slatted bow planks that are cantilevered over the bow, and stairs and ladders that must be strong enough to support your largest crewmember carrying a heavy load. Even though woodworkers guess on the high side regarding the strength of their products, some of these will call for calculations with a view to a generous margin of safety. If you once learned but have since forgotten the Strength of Materials course, check out one of many good books on the subject and make the calculations. Or you might ask a boatbuilder or architect to run the calculations for you. The hardwood dealer might assist, or perhaps suggest a place where you can get a stress analysis done. Or you can resort to time-honored boatbuilding tradition: Look around you at existing examples of the same work, to see what the standard practice is.

Now for the producer. You. You have to be healthy to enjoy boating fully!

Make sure that electric tools are well grounded, save a few that are "double-insulated," have no metal shells, and only two-wire connections.

Keep tool guards in place, and use push sticks and other extensions of your fingers for close operations.

Safety goggles are also a must for many shop operations, and a dust mask is sometimes warranted if the work generates irritating dust particles. Be aware of and heed warning labels on solvents and other chemicals used in your shop. You don't need chemical warfare at home.

This chapter has been long on background. Now it is time to act. What follows is, I hope, a combination of ideas, techniques, and designs that will be as enjoyable in the making as they are in the using.

Have fun.

2.

DECORATIVE CARVINGS

CARVING TRAILBOARDS

The most visible expressions of the marine carver's art today are the carved trailboards and transom boards that give style and individuality to many boats that would otherwise be pretty unremarkable. Traditionally, trailboards simply displayed the name of the ship. Nowadays, with the proliferation of state requirements in addition to those for federally documented vessels, a trailboard may carry anything from a simple name to an elaborately carved combination of letters and numbers, and stickers (Figure 2-1). Less visible, but also important, are registration boards, which carry the ship's federal documentation number and tonnage. Although they're displayed below decks, registration boards are often carved, due to the sheer desire for something different.

Actually, there is no technical reason for having carved trailboards; vinyl letters and numbers will do. Commercially designed characters with self-adhesive backs are readily available and easy to apply. So we don't go to all the effort of carving boards because we

Figure 2-1. *Samples of trailboard design and lettering. (a) Semicircular ends are good, with or without a rosette. (b) Ribbons may be carved in two or three dimensions. (c) Stars decorate the ends beyond the sticker plate and may be available ready-made in bronze. (d) Pad must allow for a 3" letter. (e) Gothic, or block, lettering has no ornamentation.*

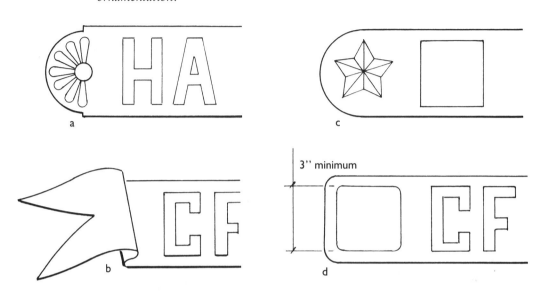

ABCDEFGHIJKLMN
OPQRSTUVWXYZ
1234567890

must; the only must is that we meet statutory requirements for such boards; they are, after all, legal documents on permanent display, and they are subject to regulations that vary from state to state.

Therefore, before we get into the actual carving, we must make sure that our design conforms to those regulations; only then can we get to the fun part—designing, carving, and finishing.

Requirements

On undocumented vessels registered in states where assigned numbers must be displayed, with or without a yearly sticker, either applied or hand-lettered characters may be used, provided they meet state requirements. The vinyl letters and numerals referred to above are available in custom-cut designs, too, so there is some scope for personal expression. However, for a little more individuality and pizzazz, we are going to consider designing and carving (*routing*) truly ornamental wooden boards and similar items. The characters on these boards may be raised (*bas relief*), recessed in full format (*intaglio*), or outlined.

It's difficult to change course once you've already begun to design and carve, so before you start to design your board, be aware of regulations in the state in which your boat is registered—they will greatly affect the design.

Each state has its own legal requirements and administration for the issue and display of vessel registration numbers. Your particular issuing agency can be traced through the Department of Motor Vehicles, which may be the issuer; otherwise, they will refer you to the appropriate department—Fish and Game, Water Resources, or Revenue, for example. Requirements generally follow the U.S. Coast Guard guidelines: not less than 3-inch block letters (*sans-serif*) and in a color, or color value, of good contrast to the background (Figure 2-1e). A state may or may not issue an annual sticker, and its placement varies by state. Some stickers trail the registration numbers on port and starboard, others always appear abaft the identification string. Your carved number board can include a routed home for the sticker (Figures 2-1c and 2-1d).

Federally documented vessels are not debarred from using boards. Even though these ships do not display registration numbers, their names can be routed on trailboards. If the hull style allows, a scroll or vine motif could add a touch of elegance, as in Figure 2-4.

A matching name board on the transom, complete with your hailing port, is another candidate for a routing project. The process is the same as that for trailboards, and there are no regulations (except good design sense) for transom boards. Just be sure that the name of your hailing port is legible and legal.

Some owners like to carve the registration number and net tonnage on a board for permanent installation below decks, in lieu of carving the data on the ship's main beam, as required for larger vessels. (Many fiberglass boats have no main beams!) Make this type of board in the same way as you would make one for the exterior.

Design

Before deciding on the details of the design, you should be aware that less-fibrous woods are best for carving. Stay away from highly figured teak crotches, stringy Philippine mahogany (Honduras mahogany is more evenly textured), and red oak (white oak has no open capillaries). Having chosen your wood, you are ready to start the design itself.

To meet legibility guidelines for registration numbers, use Alternate Gothic (Figure 2-1e) or a similar Gothic Bold Condensed lettering. Your local printer can typeset your number, or you can lay it out in characters from a sheet of press-on type available from a blueprint or art-supply store. Or you could use that set of vinyl letters mentioned earlier to lay out your template pattern, which can be enlarged as desired.

Roman-style lettering, script, and fancy scrollwork on a transom board require smaller cutters, to follow the serifs and thin strokes of the letters and flourishes. Gothic style, having neither thick nor thin strokes, is easiest to rout, using larger single- or double-fluted bits. A straight bit will yield a square shoulder at the bottom of the cut; a veining bit will cut a slight cove at full depth.

If you allot a routed or raised space for the decal or sticker, make it a little oversize to allow for future variations. Your state may change vendors, or the rounded corners may become square, or the trim size may change. If you want to avoid the problem of size altogether, you can leave a space (Figure 2-1d) for the sticker on the board; neither a recessed nor a raised platform is necessary.

With the string of numbers and letters, and the size and location of the annual sticker all decided upon, add enough length of stock for any embellishments that lead, trail, or flank this area. This will give the overall length. The depth of the cut dictates the thickness of the stock. Some end designs, such as a ribbon motif (Figure 2-1b and Photo 2-1a), may require a lot of routing or the addition of laminated sections at the ends to make them thick enough to let you rout out the design. Rosettes, stars, scallops (Figures 2-1a and 2-1c), and the like are typical elements of decor that may be added, but there is nothing wrong with nicely rounded corners (Photo 2-1b). The best design for your boat is one that complements surrounding lines. I know that's vague, but by surveying the area you will see which design complements adjacent forms and shapes. Embellished ends may be carved last but must be planned for at the outset. Fasteners should be considered in your design. These may be bunged or buttoned after installation.

Number and name boards should flex to conform to the hull. The raised-lettering style will be more pliable, because so much of the stock has been cut away from around the characters. If letters are to be recessed, the board should be slightly thinner, enabling

a

Photo 2-1.
*Finished trailboards—one with a
ribbon design (a), the other with
nicely rounded edges (b).*

b

it to conform. The actual location of the board probably will be on a more-or-less vertical surface. In any case do your best to meet legibility requirements; avoid exaggerated contours.

If you are working in relief, incorporate a hefty border or frame in your design to protect the raised image from bumps and dings. Such borders can and should be regarded as important elements of as well as protection for the design. A dividend: The ornamental carved board is easily refinished by merely painting or varnishing up to the routed edges.

Since carved boards are, in most cases, actually routed, we're going to start with the templates that are used as guides in routing.

Templates

The design and placement of templates are so bound together that we'll make no effort to separate them.

There are two options for template placement: on top of the work, which is conventional when using the portable router as shown in Figure 2-2a, or beneath the work, as a rule, when using a drill press (Figure 2-2b). In the latter position the lettering would read correctly if you could see through the board.

If you place the template underneath the workpiece, follow the image by moving the workpiece against a guide pin, which is inserted in an auxiliary table directly below the board and centered with the cutter. The pin is the same diameter as the bit. Template material can be fairly thin—for example, $1/8$-inch to $3/16$-inch tempered hardboard or plywood.

For the portable router method, place the template face up on top of the work. A veining bit with a cutting diameter equal to that of the shank will guide the cut to produce an exact duplicate of the template; i.e., one whose dimensions are exactly those of the finished carving. The template for the portable router should be of thicker material ($1/4$-inch to $3/8$-inch plywood) for the shank or template guide to ride against.

For raised lettering, individual cutouts will form your template. Each character will be spaced, aligned, and fastened individually to the workpiece or on an auxiliary backing (Figure 2-2f).

To carve recessed characters, properly spaced letters are cut in their relative positions in the template material. To make this kind of template, first drill a pilot hole well inside the character for each cutout, then insert the scroll-saw blade or thread the jigsaw blade through it. Recessed characters with islands, such as A, B, D and 6, 8, 9, require two or three bridges to the center to hold the islands in place (Figures 2-2e and 2-2f). As an alternative, you can attach separate little templates to form the islands. Bridging strands will be duplicated in routing but can be chiseled away during finishing. If you are guiding on the shank, and the cutter diameter is smaller than the shank, the size of the template image must be adjusted so that it is just enough larger than the carved-out portion to compensate for the difference in size between the cutter and the shank. When the cutter is larger than the shank—as with a double-fluted straight bit—a template guide must be attached to the router. In this case the template image must be designed to compensate for the size of the guide. Figure 2-3 shows template allowances for recessed- and raised-image routing when the shank and cutter diameters differ.

With the cutter-bit diameter and template allowance known, transfer the lettering to bond paper, or use a photocopied enlargement to arrive at the requisite 3-plus inches in character height. Trace your mark for the cut inside or outside the characters, depending on whether the letters will be recessed or raised.

If you find a design you want to duplicate in wood, have your local printer or blueprinter enlarge the pattern to the desired size for tracing onto the workpiece. The use of a square grid is another way to enlarge or reduce designs. Draw the grid over the original drawing. Note where the line of the drawing enters and leaves each square and redraw the pattern onto a grid of larger squares. (If you are lucky enough to have a draftsman's pantograph, enlargement and reduction become much easier.)

Once satisfied with the spacing, glue the paper pattern to the template material, whether plywood or tempered hardboard. Cut along the lines using a fine-toothed plywood blade. If a coarser blade must be used, tack a piece of thin wood under the template before cutting, to prevent splintering. Remember that imperfections in the template walls will be faithfully reproduced in the routed work, so take care in this first step—your efforts will be reflected in the smoothness of the finished product. Clean up transitions, radii, and straight runs before attaching the template to the work. Fillers such as epoxy putty can be used to even out slight depressions, and needle files will smooth the lines.

If your design includes a routed pad for the annual sticker, which appears at different positions relative to the numbers for the port and starboard sides, include the template form in both positions. Shift the template for alternate position.

Attach the template(s) to the surfaced board using glue and/or small brads. It must be secure enough to prevent shifting, but it also must be easy to remove without causing damage to the finished piece. Some carvers insert a sheet of newspaper between the two glued surfaces to make removal easier.

Routing

Unless you are a whiz at carving (and if so, you are envied by many), use templates and power tools to bridge the gap between the master and the novice. Most workshops contain a drill press or a portable router, or both. Either will produce good results.

Routing should be done at a high *speed* (i.e., spindle r.p.m.—not the rate at which you push the router through the work), but short of burning the wood or the bit. Optimum speed for each case is governed by depth of cut, cutter (bit) diameter, sharpness, rate of feed, and the hardness of the wood. You are working under optimum conditions when the cutter glides merrily on its charted course without overheating, chatter, or undue force.

On a drill press, speed should be at or above 5,000 r.p.m. (5-inch pulley on the drive to a 2-inch pulley on the spindle). The usual Jacobs chuck on a drill press is attached to the spindle via a taper. (A few makes of drill presses have screwed-on chucks. If you have one of these, you need take no further precautions.) Under the side loads and vibration of routing, it's conceivable that a taper-mounted chuck might be loosened and fly off, although such events are rare. One can get spindles with sockets and set screws for some drill presses; changing spindles is only a moment's work. The sockets usually accept ½-inch shanks, but there are adapters, too, so that you can use ¼-inch router bits with these spindles. Either size will turn out work as smooth and accurate as possible, given the speed of the drill press. I recommend that you use a nontapered spindle to take the side loads applied during routing, but this is not mandatory.

For ease of operation and best finish, make many shallow passes to reach the final depth: Begin with a cut of moderate depth, appropriate for the hardness of the wood and the size and speed of the cutter. Retrace the template at increasing depths. The final cut,

Figure 2-2. *Placement of templates and guide pins for recessed and raised letters. (a) Cutter shank (or template guide) traces template; portable router moves over work. (b) Drill press moves workpiece under flute. (c) A socket spindle for routing with a drill press is safe and accurate. (d) Recessed image for portable router—template on top. (e) Recessed image for drill press—template below engages guide pin. (f) Raised image—template of individual letters on top or on second sheet of plywood beneath.*

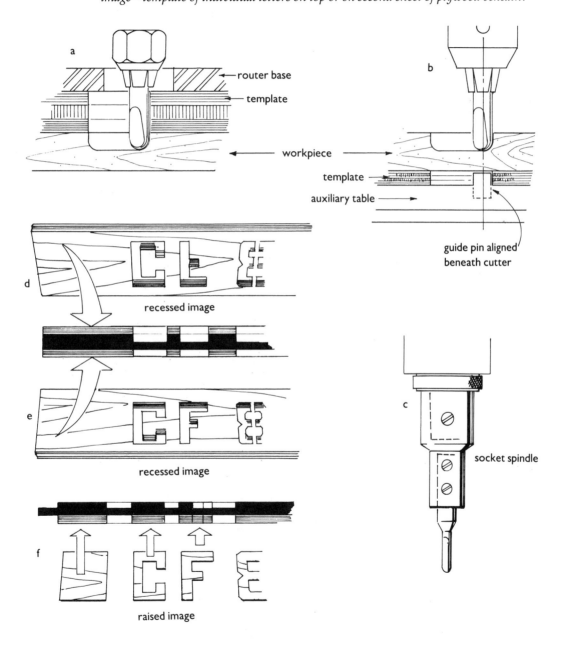

a

router base

template

b

workpiece

template

auxiliary table

guide pin aligned beneath cutter

d

recessed image

e

recessed image

c

socket spindle

f

raised image

Figure 2-3. *Allowances for differences in diameters of shank and cutter. When there is no difference, the cut duplicates the template.*

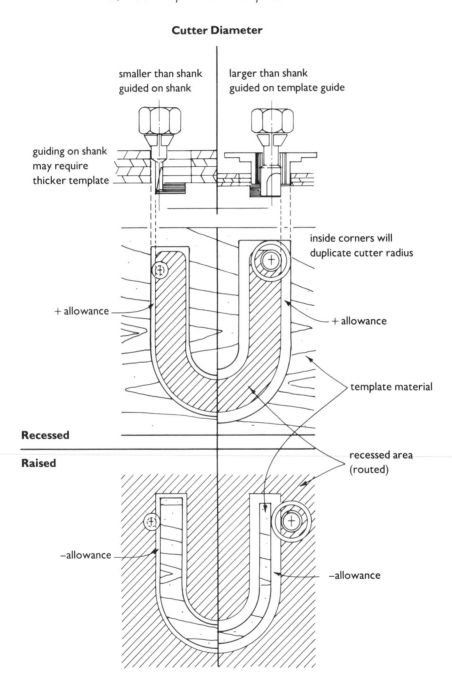

Cutter Diameter

smaller than shank
guided on shank

larger than shank
guided on template guide

guiding on shank
may require
thicker template

inside corners will
duplicate cutter radius

+ allowance

+ allowance

template material

Recessed

Raised

recessed area
(routed)

−allowance

−allowance

Figure 2-4. *Various methods of carving repetitive and nonrepetitive designs. (a) Friezes and rails can be adaptations or original designs. Concentric circles, tangents, curves, and repetition add variety and continuity. (b) A mechanical approach to carving— cut and follow template, routing up to the outline. Carve, file, and shape image into background. (c) Overlay grid on drawing. Draw enlarged grid to final size and redraw pattern square by square. (d) Recessed images are two-dimensional. (e) Raised images can be more complex with transitions, flowing forms, twists, and turns.*

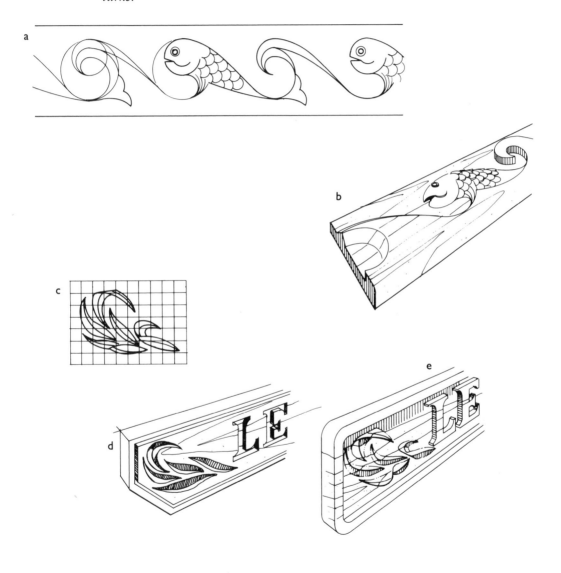

the one that reaches the design depth, should be very shallow and fast to make a smooth surface.

Either gold or silver leaf adds a nice finishing touch, and is not impossibly difficult to apply, using the shoulders of the raised or indented characters to guide the application. If you are planning to gild the work, get some instruction; there are a couple of tricky points about the right degree of tack in the preliminary sizing and in the actual handling of the leaf. It's incredibly fragile. The complete story of gilding is beyond the scope of this book. Gold leaf tends to look dark when reflecting water, especially when angled toward the water, so the contrast may not be as good as you might expect. Oiled or varnished teak, mahogany, or other deeply colored wood will darken to produce the contrasting background for gilt or painted characters.

Boards should be installed securely, preferably through-bolted to allow removal for refinishing the hull beneath the boards. Don't expect screws to hold fast forever.

Hand Carving versus Using Power Tools

Much can be done with router bits and templates, but the results may be too symmetrical and too mechanical for certain projects. What about hand carving, the way they used to do it in days of old?

Carving is an art; to master it takes years. Still, the novice can achieve an acceptable product without the flourish and flying chips. Dremel tools and needle files can replace chisel work. You may not learn to carve a balustrade in a day, but with a little care and patience you can produce fine scrollwork or other embellishments such as those shown in Figure 2-4.

A set of carving chisels, including gouges and skews and straight chisels, is handy. Keep a whetstone and a hard rubber-and-abrasive wheel close by to maintain a good cutting edge, preferably razor-sharp. A standard cabinetmaker's mallet may be used, but you might want to make or buy a sculptor's hardwood mallet; its conical head strikes the chisel squarely regardless of its orientation, allowing your attention to be focused on the carving, not on the direction and angle of the mallet head.

Carved designs can be recessed as in Figure 2-4d, or in relief, as mentioned earlier. Carving in relief is a little more difficult to visualize but can permit more intricate work (Figure 2-4e). Again, a board with a carved border might be silvered or gilded to yield an attractive combination.

A more ambitious project might consist of an American eagle carved on a plaque, a frieze cut along a shelf or rail, or handcarved trailboards and transom boards. In the privacy of your workshop, feel free to cut against a template to outline and rout excess material around the carved image (Figure 2-4b). The standing image can be tapered and faired into the background using chisels, power grinders, rasps, needle files, and abrasive papers.

Finishing

What man hath carved, he shall also varnish . . .

Designs should consist of a series of flat planes or other sandable forms so that surfaces may be easily prepared for varnishing. Exterior carvings, bombarded daily by ultraviolet rays, moisture, salt, heat, and cold, will eventually need refinishing. Restrain your ambitions—keep it simple! Interior work can be more ornate, but someday it will have to be refinished, too.

Interestingly, the hard, even-textured woods that are good for carving, are also the most responsive to good varnishing, giving durable and attractive surfaces that may be glossy or matte, depending on the varnish and the technique.

Sit right down and carve your boat a letter—or two or three. . . .

3.

BOXES

Dorade Boxes • Clock Boxes • Instrument Boxes • Deck Boxes

Battery Boxes • Tool Boxes • Work Boxes • Insulated Boxes

GETTING STARTED

Before starting on specific projects, a few words on box construction in general. We are going to consider boxes made from two principal materials: solid wood and plywood, with a glance at a lead-lined box. We'll leave a fourth kind, straight fiberglass, for the future, but we will put in a few words on the characteristics and use of fiberglass too. Each material has advantages and disadvantages with respect to its working characteristics and suitability for specific applications.

An excellent example of the moderately small solid-wood box that can be used outdoors in all weather is the *Dorade* box. That's what we will start with. Not all boxes intended for outdoor use are made of solid wood, however, as we will see.

DORADE BOXES

The Dorade box (named for the boat on which it was first used) is a ventilating device, one that has been very successful over the years. Why, then, does it appear in this chapter, rather than in the chapter on vents?

The reason is that while its function is that of a ventilator, its construction is that of a box—it fits right in with the other boxes I'll describe. Besides, it forms a very prominent feature of the boat's profile, so it's not only a box, but a conspicuous one that can add a touch of individuality to an otherwise common profile.

Most boats have a pair of Dorades, sometimes more. If additional Dorade boxes are on your things-to-do list, it is usually best to follow the design of existing boxes. You can improve the interior and function of the box without changing the exterior design.

If replacement is your goal, you must have some fairly strong dislikes for what you have, and probably equally strong ideas about what you would like to have instead. You might be thinking of embellishing the joinery with some dovetail joints or raked compound angles.

As a prominent feature atop a cabin or deck, Dorade boxes should exhibit the skill and care of the builder. The "gestalt," that is the appearance of the topsides, cabinhouse, hatch covers, handrails, and Dorade boxes, should be harmonious. At the same time the dimensions of the Dorade must fit the size and proportion of the clamshell, scoop, or cowl ventilators, especially existing hole patterns (Figure 3-1a).

Dorade boxes usually consist of two chambers. The forward chamber collects any water that enters the box. The center baffle is well bedded along sides and deck and confines the water, which drains outboard via drain holes. These drain holes are on the low side of the box and thus well below the crown of the deck. Aft of this chamber is the ventilation chamber proper, which houses the port, cut through the deck or coach roof and leading to the interior. Except in the heaviest weather, when the cowl vents should be directed away from the wind and the seas (in the very worst conditions they may be closed off altogether), a well-proportioned Dorade box gives the interior a good stream of fresh air. It also exhausts heated air from the enclosed interior by convection.

Joinery

Aside from an occasional run-in with a deck shoe, these boxes usually are not subject to abnormal stresses, so scantlings and joints may be modest but solid. Using 1-inch milled lumber (³/₄-inch net) may be sufficient for smaller boxes.

Exposed end grain will hold up if the box is well finished and kept that way. On the other hand, dovetail, box, and finger joints start out strong but tend to separate as wood shrinks and swells, unless carefully tended. Where teak is left to gray "au naturel," use miter joints to conceal and protect the end grain.

Put a good chamfer or a quarter-round on the edges of boxes for appearance and a longer-lasting finish. Sharp edges make the wood and its finish vulnerable, whereas well-rounded edges hold a finish longer and are easier to refinish, covering evenly with varnish or paint.

To make the Dorade box watertight where it meets the deck, contour the base to match the curvature of the crown. An easy way to make patterns for the parts of the box is to loft the contour onto scrap wood first. If you want vertical sides (and you should), you must maintain two planes: the horizontal, parallel to the waterline, and the vertical, perpendicular to the waterline.

First mark the scrap, using a bubble level on the vertical plane, with a vertical line representing one edge of the Dorade box (Figure 3-1b). Then, with the piece of scrap set so that this line is kept vertical, scribe the contour of the crown onto it with a compass or a pair of dividers. This contour curve is marked on the work to guide you in cutting the box itself.

If you have to deal with rake as well as the curvature of the crown, make another pattern for the rake, or use a bevel guide to duplicate the rake angle. Your objective is to keep the ventilators standing straight and tall and facing forward.

Attachment

Where you have easy access below, fasten Dorade boxes with bronze (preferable) or stainless steel (acceptable) screws projecting up *vertically* through the deck and into the sides of the box. To ensure a watertight fit put bedding compound between the deck and the box. Take care to align fasteners with the centerlines of all four sides. When fastening the vertical sides of a box through wooden or composite decks of substantial thickness, drill a vertical pilot hole from the topside down. If you are fastening a raked side, you must drill the pilot at the rake angle, as in Figure 3-1a.

Follow from below with a combination bit (screw threads, shank, countersink bevel, and counterbore) for the selected screw size, at the same angle as the pilot. After the

Figure 3-1. *Design and layout of a Dorade. It must be contoured to fit the crown of the coach roof, yet have a horizontal top for the ventilator.*

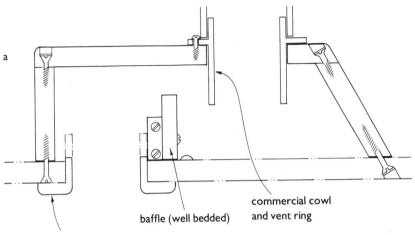

a

commercial cowl
and vent ring

baffle (well bedded)

commerical bezel finishes off
interior vent port

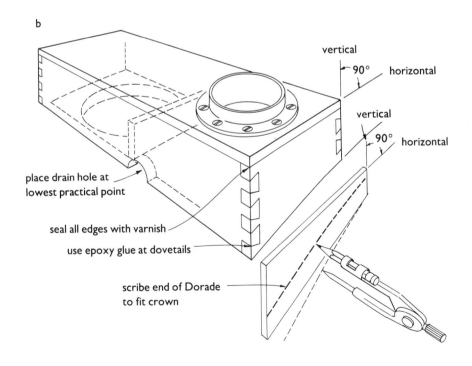

b

vertical
90° horizontal

vertical
90° horizontal

place drain hole at
lowest practical point

seal all edges with varnish

use epoxy glue at dovetails

scribe end of Dorade
to fit crown

screws have been driven home, cover the countersunk screw heads below with bungs. If there is insufficient thickness for at least a 3/16-inch countersink, chamfer the hole enough to depress the screw head, then fill and finish.

For attaching wooden Dorade boxes through fiberglass, screw heads can be depressed slightly and glazed, or oval-head screws with finishing washers, spaced in an orderly pattern below, would not be objectionable. Backing plates such as those normally provided beneath stanchions, winches, or cleats are not necessary.

If you are dealing with a vinyl overhead, drop the headliner temporarily so that you can cut the port and attach the new box. Restretch the headliner and cut a hole in it a bit smaller than the port. Then make radial cuts outward toward the edge of the hole. Tack or cement the resulting triangular segments around the inside of the port. Insert a bezel, either a commercial part or one turned to fit, to finish off the interior vent to the Dorade box.

A removable *escutcheon* (blank plate), when combined with a tube that extends well up into the air chamber, offers further assurance of keeping the interior dry. I suggest placing a small drain hole at the deck on the low side of the aft air chamber to lead off small quantities of water such as those that result from condensation.

If for some reason through-deck fastening is not practical, an alternative would be to attach cleats to the deck, positioned to fit snugly inside the box. The baffle, for example, could be attached to the deck with cleats, and the box attached to the baffle (Figure 3-1a).

Aside from its use in Dorades, solid wood is excellent for decorative additions, especially small portable ones. These may be used to hold almost any valuable, although a clock box is traditionally used for this purpose.

CLOCK BOXES

You need no excuses for having fancy clock and instrument storage boxes aboard. A front-opening case would look good mounted against a bulkhead, or semipermanently fastened to a shelf. Locked boxes keep the contents out of reach and out of sight. Cushioned inserts or profile cutouts hold the contents snugly in place. Since the item is already boxed, taking box and all to the warmth of your home at the end of the season makes winterizing a little easier.

The contents will determine the dimensions. A fitted box is a good place to keep (and hide) a signal pistol or (alas!) a revolver. It's a protective nest for a sextant, a chronometer, or a camera.

In appearance, small storage boxes all have a great deal in common, but there are two distinct approaches to constructing them: They can be made of solid wood or plywood. While we're on solid wood, let's take a clock box as an example. Later I'll describe how to construct a plywood instrument box.

Our ship's clock case (Figure 3-2) is fitted with a sliding cover stowed in matching slots at the back. They can be installed on a bulkhead-mounted rack or atop a cabinet or shelf. Teak was used for this project, but mahogany, maple, or any hard wood of choice would complement a fine timepiece, barometer, or both.

To make the diagonal grain pattern, start by cutting a rectangle at 45° to the width of a 1-inch *net* board, as in Figure 3-2a. (This will probably be called "5/4" lumber at the yard.) Using a bandsaw, resaw each rectangle to yield two ³/₈-inch boards, plane the surfaces, then butt and butterfly the two pieces to form a mirror grain pattern (Figure 3-2b). The diagonal pattern consumes about one-third more stock than does cutting pieces square to the board.

Before gluing teak or other oily wood, give the mating surfaces a good wipe with acetone to remove the natural oils. This will ensure a good bond.

Veneering a box constructed of a more utilitarian wood provides an alternative that looks like solid wood. If a lesser grade of wood is used, corners may be mitered or rabbeted, then veneered after assembly for uniformity. Natural-wood veneer and edge stripping are easy to apply, even without the heat and pressure used in commercial processing. Contact cement will hold in moist environments; 5-minute epoxy or other epoxy adhesives should hold forever. Figure 3-3 shows a number of edging and joining details applicable to both solid-wood and plywood construction.

The top and bottom of the box are rabbeted into the sides—the top member is shortened so that the sliding face can be inserted on tracks. The tracks are cut and glued in place. If your trust in teak butt joints isn't as great as mine, you can groove-and-spline, or dowel, to increase the gluing surface.

Figure 3-2c shows a *finger-lap* or box joint (in exaggerated form) produced by dadoing the interlocking fingers, but other interlocking corners, ranging from dovetails to *kerf* joints, (interlocking saw cuts or kerfs), will produce strong and attractive joints.

Felt-lined inserts conforming to the shape of the contents can be fitted into the box, as shown. A compartment containing a desiccant, such as dried silica gel, would provide protection against moisture, which causes mildew or corrosion. A false bottom could be added to cover valuables or other (legal!) contents.

PLYWOOD

Since we will be constructing boxes made mostly of plywood from this point on, let's discuss this often-maligned material before going into the details of the design and construction of boxes made from it.

Properties

Plywood is a material of convenience. It comes in large sheet sizes (commonly 4 × 8) for major projects, including enclosures, bulkheads, dividers, and cabinetry, and even whole hulls, but smaller projects also are easier when plywood is used. Quality pays off in the marine environment, so choose at least an *exterior* ply, faced with natural wood, impregnated, veneered, or covered with a layer of plastic, depending on the project.

Quality plywood is an excellent building material. It is dimensionally stable, true in thickness, and strong. These attributes justify its use in bulkheads, doors, superstructures, and even furnishings when faced and edged with hardwood veneer and attractively finished. However, both its properties and its joinery differ somewhat from those of solid wood.

The basic types of plywood you'll need to know about are listed below, from the highest to the lowest grade.

- Marine

- Exterior 6-ply

- Exterior 3-ply

- Interior X

- Interior

Table 3-1 serves as a quick reference to types of plywood and their specifications. As mentioned briefly in the introduction, avoid plywood that is graded ABX, or having any

Table 3-1. *Plywood Specifications.*

Marine EXT*	Solid, joint-core construction; strict limits on core gaps and number of face repairs.
(HDO)	High density; heavily overlaid with resin and fiber.
(MDO)	Medium density; lighter overlay. For boat hulls made of Douglas Fir or Western larch.
EXT A-A	Exterior; good both sides; waterproof glue.
EXT	Exterior; okay for outboard use. If an "X" appears after the face designation (.e.g. ABX), the ply was constructed with waterproof glue, but the inside layers are not good enough for boat use. Avoid.
INT	Interior; not recommended for outdoor exposure.

*American Plywood Association designations.

X in the designation. An X means that, although the glue used is waterproof, the continuity and finish are inferior to those of an exterior ply, marked EXT (EXT is an exception to the "no-X" rule; it's simply an abbreviation for exterior).

Joinery

A box made from exterior veneer ply can be just as satisfactory as one built of solid wood. We are going to see how three different kinds of boxes are made, for both interior and exterior use. Each will show some specific method of construction, but first let's review some general approaches that can be applied to a wide variety of projects.

Construction methods center around tucking in the edges and ends of the laminates to give the appearance of solid boards, and making corners as strong as possible—again without showing the edges of the laminates (also called veneers in the trade).

Plywood edges.   Plywood edges are either let into *banding,* as shown in Figures 3-3b, 3-3c, and 3-3d; mitered, as in Figure 3-3e, to increase gluing surface and conceal the laminates; or faced with a veneer, as in Figure 3-3a.

Two methods of banding (Figures 3-3c and 3-3d) appear as distinct differences in the grain near the edges. In both cases the plywood is milled to accept mortised or rabbeted strips, forming tongue-and-groove joints, and the parts are glued together.

Another technique, shown in Figure 3-3b, is first to cut a beveled strip in the sheet of plywood at 45°, so that its cross section forms a right-angled triangle. Then cut again, bisecting the right angle. This yields a smaller right-angled triangle. The piece now has one face carrying the surface grain pattern of the original sheet. Make a corresponding right-angled V-groove, with two opposite saw cuts or with a molding cutter, in the edge of the workpiece at 45°. Glue the strip into the V. When the strip has been glued in place, the edge repeats the grain pattern of the plywood surface, not the edge grain.

The solid-wood edge (Figures 3-3f and 3-3g) offers many choices, such as a wooden corner brace, a framed outline, or a simple flush edge.

Plywood corners.   In plywood, butt joints have a propensity to pull out; a simple rabbet or box joint is much stronger because of the increased gluing surface. This takes maximum advantage of the material's inherent strength.

Where fasteners go through a plywood face into a butted edge, align them on center, but angle them alternately above and below the horizontal. Perfectly aligned fasteners will pull out more easily than will angled ones—they take the pull-out force lengthwise, while angled fasteners direct part of the force crosswise to the grain.

Bottoms of boxes should be set in slots let in about one-third the thickness of the sides, then liberally glued and fastened with nails or screws.

Figure 3-2. *An elegant clock case of solid wood. The cover design is based on use; here, a sliding lid is stowed in a slot below. Orient the box on edge to display a ship's clock.*

a

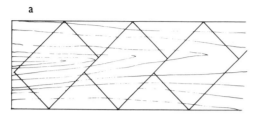

cut diagonal pieces at 45° to grain of figured stock; you'll net about ⅔ of the board length

b

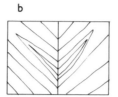

resaw thick board, butterfly, and glue; butt, dowel, or tongue-and-groove the joint

valuables can be covered by false bottom

pillow the contents with a shaped wooden block, covered with felt

c

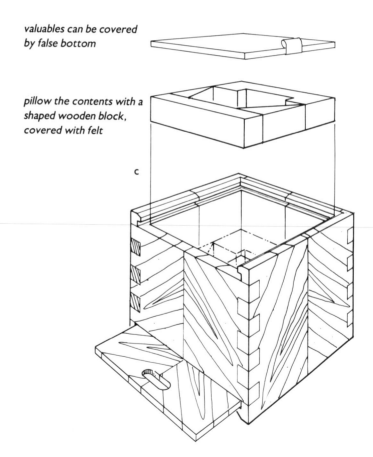

Photo 3-1.
A finished solid-wood clock box.

INSTRUMENT BOXES

Our plywood box (Figure 3-3) is constructed with mitered corners, with the top and bottom let into the inside face of the ply. Within the box is a plywood insert (to hold a chronometer and barometer set) that can have unfinished edges butting to the inside of the box.

If the box is small, the sides, top, and bottom can be assembled as a fully enclosed case, glued, and allowed to set. The top would be cut free later. The exposed ends and edges of the laminates should be planed and covered with veneer edging.

Plywood edge treatments can be more substantial, resembling the decorative trim on a partition, or a shaped fiddle edging on a tabletop. These methods can be applied to the box project by framing the sides with molded and angled wooden strips, thus embellishing the corners with a nice diagonal, semicircular, or other decorative shape, again as in Figures 3-3f and 3-3g.

Let's move on to boxes used on deck and those used for various nondecorative purposes.

Figure 3-3. *A plywood instrument box has all raw edges hidden by banding and strip veneering. (a) Edge veneer—roll or delaminate veneer from scrap and glue to edge or (b) band edge with a triangular piece, cut from scrap or the working sheet. You also can (c) let a tongue-and-groove band into plywood edge, or (d) let plywood into a tongue-and-groove band, or (e) miter the corners. (f and g) Hardwood edges can act as trim, frame, or fiddle.*

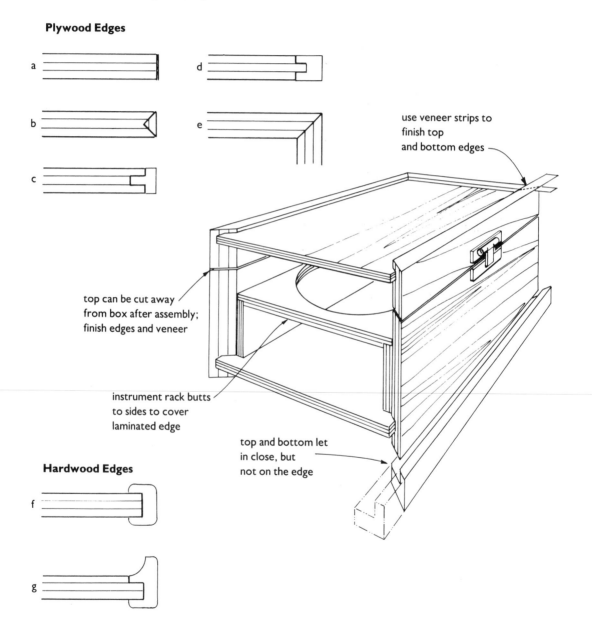

Plywood Edges

a

b

c

d

e

use veneer strips to finish top and bottom edges

top can be cut away from box after assembly; finish edges and veneer

instrument rack butts to sides to cover laminated edge

top and bottom let in close, but not on the edge

Hardwood Edges

f

g

Deck Boxes (For LP and CN Gases)

Cooking and heating fuel on board requires taking precautions against hazards. Caution is required when stowing, handling, or using any fuel, such as alcohol or kerosene, but the requirements for LPG (Liquefied Petroleum Gas) and CNG (Compressed Natural Gas) are quite specific. It may be wise to confer with the local inspector or yard when undertaking this project.

Terminology and Requirements

Both LPG and CNG are gases at normal room temperature and atmospheric pressure, liquefying under moderate increases in pressure and readily vaporizing when pressure is released.

LPG is a term given to products comprising propane, propylene, butane, butylene, or a mixture thereof. It is a two-phase (liquid/vapor) fuel of higher caloric value (it produces more heat per pound) than CNG, and is stored at lower cylinder pressure. LPG is heavier than air and will fall or settle if released. (Familiar, isn't it? Just like gasoline vapor.) CNG is lighter than air and will rise and dissipate into the atmosphere through overhead ventilation.

Both LPG and CNG are nontoxic, odorless, and invisible in their natural state, but have odorant added for leak detection. LPG's odor concentration can vary depending on the volume of fuel remaining in the cylinder; CNG is always in vapor form, so its odor concentration does not vary.

The U.S. Coast Guard regulations are both general and specific. Let's take the general ones first.

Manufacturers must meet certain standards when producing appliances certified for marine use. Specific requirements are incorporated by reference in publications of the American Boat and Yacht Council, Inc. (ABYC) and the National Fire Prevention Association (NFPA).

The use or stowage of stoves with attached CNG cylinders is prohibited, which brings us to the topic of seamanlike and legal placement of the separate tanks. Carrying on to the next paragraph of the U.S. Coast Guard/DOT saga, we learn that if the fuel supply of an LPG or CNG system enters an enclosed space on a vessel, a remote shutoff valve must be installed near the appliance. The valve must be located between the regulator and the point where the fuel-supply line enters the enclosed portion of the vessel. Manufacturers' installation instructions will show approved hook-ups.

LPG installation requirements. How and where you install LPG tanks is based on the following requirements, somewhat paraphrased from the official guidelines.

- Each LPG tank must have a shutoff valve threaded directly into the cylinder outlet, equipped with an attached hand wheel for operation without the use of a separate wrench. All cylinders must be provided with a safety-relief valve, specifically designed for LPG (DOT regulations).

- Discharge of the safety-relief valve(s) must be vented away from the cylinder and its compartment into the open atmosphere. The point of discharge must be at least 2 feet distant from any opening to a cabin or hull interior, or from engine exhaust that is below the level of the vent discharge. The outlet must be located and designed to prevent water from entering the relief-valve port.

- LPG gas cylinders and regulating and safety equipment must be substantially secured, readily accessible, and located where escaping vapor cannot reach the bilges, machinery spaces, accommodations, or other enclosed spaces. Such locations must be confined to open decks, cabin tops, and areas outside cockpits or semienclosures but protected from climatic extremes by a housing vented to the open air and unrestricted, with at least two vents having an aggregate free area equal to 1 square inch for each 7 pounds of the total LPG capacity of the cylinder(s), the vent area being equally divided, top and bottom. The bottom edge of the lower vent(s), if in the door or walls, must be at floor level of the housing.

If boat construction or design prevents the above, the cylinder and equipment must be:

1. mounted in a locker or housing;
2. vapor tight to the hull interior;
3. located above the waterline;
4. constructed or lined with corrosion-resistant materials;
5. opened, without tools, only from the top, with a cover seated on a gasket;
6. conveniently located and have easily accessible valves and gauges for operating, testing, and checking.

Two variances from these regulations are allowed for CNG: The storage locker or housing-access opening need not be in the top; and the locker or housing need not be above the waterline. Vents for CNG are high up since the gas is lighter than air. According to a marine surveyor, installation is the same as that for LPG, except everything is upside down.

Onboard tanks usually have a fairly small capacity, since LPG cannot be recharged while on the boat, and CNG cylinders are exchanged rather than refilled. Cylinder sizes are given in Figure 3-4.

Aluminum cylinders might be preferred, depending on their location on the boat. If the mild steel of a standard cylinder is close enough to the compass to cause the needle to deflect, you should use aluminum. Warn your checkbook that aluminum cylinders will be two to three times the cost of comparable steel tanks.

Hold-Downs

Gas cylinders have either a ring or feet on the bottom. The configuration determines the design of the saddle or holder. Whatever the configuration, you must keep the cylinder dry, not sitting in a pool of water. Design saddles so that water does not collect anywhere against the body or the base of the tank, causing corrosion.

The most common hold-down consists of a hefty vertical rod, threaded for a wingnut. If only one tank is installed, one or both sides can be cinched down. For a pair of tanks, a yoke arrangement with a threaded rod between the tanks will hold them in place (Figure 3-4).

Housings

The deck box, locker, or housing for gas cylinders must comply with the above regulations. A top-opening, watertight, vaportight box, vented at the top and bottom, and located above the waterline, really isn't too much to ask. Here's our box, in Figure 3-5, to prove it.

Our gas-bottle box is an attempt to balance the requirements with a sense of belonging to the boat. Clues for your design will come from the surroundings; match the joinerwork, materials, shape, and form. Produce a noninterfering structure (if possible) that could double as a sunning platform for your bikinied crew, or divide the box into compartments and use part of it for stowage.

Although whatever you produce must be vapor- and moisture proof, above the waterline, etc., it doesn't have to be ugly. In essence, a box for a gas cylinder is just another box, but you may have to pick a smaller cylinder than you would like, in order to preclude a mighty box growing like a huge excrescence out of the deck.

Do note the details of the hold-downs in Figure 3-4 and the general construction, gasketing, and sealing, in Figure 3-5.

Figure 3-4. *Gas cylinders and their retaining systems. Retainers may be built in as part of the box or kept separate for ease of maintenance and repair. A central, dual-tank yoke captures both cylinders at once. A single-tank yoke must retain the cylinder without interfering with valves, regulators, etc.*

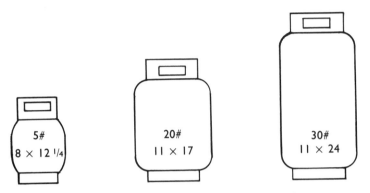

5#
8 × 12 ¼

20#
11 × 17

30#
11 × 24

LPG tanks have common characteristics—similar valve-guard configuration, 8" diameter, base ring, etc. If capacity is too small, tanks are not economical (minimum refill charges). Containers that are too large are difficult to transport for recharging.

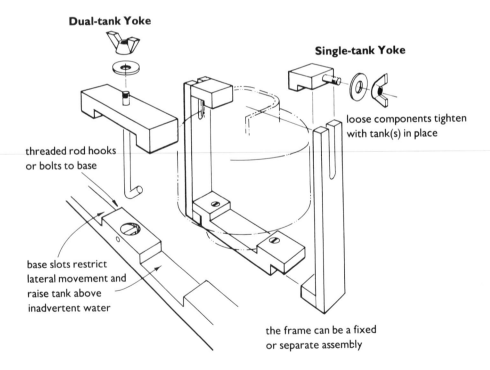

Dual-tank Yoke

Single-tank Yoke

loose components tighten with tank(s) in place

threaded rod hooks or bolts to base

base slots restrict lateral movement and raise tank above inadvertent water

the frame can be a fixed or separate assembly

Figure 3-5. *Construction of a plywood gas-cylinder box. Vapor-tight, watertight compartment requires sealed bottom, joints, and gasket around lid. The brass edging is designed to meet the gasket in a gas-tight seal. Vents should be at least 2 feet away from cabin and hull openings, and engine exhaust. Both deck-mounted and through-deck installations must be above the waterline.*

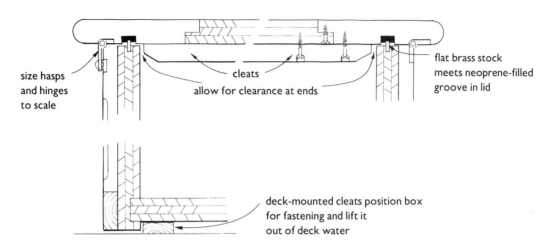

size hasps
and hinges
to scale

cleats
allow for clearance at ends

flat brass stock
meets neoprene-filled
groove in lid

deck-mounted cleats position box
for fastening and lift it
out of deck water

with through-deck installation,
deck profile appears lower
than when box is mounted on deck

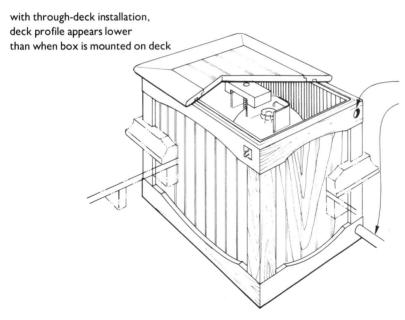

To determine vent size, allow 1 sq. in. for each 7 lbs. of tank capacity and divide between the top and bottom vents, with the bottom vent at the lowest level. (For example: One 20# tank ÷ 7 = 2,857 sq. in. of vent ÷ 2 = 1,429 sq. in. per vent, or two 1 3/8-inch diameter vents at the top and bottom.)

Battery Boxes

Another project that doesn't require a furniture-grade material or finish is a battery box, shown in Figure 3-6. It may be constructed using ordinary exterior- or marine-grade plywood, unedged. After all, the box will be kept in an engine space or down deep in some locker. Either of these grades of plywood will hold up well. Marine-ply has greater density (fewer voids and a lesser knot count) than lower grades, to meet stringent specifications for hull construction. Onboard projects made of plywood seldom require the maximum density, but the little extra insurance it affords—due to possibly better glues, no voids, and so on—could lengthen the life of the box.

Joinery

The joinerwork is simple. The drawing shows a box made with plain finger or box joints, preferably cross-doweled. Various corner joints are also shown, along with their relative strengths. The figures clearly show why I have chosen finger joints.

The box has to have a cover and a means of keeping both the box in the boat and the battery in the box—vents in the cover and a very strong bottom to hold the weight of the battery. Otherwise, the details are up to you. There are so many different batteries and places to install them. A battery is massive, and the effect of its weight is multiplied in a rough sea: Use a heavy plywood for the bottom, let it in all 'round, and fasten with screws as well as glue. So much for the woodwork. Battery boxes, like CNG storage boxes, are subject to official requirements.

Requirements

Whether fancy or plain, a battery box must meet certain regulations. To quote (approximately) from the U.S. Coast Guard requirements for commercial vessels:

> ". . . on-board acid batteries shall be secured in a
> lead-lined tray or box, which is, itself, fastened in place,
> with the batteries strapped or otherwise captured in position.
> If the battery box is enclosed, the exterior casing is
> to be vented at the top for escape of hydrogen gas. "

The lead-lined battery box, mandatory on commercial vessels or vessels for charter, is recommended for private vessels as well. If lead sheathing is not readily available, fiberglass-and-plastic may be an alternative for use in pleasure vessels.

Lead sheathing, available in weights and sheet thicknesses of $1/32$-inch (2-pound, or 2

Figure 3-6. *(a) Relative strengths of corner joints, based on the butt joint. The finger-lap, or box, joint combines strength and ease of construction. (b) Battery boxes must be secured in place, restrained from above, and vented on top if a cover is added. In commercial vessels, they must be lead lined; in pleasureboats, reinforced plastic may be used in place of lead. This one has heavy, plywood finger joints. The bottom is let in, glued, and fastened with screws.*

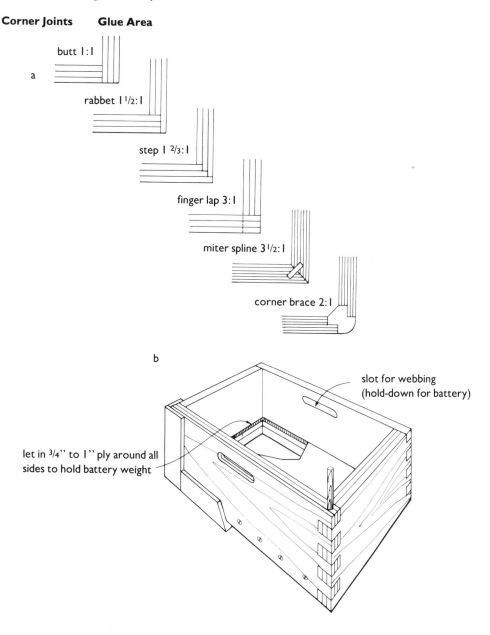

Corner Joints   Glue Area

butt 1:1

a

rabbet 1 1/2:1

step 1 2/3:1

finger lap 3:1

miter spline 3 1/2:1

corner brace 2:1

b

slot for webbing
(hold-down for battery)

let in 3/4'' to 1'' ply around all
sides to hold battery weight

pounds per square foot), $1/16$-inch (4-pound), and $1/8$-inch (8-pound), is fairly easy to work. At the time of writing it cost about $4 per square foot for the $1/16$-inch thickness, which is the one I prefer.

Before concerning yourself too much with how to design and fabricate the liner, make sure that cut sheets of lead, of the right thickness and in the small size you will need, are available. Make a pattern of the box liner (heavy paper is good material for the pattern) and cut the shape to make the corners either meet, overlap, or fold. Let's suppose you decide on folded corners; folded corners can be sealed with a bead of solder along the seams.

Cut and fold the lead. Solder with an iron and an acid-flux solder. This will form a good seal. (Unlike electrical components, lead calls for an acid-flux or an acid-core solder. Ask a plumber or the friendly hardware man. . . .) After the job is done, wash off the acid carefully with a dilute solution of baking soda and rinse a few times with plain water.

Tool Boxes

Projects that provide a change and relaxation from built-ins and elegance are tool boxes—simple and complex—but all extremely useful, whatever their degree of complexity. Here are some examples.

Although the common purpose of the tool box is to stow tools on board, its design can range from accommodating every tool owned by the liveaboard to stowing only those needed by the commuting yachtsman for light maintenance while underway. The third category, similar to the commuter, is the trailer boatman, who has the advantage of taking the boat to the workshop.

The onboard complement includes tools for minor work on the engine(s), plumbing, electrical components, plus gauges and rules, and a good assortment of hose clamps, crosby clamps, plugs, screws and bolts, cotter pins, electrical tape, and a variety of lubricants, cleaners, and polishes.

The collection probably includes a hammer, vise grips, adjustable and box-end wrenches, channel-lock pliers, snips, cutters (including a pair of double-action cutters), metal and wood saws (or saw blades), chisels, hand drills, Allen wrenches, etc.

This list forms the basis for planning the quantity and variety of tools to be stowed, as well as their individual and collective sizes. Large items, such as a pry bar or cable cutter, may be stowed apart from the majority of the smaller hand tools, their locations depending on space constraints and convenience.

Location also may be a consideration in your design, dictating size, proportion, and even a peculiar shape for the tool box where the available space is equally peculiar.

The more portable the box, the more useful. The base should be mar-proofed with pads or other protectors so the tool-laden box may safely be placed atop your most cherished brightwork.

Three versions of this onboard tool box show a range of useful designs, from the basic model to the ultra-deluxe.

The first box (Figure 3-7a) is for small hand tools stowed in a small compartment. Frequently used tools tend to surface, always (well, mostly) providing quick access.

The second version, more along the design of a carpenter's box (Figure 3-7b), can be larger, yet is easily carried one-handed from its location to the job site—maybe a distance of 10 to 20 feet. This design also can serve as a traveling work box. A fancier version is shown in Figure 3-7c.

This deluxe tool box can be as deluxe as you like. It can be cleated to a workbench or rack, or stowed in a locker. Drawers equipped with lift stops can be customized with routed blocks to house a drill-bit set, a drilled block or two to hold small bits or burrs, or just to hold the small items that normally filter to the bottom. Drawers can be the full depth, under a false bottom, or short, housed within a shallow compartment.

In this version a double-hinged lid allows full access to the top tray, the home of the most frequently used tools. The tray is designed to slide back (after a slight lift to clear a stop block that keeps it in place), for removal, or just for access below. The second hinge at the back of the cover folds the entire lid away so that one can reach the torque wrench or double-action cutters.

Vent and drain holes drilled through the bottom will allow air and water to leave. Holes should be small but plentiful. Rust protection, aside from treating the metal parts with oil or WD-40 can be increased by including an oiled canvas-cover flap, or even a lining inside the box.

If you use oil, avoid automotive oils, because most such oils contain agents that attract water, which is just what you don't need. Sprays such as WD-40 are made to repel water. Even high-grade salad oil is better than auto oil!

WORK BOXES

Owners of vessels equipped with workbenches will have little need (or little occasion for that matter) to use the following design. But for the boat owner who must do his maintenance at the dock, or in the boatyard during a yearly haulout, the project could make repairs and maintenance a good bit easier.

Lacking an onboard workshop, we do-it-yourselfers have to carry with us the tools needed to tackle whatever repairs are on the agenda—or not on the agenda, which is tougher. A simple box could be sufficient, but a carrying box that could double as a small workbench, as in Figure 3-8, might be much more useful.

Every craftsman has his own way of working, therefore, the description of this partic-

Figure 3-7. *Three tool boxes of increasing complexity. (a) A box for small hand tools stows readily in many areas. (b) A carpenter's box will stow and tote longer tools and parts. (c) This box will hold numerous tools.*

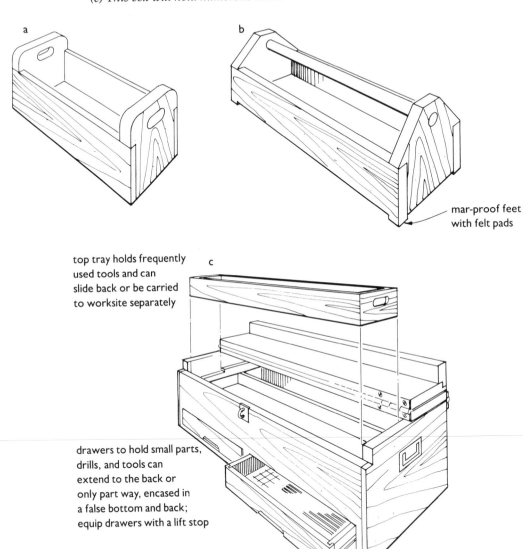

a

b

mar-proof feet
with felt pads

top tray holds frequently
used tools and can
slide back or be carried
to worksite separately

c

drawers to hold small parts,
drills, and tools can
extend to the back or
only part way, encased in
a false bottom and back;
equip drawers with a lift stop

Figure 3-8. *This box is a combination of a small workbench with a vise and a box for small tools. Position the dog, shim, and wedge the workpiece in the vice for drilling, cutting, planing. A flat bottom adds stability; make the box as wide as you can easily carry.*

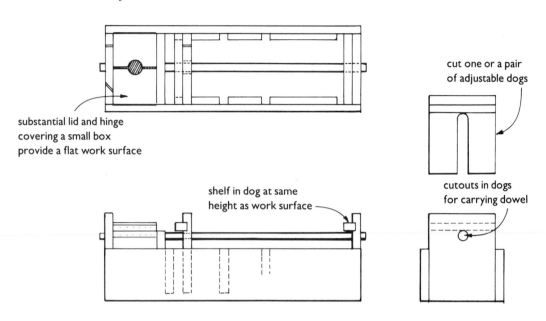

substantial lid and hinge
covering a small box
provide a flat work surface

cut one or a pair
of adjustable dogs

shelf in dog at same
height as work surface

cutouts in dogs
for carrying dowel

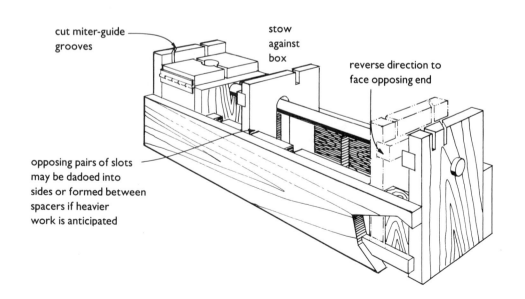

cut miter-guide
grooves

stow
against
box

reverse direction to
face opposing end

opposing pairs of slots
may be dadoed into
sides or formed between
spacers if heavier
work is anticipated

ular box should be thought of as only the beginning of your ultimate design to fit your specific needs. The design includes high ends, one with a small work surface atop a hefty cover, over a built-in compartment. This end compartment is a good place to keep small parts, fasteners, drill bits, and the like temporarily, while at the job.

The opposite end is of equal height: Note how it carries a horizontal member let in at the same height as the compartment lid. Slotted adjustable boards form the jaws of a vise. Each of these also carries a crossmember at the same height to support the work in the vise.

Paired vertical slots are either dadoed or built up along the inside of the box to position the vise face, to fit the piece held. Spacers and wedges are used to hold work firmly between the jaws for drilling, sawing, planing, etc.

Ends also can be made into a quasi miter box by precutting grooves—saw kerfs, usually—at 90° and 45°. Whichever box you choose to make, choose the materials appropriately. Pine or fir would be adequate if you use the box as a tote, but oak or other hard wood would hold up better under heavy use. Ironbark and lignum vitae for the vise part would constitute overkill—but you get the idea. When not serving as a workbench, the vise end could be stowed in the slots along the sides of the compartment. Contents may have to be rearranged to clear a space to insert the vise end where needed.

The size of the box and the anticipated loads on the parts will help you decide whether or not to dado the slots down the sides, or to build up these slots by laminating a second thickness of wood to form the grooves for the cheeks of the vise.

If the two-ply method is used, the inside surface of one or more of the inner blocks could be dadoed to fit your set of wood chisels, files, or whatever else could be stowed and carried in vertical slots. Otherwise, strips of leather stapled or screwed to the sides will form tight and loose loops to hold the chisels. Either method will hold the tools at the ready for a quick draw.

INSULATED BOXES (A FIBERGLASS PRIMER)

It's often necessary to insulate a box so that it can be used as an effective refrigerator, or even as a good portable cooler. The more-than-weekend boatman probably will welcome the addition of a built-in insulated box.

Because cooling boxes often get damp, many users like reinforced plastic construction, which leads us to our next topic.

Reinforced Plastics

GRP stands for Glass Reinforced Plastic. It means the same thing as reinforced plastic and, in this context, fiberglass. (Not "Fiberglas," which is a registered trademark of Owens-Corning Fiberglas Corporation.)

Fiberglass is a preferred material for many boat projects, whether by itself to form a housing or shell, or in combination with wood. It's basically very strong and nearly impervious to moisture, and it is easily worked into almost any shape, including curves, with little or no machining.

Fiberglass-and-resin combinations have other valuable attributes as well. They may be used as adhesives, insulators, or moisture and corrosion barriers. They also are extremely good electrical insulators.

Because reinforced plastics are so popular in the construction of all kinds of small containers, notably those that must be insulated—whether the plastic is used to form the box proper or just the waterproof lining—a few words about this material and its handling seem to be in order.

I have included a short primer on fiberglass-reinforced plastics to acquaint the pure woodworker with some basic characteristics and applications, and with some questions that need to be asked of those purveying fiberglassing supplies. He should listen to you and supply you according to your needs. Otherwise, you yourself will have to specify in detail exactly how and where the fiberglass and resin will be used, and the characteristics you seek.

You should leave the vendor's establishment with the most suitable kind of treated fiberglass—the right resin and hardener or catalyst combination, in a workable viscosity, to ensure proper waterproofing qualities and working characteristics. You'll also have to get whatever else is needed to bond parts, to lay in fillets, to release the part from the mold, and to clean and finish the surface. Don't leave without suitable gloves and solvents to protect and clean your own surfaces, too.

Small projects suitable for fiberglass construction include cold boxes, battery-box liners (though lead must be used in a commercial vessel as outlined above, a yacht may substitute fiberglass), and backing plates for deck-mounted fittings.

More extensive projects might include the addition of bulkheads, bunks, or other members fitted into molded interiors. These topics are covered more completely in *The Fiberglass Boat Repair Manual,* by Allan H. Vaitses, International Marine Publishing, 1988.

Fiberglass construction is applied to so many different kinds of things that it would be a huge task to illustrate all, or nearly all, of the most important ones, even though everyone knows about its use in hull building.

Instead, I have designed the ultimate device, illustrating a great many of the techniques important to the DIYer, and good for absolutely nothing. You may call it what you will: I trust that it will be a name suitable for use on a family cruiser. You will find a drawing and description of this unique machine in Figure 3-9. Study it, for it shows and tells a lot about where fiberglass techniques may be used to advantage.

Built-up shapes may be made of glassed-over plywood: Rapid-curing resins may be used in a little less viscous composition, because they will set before they sag. Don't put polyester resin over an epoxy—it won't stick well. The other way around is fine. Epoxies are excellent adhesives. For some projects, you might choose epoxy altogether, but be

Figure 3-9. *The unique, incredible Graves machine. It does nothing but show some of the things you can do with reinforced plastics. Epoxy resins may be applied over cured polyester; polyester will not stick well to an epoxy surface.*

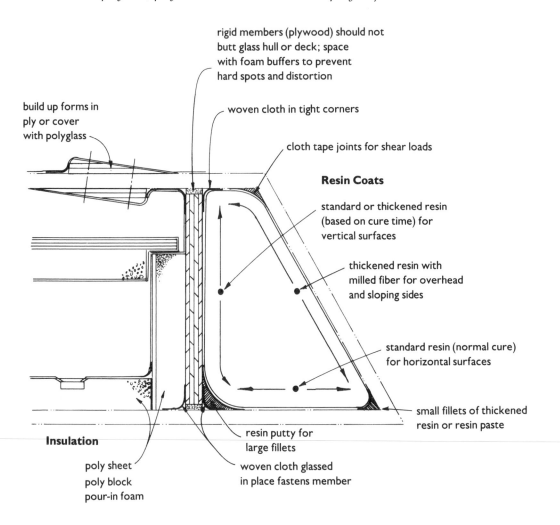

rigid members (plywood) should not
butt glass hull or deck; space
with foam buffers to prevent
hard spots and distortion

build up forms in
ply or cover
with polyglass

woven cloth in tight corners

cloth tape joints for shear loads

Resin Coats

standard or thickened resin
(based on cure time) for
vertical surfaces

thickened resin with
milled fiber for overhead
and sloping sides

standard resin (normal cure)
for horizontal surfaces

small fillets of thickened
resin or resin paste

Insulation

poly sheet
poly block
pour-in foam

resin putty for
large fillets

woven cloth glassed
in place fastens member

advised that it is more expensive than polyester. When trying techniques new to you, take the time to familiarize yourself with the process and material's characteristics before you spread the goop or pour the foam over the final project.

Here are some notes on the characteristics of the stuff we're talking about.

The resins are more-or-less viscous liquid systems, which, when properly mixed, cure without the use of a heat source (unless one is in a big hurry or the weather is very cold). There are special instructions covering this situation. On the contrary, the curing reaction is *exothermic*—it generates heat.

Work at an ambient temperature, somewhere around 70° Fahrenheit, and don't make big, thick objects, because if the stuff is too thick, the heat can't get out fast enough. This leads to all kinds of embarrassing consequences, such as masses of unrecognizable junk instead of the neat project that you expected.

All of the resins used in the composite construction nowadays are two-part systems. Depending on which base resin is used, the second component may be either a catalyst, which doesn't form part of the final product, or a hardener, which does.

- Epoxy resin: If combined with a fast hardener, epoxy requires 12 minutes to cure at 70° Fahrenheit; a slow hardener will require 30 minutes to cure at the same temperature. Epoxy provides superior adhesion.

- Polyester resin: The cure time for polyester varies from 5 minutes to 1 hour. A favored catalyst when working with polyester is methyl ethyl ketone peroxide. Alternatively, you can add an accelerator directly to the resin before application. Polyester does not adhere as well as epoxy, and it will ignite at a lower temperature. (See the material safety data sheet for information on the flash point.)

Acetone or methyl ethyl ketone are effective solvents to use when applying resin.

The starting materials for the polyester series are not usually composed of straight ester. They nearly always contain a certain amount of styrene, too, to yield certain properties. Since the esters are fairly viscous, while the styrene runs like water, it is possible to get mixes with a variety of viscosities to start with.

While you can control the time and completeness of cure to some extent by varying the amount of hardener or catalyst added, don't stray too far from the manufacturer's straight and narrow, or you may be greatly disappointed in the result.

Thickener may be added to any of these resins to increase the viscosity and improve some of the physical properties, such as retention of shape after application. Typical thickeners are milled (very short) glass fibers used for preparing a putty, and glass microballoons to add volume, viscosity, and minimum weight. The putty is commercially available. The glass is chemically treated for use with these resins; it's usually called *chromed* glass.

Fiberglass is available in various forms:

- Cloth: Woven cloth in various widths and lengths and weaves.

- Roving: Long strands of fibers, loosely twisted.

- Mat: Randomly oriented short strands.

- Tape: Narrow strips of woven cloth with selvage.

- Chopped or milled: Machine-chopped strands, often added for local reinforcement, as in fillets.

In the construction of relatively thick structures, fiberglass skins over lightweight cores are the preferred combination wherever possible. The reasons are straightforward: The structure is nearly as strong as solid fiberglass would be, and very much lighter. In addition, a thermally insulating core will yield a thermally insulating sheet of almost any desired shape, so that it becomes very easy to construct a refrigerator or cooler, or even a deck or bulkhead. Most such structures don't transmit sound very well, either. Popular core materials include polyurethane foam sheet (not polystyrene!), which is solid, and two-component, pour-in-place liquid foams.

These are the lightest, used for flotation and insulation. Fiberglass-over-plywood is more often—but not always—used for primary construction. It's a little outside our scope here. Much the same applies to balsa-core, which has long been popular for decks and to some extent for hulls.

There are lots and lots of ramifications of fiberglass techniques; refer to Allan Vaitses' book, mentioned above.

Meanwhile carry on with all that good woodwork.

4.

HOLDERS, CASES, AND SUPPORTS

Gimballed Glass Holders • **Cockpit Trays** • **Flashlight Holders**

Fire Extinguisher Holders • **Rod Holders** • **Boom Crutches and Gallows**

A boat needs holders and cases of all kinds—to hold drink glasses, conceal ugly items below decks, and to restrain spars in heavy weather.

This chapter introduces a new technique for the small items—laminated construction. The box-like cases for use below are different, too, with windows or tambour closures. The heavy-duty, on-deck items, while not very complex in design, allow free-form shapes to some extent, and, primarily, strong construction for use in almost any weather.

GIMBALLED GLASS HOLDERS

As practical as gimballed glass holders are in terms of convenience, safety, and prevention of spillage, current designs leave something to be desired. Still, going without holders means that three-quarters of a nice cold drink will go over the side someday or, worse yet, spill onto your cockpit cushions.

If you don't want to buy those little ship's-wheel coasters, take some time to make gimballed ones as described below.

Thin strips of wood (*veneers*) laminated with a resin—polyester or epoxy—can be formed into a variety of shapes. The convenience of forming to shape and the slight flexibility of the laminate lend themselves very well to designing and constructing the rings and yokes required for drink holders. The material's nearest relative is the plywood sheet, and it's not a very close relative at that. Two types of drink holders are shown in Figure 4-1, both using the same lay-up process.

The design shown in Figure 4-1a is intended to combat heavy pitch and roll. It consists of a ring and two yokes. The ring and inner yoke are glued together and hung from a pair of pins that swing in the outer yoke. The outer yoke is attached to another pin that rotates in a bearing block and is captured at the end with a plate, preventing the pin from slipping out. The bottom of the block carries a dowel that is inserted into a mating hole in a bracket for use, and removed for stowage. The bracket itself is permanently fastened to a bulkhead.

A second, two-piece design is for lighter conditions and has less gimbal action. This version has a bearing plate, built up on the ring, formed and grooved to fit into a mating bracket. These will stow neatly in a row (Figure 4-1b).

The dimensions of the holders will be based on your serving standards. Design the holders to fit loosely around a naked can, a sleeved can, glassware, or whatever your galley provides.

Teak, oak, alder, mahogany, or whatever matches or complements your yacht's appearance can all be resawn into strips of a thickness suitable for lamination. Using a 1/16-inch-thick strip, a 4-ply laminate would be ¼ inch plus thick. Given the added strength of laminates—due to the grain direction—this should be adequate for the biggest drinks.

Both types are built up on molds, for yokes and rings. The height of each mold will depend on whether you want to lay up the rings one at a time, or to laminate blanks that can be cut apart into a number of pieces. The throat dimension of your bandsaw and the hardness of the wood may dictate how many multiples you can cut and clamp.

The ring may be formed around a large dowel or turned spindle, coated with a releasing agent containing wax. (carnauba wax is fairly common and works well.) Dry-fit the first two laminates for butt joints; thoroughly impregnate the wood with resin; and wrap the strips around the spindle, holding it in place with a sheet of thin tin or aluminum—also coated with a releasing agent—that will bend to conform to the curvature of the circumference. Clamp with even pressure around the wrapped assembly using bungee cord, rubber tubing, or strips cut from a bicycle inner tube.

Repeat the process for the remaining layers, omitting the releasing agent on the inside so that all of them will stick together. Stagger the joints so that they will not fall on top of one another. Once the blank has been formed and cured, clean off the residual agent from the inside and outside surfaces and coat with more resin. Postpone this last step if you are cutting multiple parts from along blank layup, so that the edges too can be treated with another coat of resin.

Follow a similar procedure to form the yoke. In this case you would mount a male or inside mold on a base block and clamp the laid-up strips to it with three pads, as shown in Photo 4-1. The combination of inside male block and outside pads essentially constitutes a pair of inside/outside molds that forms the shape you want, regardless of small variations in the thickness of the work. Then trim, drill, and edge-finish each piece. Not much need be said about drilling, except that you should measure carefully and be sure to drill straight across the diameter of the ring, so that the pivot pins will be in line and square to the surface.

There is some spring to the yokes, so they can be fitted over the pins. For a more natural finish, don't float resin over the surfaces but sand and varnish as with any wood. Don't get varnish on the surfaces of the pins and bearings!

The lighter-duty holder (Figure 4-1b) is made in much the same way: The nonlaminated structure, the thwartship swinging block, and the mounting assembly are fairly conventional.

If you need a wedge to give you a truly vertical mounting bracket, be sure to make it to the exact angle of the bulkhead. Otherwise, you might not get that swing!

COCKPIT TRAYS

A more formal array of drinks can congregate with the drinkers around the wheelhouse, bait tank, binnacle, or mizzen mast. Our project here is a cockpit-center drink holder that can be mounted on protective bars or grab bars for convenience. However, legislation is afoot in many states to keep alcoholic beverages out of reach of the helm station. Be familiar with regulations on your local waters, and steer clear! Happily, legis-

Figure 4-1. *Two basic designs for gimballed glass holders. (a) Fully gimballed for pitch and roll, this holder has a simple dowel suspension. (b) Semi-gimballed holders won't rotate as freely, but they are adequate for most outings.*

a

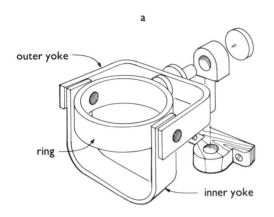

outer yoke

ring

inner yoke

b

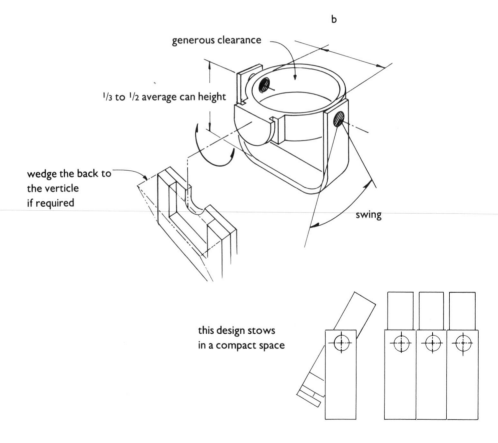

generous clearance

1/3 to 1/2 average can height

wedge the back to the verticle if required

swing

this design stows in a compact space

Photo 4-1. *Laminating the veneers. The process is explained on page 59.*

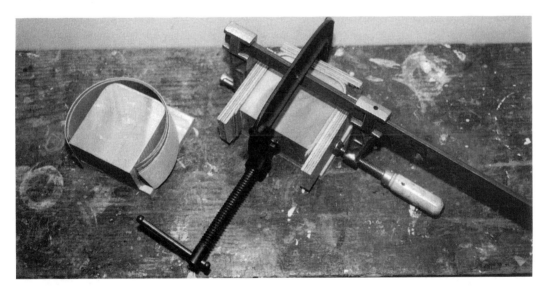

lators are not yet prohibiting imbibing sodas, so . . . "This Offer is Limited to Use With Non-alcoholic Beverages." So to speak.

Strive toward sturdiness, since the cockpit experiences the heaviest traffic and responses may be quicker than normal in times of adventure. You don't want to worry about breaking this accessory!

The design shown in Figure 4-2, developed for a dockmate's Bristol sloop, had a relatively small envelope to work in, so it consisted of a simple two-drink holder. Slots were cut in the upper and lower plates to fit the 1-inch stainless grab bar, with the legs spread at a 10° angle. (Note that the ends of the slots are at the same angle to give a neat fit.) Thus the holder could be slipped over the bar, where it would slide down, staying put at the desired height.

Holders may be split and reattached around a convenient support. A two-piece wooden clamp with one-half attached to the tray and its mate bolted into it, holding it to the bars, also would do the trick (Figure 4-3).

If the bar has an odd diameter, or if you want to make a slightly undersize hole for a better grip, consider grinding an old spade drill to the proper width to make a hole of the desired diameter. (If the bar diameter is even, for example 1-inch or 1⅛-inch, and you have a Forstner bit of that size, it makes an ideal way to cut the holes at the desired angles with no danger of having the bit walk away from its intended path.) The diameter of the bar, its angle of divergence, and the distance down the legs, all figure into the designed position of the clamp.

Remember to design your cutouts to fit your habits, whether you serve beverages in unsleeved aluminum cans, jacketed cans, cups, or glasses. A slight clearance diameter, and perhaps a slot to house a cup handle, ought to do. The lower rest, or stop, may be suspended on blocks—square, rectangular, or sculpted—to form smooth transitions. All corners should be chamfered or well rounded. A fiddle will add a finishing touch to the project, especially if the core wood is ply veneer.

FLASHLIGHT HOLDERS

Homes for flashlights (torches, if you prefer) and auxiliary or emergency lights (independent of the boat's battery or generator) can be made by placing a few flashlight holders at strategic locations about the cabin, engine compartment, etc. Individual flashlights can be fetched when needed, or turned on in place for illumination.

A holder (Figure 4-4a) might consist of top and bottom lugs spaced by a single backing piece or by two vertical members that straddle the flashlight. The height of the holder is a matter of choice, depending on the size of the flashlight. Lugs can be closer together to accommodate only the barrel, or spaced apart to take the full length of the flashlight including the head. The bottom should have a shallow hole, counterbored to take the barrel. This will keep the end of the flashlight from whipping around.

If this is a utilitarian project only, the design is complete at this stage. If you want to sheathe the assembly for a more finished look, add a tambour (Figure 4-4b) to cover the lugs and flashlight. If you elect to add a cover, bore a finger hole through the bottom to help you remove the flashlight. The tambour, movable when used for rolltop desks and some sliding doors, can also be made as a fixed feature, conforming to a variety of arcs and planes.

To make our fixed tambour, rip narrow strips to make slats of the selected wood (teak or mahogany is suggested), bevel both outside edges of the slats, and cement to a piece of duck or other heavy fabric. The width of the slat will determine the radius it can follow. Rounded corners on an otherwise rectangular shape, as in the drawing, may call for narrower strips than would be required to conform to a full-radius cover.

The drawing shows two alternative ways of capping the ends of the fixed tambour. Either its thickness (slats plus duck) can be let in around the top and bottom lugs, or the ends of the lugs may be covered by means of glued-on, oversize caps. This calls for less effort but gives comparable results.

FIRE EXTINGUISHER HOLDERS

Here is a box that is not a box, but a holder. (Trust me on this!) Fire extinguishers are a must, but they needn't be eyesores. A case with an acrylic cover can be most accessible yet unobtrusive in otherwise pleasant surroundings. Be sure crew and guests know what's inside—use a transparent, colorless, or tinted cover. If you use solid wood or other opaque material, advertise the contents with silkscreen lettering or vinyl letters.

The holder can include a ring, located about one-third of the distance up from the bottom, to restrain the bottle—as shown in Figure 4-5—or the hanger that came with the extinguisher might be fastened inside. One benefit of the commercial hanger is that it allows you to place a top over the holder. Otherwise, the case top should be left open, or built with the top and face as one unit.

Keep everything loose in this assembly—plenty of clearance for the acrylic cover, good clearance between the holder and the extinguisher itself, and so on. If you ever need that extinguisher, the last thing you want is a struggle to remove it from its case.

Although Halon extinguishers *must* be stored vertically, dry chemical extinguishers may be laid horizontally. This position is not the preferred one, but it may be necessary if one wants to tuck the extinguisher away under a shelf or companionway ladder, where there is little vertical clearance. A horizontal rack is also shown in Figure 4-5.

Some of the active chemical powder may remain caked on the low side of the cylinder, and the propellant will not be able to deliver all of it. Thus a horizontally stored cylinder should be checked monthly for adequate pressure, and it should be tapped smartly with the heel of the hand on bottom and side to loosen any caked material. (This suggestion is courtesy of a Coast Guard Auxiliary inspector.)

Figure 4-2. *A simple two-hole holder that fits over the splayed legs of a protective rail.*

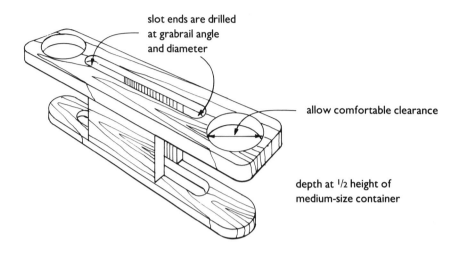

slot ends are drilled
at grabrail angle
and diameter

allow comfortable clearance

depth at ¹/₂ height of
medium-size container

the design for this drink rack is
fairly confining—wheel/binnacle post
abaft, mainsheet tack forward

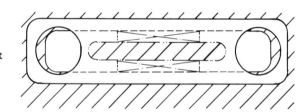

with a 10° splay on the bar,
two horizontal members with slot
widths to match design height
will hold tray in place

10°

Cockpit trays need to be sturdy since the cockpit is a high-traffic area. Be sure to size the cutouts fit your galley habits—cans, jacketed cans, glasses, or cups.

Figure 4-3. *A clamp-on drink holder that fits splayed legs. Design the shape to attach to anything within reach of guests or crew.*

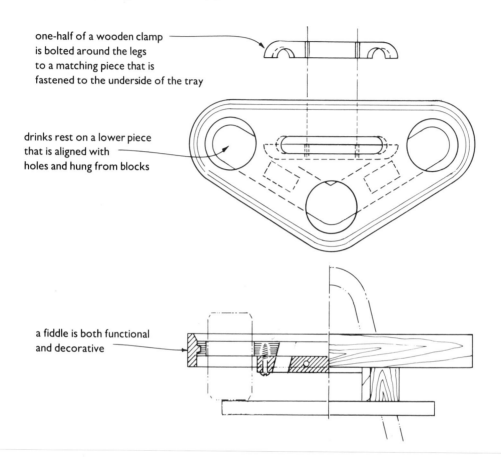

one-half of a wooden clamp
is bolted around the legs
to a matching piece that is
fastened to the underside of the tray

drinks rest on a lower piece
that is aligned with
holes and hung from blocks

a fiddle is both functional
and decorative

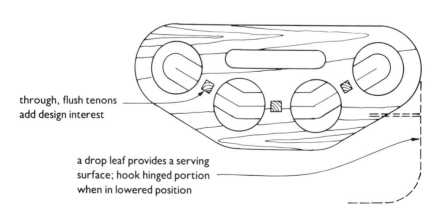

through, flush tenons
add design interest

a drop leaf provides a serving
surface; hook hinged portion
when in lowered position

Figure 4-4. *A simple flashlight holder (a) and a more elaborate one (b) with a tambour cover. The basic structures are the same.*

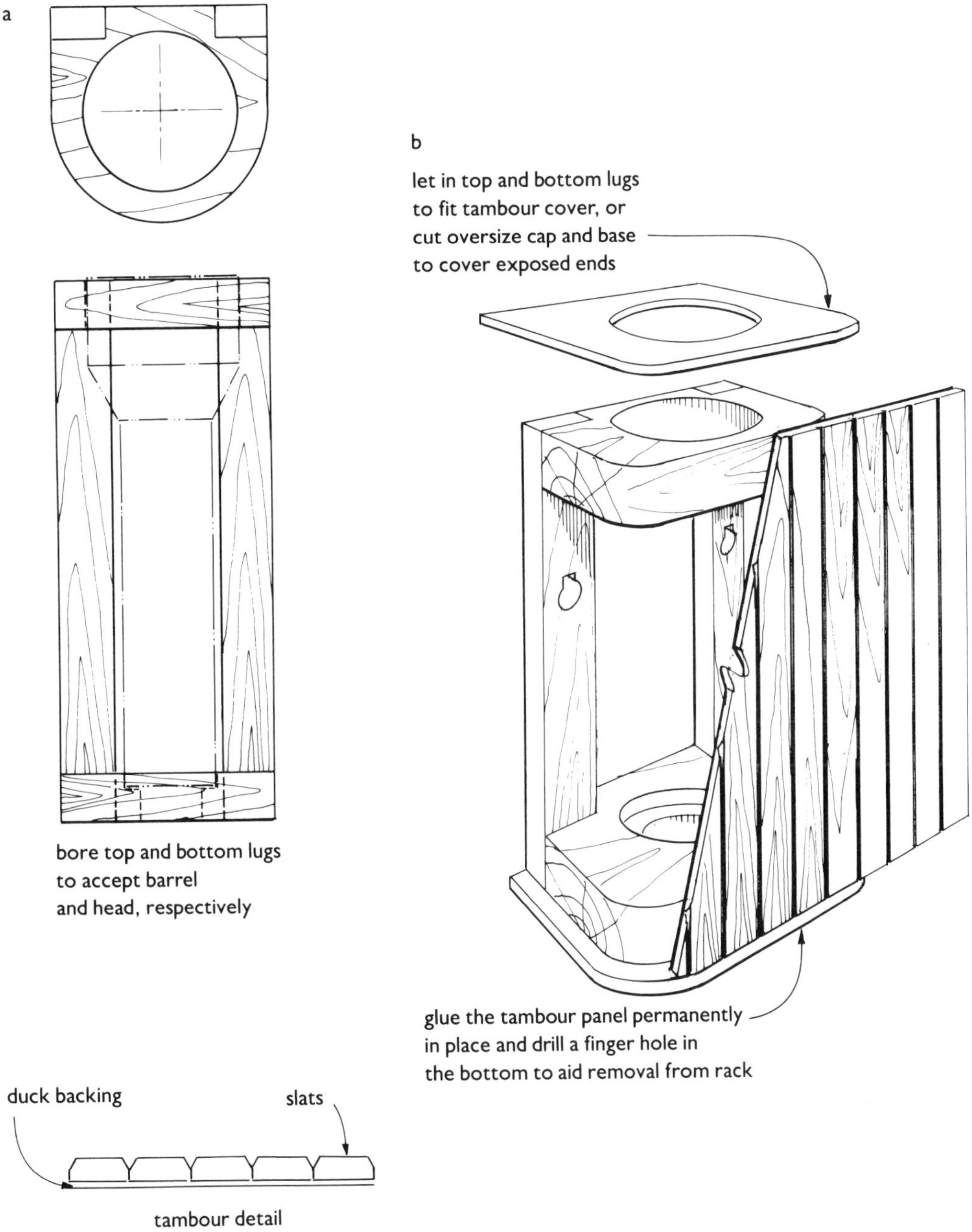

a

b

let in top and bottom lugs
to fit tambour cover, or
cut oversize cap and base
to cover exposed ends

bore top and bottom lugs
to accept barrel
and head, respectively

glue the tambour panel permanently
in place and drill a finger hole in
the bottom to aid removal from rack

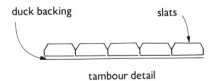

duck backing   slats

tambour detail

Figure 4-5. *A case and a rack for a fire extinguisher. Solid chemical types may be stowed horizontally or vertically. Construct a case that complements the design of the cabin area, yet allows access.*

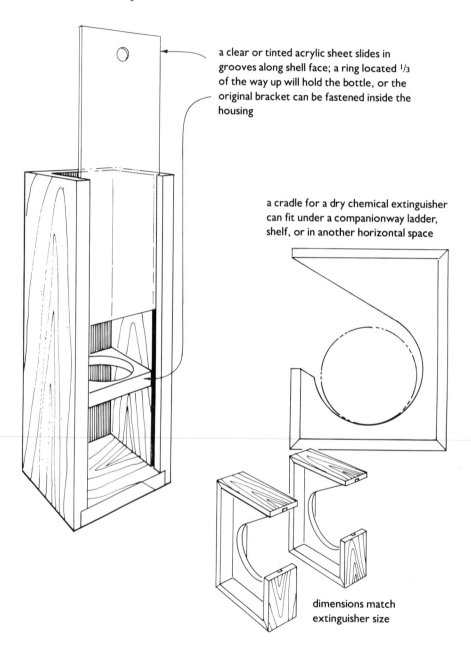

a clear or tinted acrylic sheet slides in grooves along shell face; a ring located $1/3$ of the way up will hold the bottle, or the original bracket can be fastened inside the housing

a cradle for a dry chemical extinguisher can fit under a companionway ladder, shelf, or in another horizontal space

dimensions match extinguisher size

Rod Holders

This project falls into the "build a better mousetrap/beat a path" category. It's hard to improve on the universally accepted design. If the standard pattern is to your liking, but you would rather build than buy, I suggest some R & C (research and copy) activity. Otherwise, here are a few alternative designs, suited to the one-, two-, or four-pole enthusiasts.

The design is a variation on the commercial version—same concept, different pattern—for a departure from the mail-order look. The pattern (Figure 4-6a) can be drawn on two boards, each of which is then cut individually, or it may be lofted on a board of double thickness, then resawn down to the finished thickness. The sawn, opposing pieces are flipped end for end so that the centerlines of the cutouts for the whips and handles are aligned.

The wood grain should be random for greatest strength. Vertical grain can split if weakness occurs across the narrow portion of the supporting hook. All corners may be bullnosed for a sculptured look, but they should be least rounded or chamfered. Cut crossmember pieces from the same stock, dado slots to accept the supports, glue and screw the latter to the crossmembers, and mount the assembled T-shape to the overhead.

If only the skipper likes to wet a line on occasion, a single pole can be hung from either two "Js" aligned overhead or under a shelf, or from a hole and a "J" as shown in Figure 4-6b. A pair of poles can hang from the same internal pattern, cut at the ends of wider stock, with enough clearance space allowed between the reel and the adjacent whip.

Boom Crutches and Gallows

Powerboaters, take a break! Without a boom to hold down or worry about, you scarcely need the following discussion—unless we can entice you over to the rag side of the sport.

There are occasions on sailing vessels when the boom gets in the way, but in today's high-aspect-ratio rigs, the boom is usually goose-necked well up the mast, which may make this discussion as irrelevant for high performers as it is for powerboaters. Still, there are many boats whose booms are rather lower down, in the more-or-less old-fashioned way, and for these, as for the long-distance or offshore cruiser, crutches and gallows may become very relevant indeed.

Heavy-weather considerations aside, if a sailor spends much time at anchor enjoying the surroundings, one worthwhile convenience may be a boom crutch or gallows where the boom rests firmly out of harm's way (or if Harm is not on board, at least away from the center of the cockpit and the heads in it). Such additions also reduce depen-

Figure 4-6. *Single- and multiple-rod holders. (a) Note how space is saved by alternating whip ends and handle ends. The diameter of the largest pole handle determines the dimensions; align heel and whip on centerline. Allow clearance to suit pole with reel, if necessary.*

a

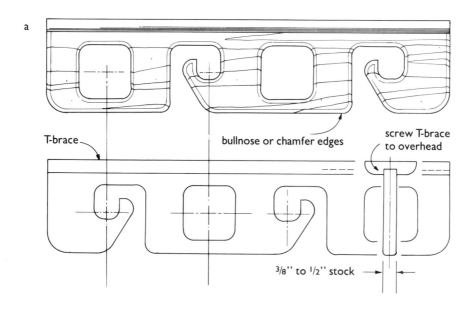

T-brace

bullnose or chamfer edges

screw T-brace to overhead

3/8'' to 1/2'' stock

b

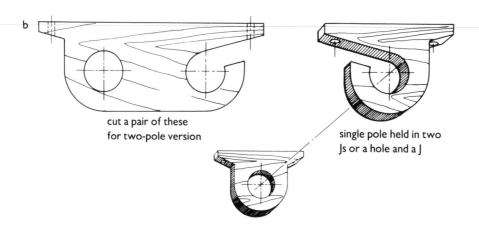

cut a pair of these
for two-pole version

single pole held in two
Js or a hole and a J

Figure 4-7. *A boom crutch (a) ready for shaping and details of a gallows (b). Both projects will look best if highly sculpted. Avoid square forms.*

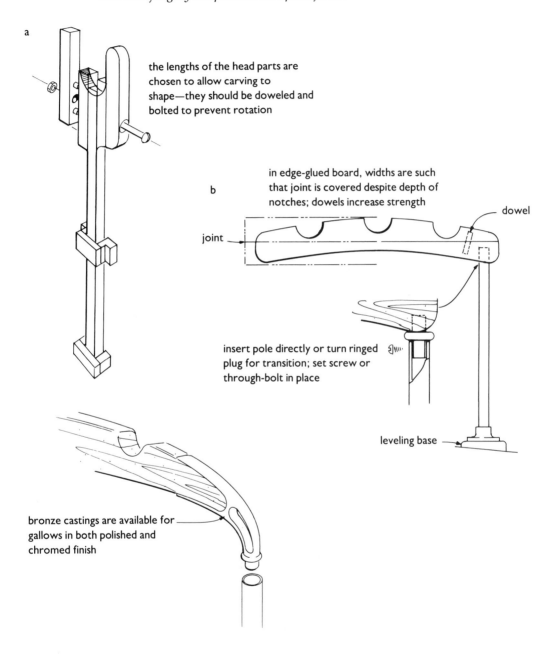

a

the lengths of the head parts are chosen to allow carving to shape—they should be doweled and bolted to prevent rotation

b

in edge-glued board, widths are such that joint is covered despite depth of notches; dowels increase strength

dowel

joint

insert pole directly or turn ringed plug for transition; set screw or through-bolt in place

leveling base

bronze castings are available for gallows in both polished and chromed finish

dence on a topping lift, and/or pigtail, to hold the boom at a safe, convenient height when not in use.

A crutch can be simple, but, rigidly braced against a bulkhead, it must be sturdy enough to hold the weight of the boom and sail despite the roll of the boat. When designing the length and placement of the crutch, consider its stowage too. A fork made from edge-glued boards can be formed into a pleasing crutch shape. To ensure strength, the glued-up pieces should be doweled or mortised, then through-bolted to withstand side loads. Bolt heads and their opposing nuts and washers are countersunk and bunged prior to forming (Figure 4-7a) the curves.

A router and/or rasps, or possibly a Surform (R Stanley Tool Company) can make quick work of transforming sharp corners and edges into sculptured shapes.

If you want more options on where to place the boom at rest, a gallows arrangement might better suit your needs. The gallows provides various positions for the boom to sit in—to say nothing of looking very salty on the right boat! They're the ultimate in strength at sea, too.

Gallows present a sizable project. You could get bronze fittings from such sources as Bronze Star, San Diego, or you could fabricate all of the pieces to form the finished gallows.

The curvature of the gallows may require that two or more boards be fastened on edge, making one wide board from which to cut the arc. When selecting board widths, the upper board should be wide enough so that the notches don't extend into the joint. This protects the joint from the weather, since it is buried all along its length. Not mandatory, but preferred.

Gallows have to be strong; you may have to think of 1-inch wood—5/4-inch dressed down.

Stock can be assembled using drift pins (treenails, or *trunnels*, may be better since their ends may be formed to the contour) wood screws, lag screws, or bolts, depending on the project.

Supporting stanchions made of bronze or of stainless steel pipe can be secured in threaded flanges attached to bases, shaped to compensate for the crown of the deck. Obvious observation: The height of the gallows on the stanchions must be low enough to clear the swinging boom when the mainsail is hoisted! At their upper ends, the stanchions may be inserted into corresponding holes, drilled in the underside of the gallows beam (Figure 4-7b), or attached by an auxiliary plug—one end of which is designed to fit inside the pipe, so as to provide a dowel between the pipe and the cross piece, and the other, smaller end glued into the underside of the wood. Perhaps this latter method is more suited to use with a thicker beam, because you can insert a thicker dowel.

One enjoyable feature of this project is the amount of free forming required. No sharp edges, anywhere. Also, the offcenter notches for the boom must accept it at an angle to the centerline, whether it rests in the port or starboard notch. This consideration also applies to a boom crutch situated offcenter. So you can have the fun of hand-working the notches to fit.

5.

RAILS AND POSTS

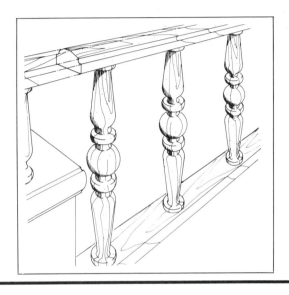

Grabrails • **Driprails** • **Fiddlerails and Posts**

• **Large Posts**

GRABRAILS

Grabrails seem to exist only to be sanded and varnished, or masked for painting—right up to their little stanchions. But they stand ready while you, or your crew, navigate a pitching deck.

Nicely formed rails add an attractive element to a coach roof, cabin trunk, and to the space below decks as well—along the overhead of a beamy cabin. What makes them attractive, not withstanding their basic design, is the care taken in forming the rails and the risers or stanchions. They should appear sturdy but graceful. With a little coaxing, straight grabrails will bend to conform to a gentle curve on the side of the cabin.

Traditional rails are sculptured, whereas contemporary grabrails are more angular. In either case they must be nicely shaped and neatly rounded. Both varieties must possess similar practical attributes: 1) comfortable grip diameter, 2) adequate clearance from the deck, and 3) a sufficient number of stanchions—attachment points—for rigidity and, above all, for safety. Their length and placement should complement your craft's overall design. Figure 5-1 illustrates some of the different designs and shows how the edges are rounded over.

Interior and exterior rails aren't all that different in design and construction, so we'll tackle them more or less together, recognizing that there are any number of sizes and locations where rails are needed—and look good too.

Design and Construction

Overall placement of the rails, especially their attachment points, must take into account the configuration of the accomodations below decks. Space the stanchions equally over the length while avoiding deck beams, bulkheads, and cabinets. Such interferences could have quite an effect on both the pattern and the method of attachment.

Openings between the stanchions allow water to run off. If you get a little fancy with exterior rails and incorporate a run of solid material along the deck, remember to cut a few drain holes.

Most grabrails are made of teak or mahogany and are cut out and finished with much the same tools as are many of the preceding projects, so we won't go into that again. I'm sure it would be safe to say that you are used to measuring and measuring tools, so we won't go into that again, either, except to emphasize the need for accuracy when you're fitting exterior and interior rails with a coach roof in between.

Below decks, one might use white oak or perhaps maple or other light, dense wood, but teak is still the favorite.

The fasteners you'll use for this project are stainless steel or bronze bolts and wood screws, and finishing washers. Attaching rails to and/or through the coach roof calls for a few remarks—it's a little different from ordinary woodwork.

Attachment

My preferred method of attaching a grabrail is to set 3-inch, #10 stainless steel or bronze screws from the inside up, and well into the stanchions, as in Figure 5-1a. These screws should be oval-head, slotted, or Phillips, with a finishing washer. Screws or through-bolts inserted from the top require that the holes be countersunk and bunged, which isn't all bad, but future problems can be prevented by going in from the bottom. Also, it's unlikely that there will be enough solid strength in the cabin top (even using a substantial backing plate) to hold the rail firmly when attached top-down.

Some schools suggest using a through-bolt at each end for a measure of safety, which seems like a very good idea. Whatever the shape and size of your rail, and however you fasten it down, be sure to bed it in well—a leak at a rail is a great nuisance to repair.

Figure 5-1. *Details of grabrail design and construction. Traditional and modern designs differ mainly in the way they are sculpted.*

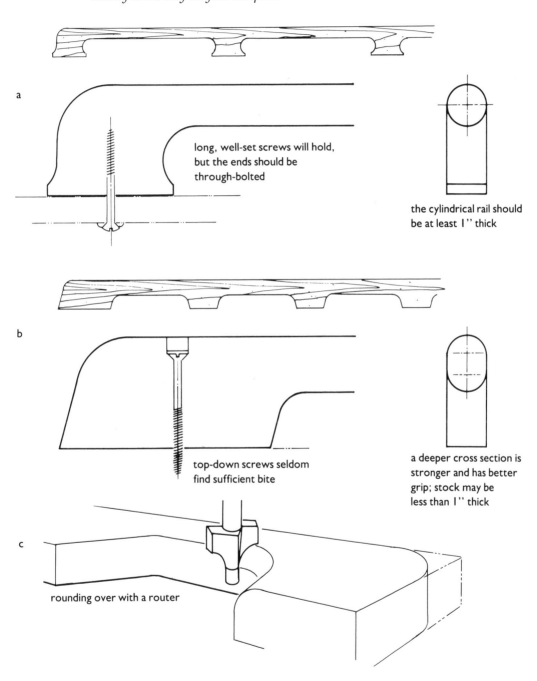

a

long, well-set screws will hold, but the ends should be through-bolted

the cylindrical rail should be at least 1" thick

b

top-down screws seldom find sufficient bite

a deeper cross section is stronger and has better grip; stock may be less than 1" thick

c

rounding over with a router

If your plans include backing the external grabrail with an internal handrail, a common through-bolt or long screw through the interior rail into the topside rail makes a cleaner installation than using backing plates, which are simply ugly and show on the overhead below decks. Without the backing plates, you see only the attractively finished and useful overhead rail.

Interior Rails

Overhead grabrails may be very desirable in larger cabins on vessels—especially beamy ones—that see more than the peaceful Sunday-afternoon excursion.

A matching set of inside handrails can be cut from a wide board. Make symmetrical cutouts, then rip down the center to form the pair, as in Figure 5-2. In fact, this is a logical way to make any matched pair of rails.

If there are to be no rails below, and you must use backing plates for the rails on the coach roof, here's a way to prevent having to replace something ugly on your nice, lined overhead.

Drop the liner temporarily rather than run your fasteners through it. If possible, use an unobtrusive backing plate under the coach roof, fasten the rail, and then replace the liner. Or you can glass in a backing plate, replace the liner, and then fasten the rail with screws and nicely finished wooden washers, or an ornamental batten matching the length of the outside rail.

A steep companionway leading to the main cabin may require siderails and/or some kind of athwartship rail or handle. It might be mounted on the sliding companionway cover or on a handy beam (Figure 5-2).

Short rails can serve many purposes. For example, a grip between windows can double as a center bracket for curtain rods. These smaller units can be more decorative without being obtrusive. A good place to show your carving talent! Figure 5-2 shows a number of these short rails and special shapes.

Rails may be installed waist-high along passageways, and in the main cabin and stateroom(s), too, if offshore cruising is anticipated. Here is an application for the brass-and-wood combination (or brass only if you have a crew member who thrives on elbow grease and metal polish).

DRIPRAILS

The inside of the cabin trunk may get wet if a hatch or port is closed too slowly. "Sweat" on a foggy night, announcing its presence by dripping down someone's neck or onto a settee below decks, can also seep through hatches and portholes. A well-designed driprail melds with the surroundings while keeping bunks and settees dry. It earns its

Figure 5-2. *Long, matching rails may be cut from a single board. Interior rails may be installed overhead or along passageways, ladders, galley, and head.*

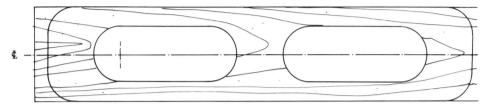

matching rails may be cut from a single
board, edges rounded, then ripped down

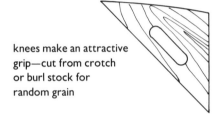

knees make an attractive
grip—cut from crotch
or burl stock for
random grain

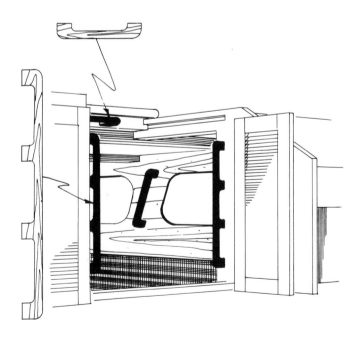

keep best in the vicinity of hatches or portholes. At the same time, it makes a pleasant cabin trim.

Driprails are good milling projects—their design includes a trough to catch water just where the cabin trunk meets the deck, and the outer edge should be nicely shaped as well. Driprails are very often made from hardwood dowels, such as closet-rod stock. Figure 5-3 illustrates some milling techniques and shows some of the potential applications of driprails, with their odd profiles.

The trough may be finished flat or coved, but nothing fancy that would trap moisture and cause future problems. If the driprails are large, finish the inside troughs so that they provide comfortable handholds; be assured they will be used that way—it's second nature.

At the transition of deck to cabin trunk, determine the cross section that will best fit your design and installation. This could include, for example, a lip molding under the deck (Figure 5-3c), or a nicely formed extension inboard, milled with a trough to catch the drips.

The rail must bend with the curve of the sides, so thickness enters into your design considerations. The more severe the bend, the thinner the rail must be. Terminate rails where collected water can escape, directing the flow toward the bilge. A driprail is not a downspout to handle the runoff from a whole roof, so a major diversion is not required. Do ensure that the point of exit is in a spot where the drip will cause the least discomfort if the area beneath it gets a little damp.

A wide trough is easiest to keep clean. If possible, round the bottom of the trough to keep moisture away from the joint along the cabin sides. However, a square trough is better than a reversing pattern that would invite water into the joint; bedding compound will keep water out of it.

The rail design could be continued athwartship, tying in with the design of the sides. If this is an area that doesn't get wet, it might harbor a handy bookshelf. Whatever you use the shelf for, duplicate the driprail profile along its face.

Two approaches to milling round or half-round doweling into a driprail are shown in Figures 5-3a and 5-3b. Commercial molding can be adapted to this application as well, or you can break out the shaper heads to produce a cross section of your own that will suit the boat's interior.

FIDDLERAILS AND POSTS

A fiddle, by definition, can be any slat, board, or light railing used to keep plates on a table or items on a shelf. The addition of solid fiddles needs little discussion, except to say that the edges should be nicely finished and the corners left open for for easy cleaning.

Figure 5-3. *Fashioning a driprail from closet rod or large dowel stock. Hardwood and softwood call for different methods. Sometimes commercial moldings are available, or one can start with square stock.*

The dado method for hardwood.

a

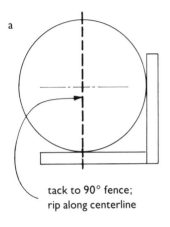

tack to 90° fence;
rip along centerline

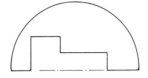

on the flat, dado
a rabbet for a shelf
corner and a deeper
cut for a trough

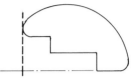

use an auxiliary slat
to keep the
half-round level
and remove the
support tab

The kerf method for softwood.

b

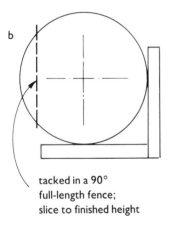

tacked in a 90°
full-length fence;
slice to finished height

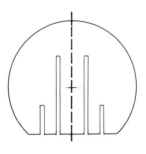

on the flat, kerf
to design depths;
rip along centerline

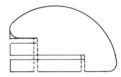

kerf to meet earlier cuts;
use an auxiliary support
to level for cutting

radius upper and lower
edges; install along
deck shelf

bedding compound

c

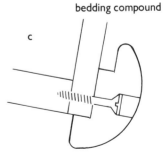

A railing, by definition, consists of a horizontal member supported by a series of uprights or posts, commonly in the form of spindles or turnings. Clearly, there's much more to the design and construction of railings than to that of fiddles. Not all boat interiors will be enhanced by the addition of spindles, but many will. Even the ultra-contemporary designs—the Spartan go-fasts—have niches or spaces that would be improved by spindle rails. A library shelf is a prime candidate for this addition. The appearance of the surroundings might be improved by continuing a light railing, which would retain items stowed nearby, to various levels and components (see Figure 5-4).

Before we begin to construct some railings, take note that almost any wood-turning lathe will serve for making short spindles—even quite small "hobby" types.

Spacing spindles properly is the key to designing railings. Too many or too few spindles drastically affects the look. Sketch the area to get a general idea of the spacing and thus how many spindles you will need. For best appearance or symmetrical spacing, you can always add or remove spindles when you're ready to assemble.

A continuous railing offers opportunities to turn corners, vary heights, and tie areas together, applying good, imaginative design and craftsmanship. To change the height of a railing, you can use only the lower portion of a symmetrical turning, thus continuing the railing on a different level.

Just a few thoughts on design. A one-of-a-kind spindle can be ultra-ornate, but a set of spindles should be appropriate for the adjacent design, and, ideally, they should be easy to reproduce. If multiple spindles are required, shy away from tricky, fluted shapes. Straight tapers will be just fine, thank you, and much easier to duplicate.

Spheres and ellipses should be turned to full form, and they should have a natural "sweep" to adjacent elements; the sweep is generally tangent to the arcs. Abrupt transitions should be kept overtly abrupt: A 90° cut to an adjacent diameter, or a 45° chamfer, looks good in turnings. Raised rings and grooves will add more old-world character to spindles if they complement the interior scheme.

Square ends provide a natural transition from spindle to rail. Shapes that are symmetrical above and below mid-height can be drafted on a folded piece of kraft paper, cut to shape, and opened to provide the duplicate half. The full design can then be transferred to a uniform batten, for example, which is then cut to make a working template, as in Figure 5-5. Once you've considered the area and designed the size and profile of the spindles, you can cut the templates and you're off and turning.

Before you start, outside calipers or micrometers are a must—preferably several, each one set to a particular control diameter. This will eliminate continual readjustments and reduce the potential for error.

Turn the square stock to a rough cylinder (Figure 5-5). For multiple turnings, rather than measure each piece, notch a spacing template for marking major control diameters. With a parting tool or skew, cut grooves to a diameter slightly larger than the desired dimension as set on the calipers. Turn as usual. As the form takes shape, keep all diame-

Figure 5-4. *Details of fiddlerail design.*

position spindles so that the spacing is agreeable;
a 2:1 ratio of space to solid wood is attractive

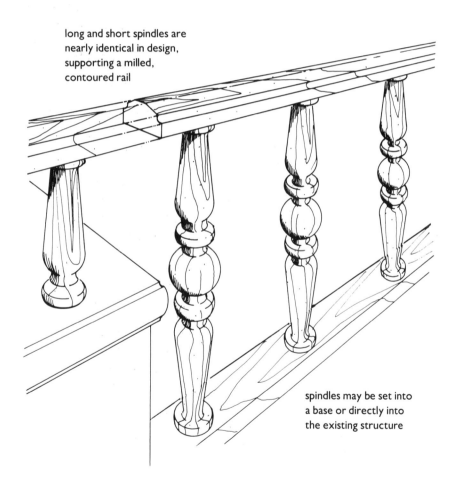

long and short spindles are
nearly identical in design,
supporting a milled,
contoured rail

spindles may be set into
a base or directly into
the existing structure

Figure 5-5. *Use templates and calipers to produce multiple spindles.*

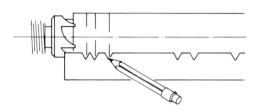

turn stock to a rough cylinder; using a
notched marking template, scribe positions
of key diameters

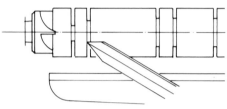

groove marks to rough depth with parting
tool and caliper

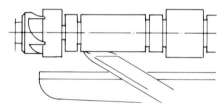

cut away to rough diameters using gouge
and skew

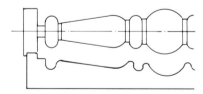

turn to final shape using template and
calipers; finish-sand and cut off

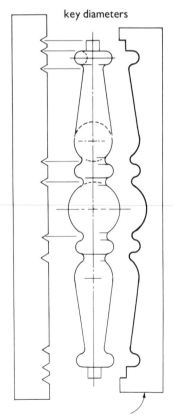

key diameters

full-length symmetrical template

ters slightly oversize. Your final cuts and sanding will bring the spindle to the profile. Finish-sand with 400-grit, reversing the turning direction if possible.

One's done—on to the next . . . and the next!

Large Posts

From the small spindles of a fiddlerail, we move up in size to rather larger turnings for the taffrail, and to long members used as cabin posts or as stanchions for fiferails.

A lesson I learned from the builder of California's flagship, *Californian*, is to prebore long stock that you plan to through-bolt in place after turning (to support a fife rail). Most craftsmen wouldn't approach a project the size of this 1846 revenue cutter, but the concept might fit a project of more moderate proportions.

In this method the critical step is done first. The rough stock is prebored, then squared parallel to and concentric with the centerline. The squared stock is mounted on the lathe and centered on the predrilled hole. This approach prevents completing a set of taffrail posts, only to have one or more ruined if the drill bit deviates offcenter.

Another approach to preboring, especially if long pieces are to be built up in thickness anyway, is to dado a slot along the centerline in each mating side before gluing them together, slot facing slot.

Cabin posts may or may not need this preboring technique, depending on their size and installation. Whatever their construction, they should not be skimpy. A post should be strong enough to handle its assignments, and should look the part. The design may incorporate traditional turned shapes, or, for a little variety, they may be faceted, fluted, or cut in a helical pattern. It is best to carry on the pattern of any existing functional or decorative balusters in the vicinity.

In Figure 5-6 there are some details on the design and turning of more ornate products—the limitations here are mainly those of your imagination and patience. A taffrail post (Figure 5-6a) has to be both longer and stronger than a fiddlerail below decks. Yet note how the design makes for agreeable proportions.

A truly elegant variation on the traditional cylindrical turning is shown in Figure 5-6b. Here we have two versions. The upper one has an octagonal section, with a transition to a circular ornament, and so on. Make this in two operations. First mill the work to the octagonal shape on a jointer, or cut it on a bandsaw or a table saw. Then center it in the lathe and turn the circular parts in the usual way.

The fluted version in Figure 5-6c is made with a router. Routing on the lathe calls for an accessory. The workpiece is centered in the lathe and indexed as desired for the number of flutes, either using the lathe's own index plate (if there is one) or the one on the accessory. Then, with the lathe idle and the workpiece firmly in place, the flutes are routed using a suitable veining bit.

Figure 5-6. *Some elegant spindle designs. (a) Taffrail posts are short and portly. (b) A post may combine cylindrical and angular elements. (c) A fluted version, made using a routing accessory with a lathe. (d) Laying out a helix (heavy line) on a rough-turned cylinder.*

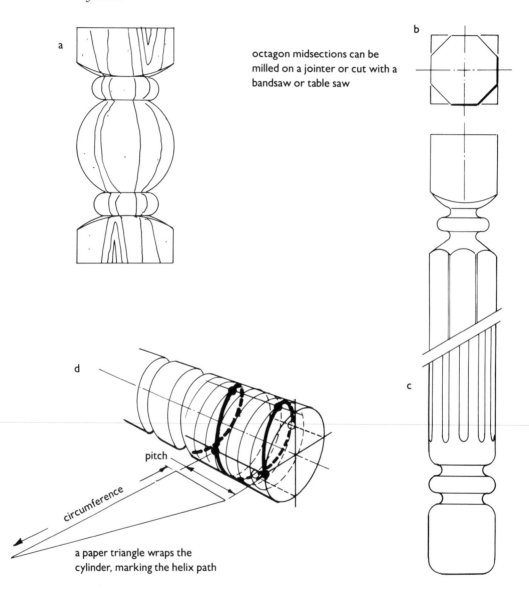

octagon midsections can be milled on a jointer or cut with a bandsaw or table saw

pitch

circumference

a paper triangle wraps the cylinder, marking the helix path

There are accessories available that will guide you in cutting a helix, but you can make a helical design by hand, using ordinary tools, as seen in Figure 5-6d.

Rough-turn the workpiece to a cylinder and square the ends. Mark off quadrants on an end, and at the ends of each of the diameters so made, pencil a line along the surface (see the figure; this takes almost less time to do than to describe). Lay off a distance equal to the desired pitch, along the length of one of these lines. Now make a paper pattern in the shape of a right triangle, with the base equal to the pitch and the height equal to the circumference of the cylinder. Mount the piece in the lathe, and, rotating it by hand, wrap the paper around the work with the base on the laid-off line. Trace along the edge, marking each spot where the hypotenuse crosses one line after the other. Move the paper along one pitch after each wrap. This lays out a continuous guide for a uniform helix of any length.

Now set an index pin, or otherwise secure the spindle, and start cutting the helix to a constant depth with a very sharp back saw. Follow with a rasp or files, or, if you are a good carver, with appropriate small gouges, and finish by sanding.

6.

GRATES AND SOLES

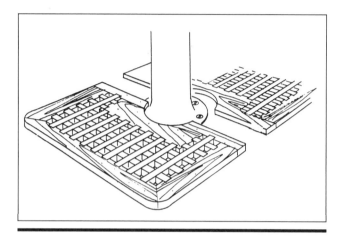

Rectangular Grates • **Triangular Grates and Grids**

Planks • **Cabin Soles and Hatches**

GRATES

Classic cockpit grates are composed of evenly spaced wooden stringers intersecting at cross-lap joints, mortised into a surrounding frame. They are practical, efficient, safe, and strong (sounds like a Scout Creed, doesn't it?), not to mention comfortable, attractive, and easy to maintain. Their design is an illustration of how form and function have been integrated and perpetuated by generations of yacht designers and builders.

Grates are for areas where feet tread; for example, in the cockpit wells of powerboats and sailboats, daysailers and long-distance cruisers. They're found in various locations aboard large vessels, too, but that's a little outside our scope. The grid arrangement provides firm footing, since it is raised above any minor layer of water taken aboard. For large expanses needing traction, ventilation, and water removal—such as decks and powerboat cockpits—grates may be integrated into the deck structure.

Most grates are rectangular, more or less, so we'll concentrate on grates of this shape. However, there are other shapes, notably triangular ones, and we'll deal with those, too. The joinery for both types is similar, so only the differences will be treated anew.

I'll also describe the design and construction of such less-common items as gridwork bowsprit planks, which have some special features of their own.

The design of a grate must be structurally sound; i.e., the spans between the supporting edges or frames must be able to meet the pressure of anticipated loads. One must strike a balance by selecting the optimum cross section and by spacing the stringers and the width of the frames properly. All of this depends on the material—the wood from which the grate is made.

Materials and Tools

The properties of wood vary greatly, and it is these unique properties that determine the selection of the best wood for a particular project.

The shock resistance of teak and other hardwoods is good, because these woods combine a relatively high degree of flexural strength with elasticity. Elasticity is important because it defines the ability of the wood to recover its original shape after being bent. Elastic woods will not sag as freely as others do.

In short, these dense woods have desirable deflection characteristics. We like teak for its natural oils and self-sealing properties, which give it outstanding weather resistance, but we also like it for its physical properties of hardness, shock resistance, and just the right amount of "give." Consequently, although other woods could be considered for the projects in this chapter, we will rely on teak.

All adhesives must be waterproof (as much as they can be—some are remarkably good, none are perfect). Among these, epoxy types are the best. Note the setting times before using them; there's a fairly broad range. And remember that where there are adhesives, there must be solvents for cleanup. Acetone, methyl ethyl ketone (MEK), and mineral spirits are the best known, but there are quite a few others. Make sure that you have the correct solvent for the particular adhesive you pick.

The screws we use are generally of stainless steel, but if you can get them, bronze (never brass!) screws actually will be more corrosion resistant. Stainless requires oxygen to remain stainless—it can't take on oxygen when buried in wood. Bronze doesn't seem to mind. Phillips heads are desirable because they auto-center the screwdriver and reduce the chance of its slipping out.

Each of the projects I will describe calls for tools generally found in every craftsman's shop—a table or radial-arm saw, fitted with dado blades (or a router), a smooth or jointer plane, or the mechanical equivalent such as a jointer, sanders, and the usual selection of hand tools for fine-tuning. Of course you'll also need good measuring tools and the patience to use them, because any error in measurement for repetitive structures will accumulate—with disastrous results.

RECTANGULAR GRATES

Design

Making strength a factor in the design of a cockpit grate is more forgiving than calculating the flexural strength of the wood used; nevertheless, we don't want the grate to give way under our guests' feet, nor may the spacing between planks be so big that their toes go right through! . . .

Weight placed on a horizontal member or beam will cause it to deflect or bend. The strength of a beam in a rectangular cross section (such as the stringer of a grate) varies directly with its width and the square of its depth, whereas its stiffness varies directly with its width and the cube of its depth. Therefore, it is advisable to make stringers thick as well as wide. The total load on the grate is distributed among multiple interlocking members of the lap-jointed structure, so scantlings need not be excessively massive. Yet using a fairly large cross section will prevent your having to rabbet every little joint in the grate's frame, where the let-in stringers support the full load. By increasing the scantlings, and therefore the strength of each stringer, you can alternate rabbet and dado joints (the latter being easier to make, but inherently weaker) in a frame that has to carry the full burden. Figure 6-1 is a close-up of these alternating rabbets and dado joints.

You would think twice about crossing a creek on a felled sapling but would trust a substantial log. The same principle is true here. Don't span an impossible distance with light scantlings.

Most woodworkers will estimate the required strength of scantlings and calculate on the high side, thereby exceeding load requirements. Design for the heaviest loading conditions, then double or even triple that factor. This doesn't mean that huge beams will be required, but thickness greater than that of standard milled lumber or braces and supports can strengthen the member to meet the ultimate loads. If the scantlings cannot be upsized, add supports below, or build up existing deck beams to meet and support the grate over an open span.

We can't expect to support four, 200-pound bodies on a 1-inch stringer, and it is a mathematical nightmare to calculate for the solids and holes in a grate, so I am bailing on this, offering instead some margin of safety over plywood strength, based on calculations from the American Plywood Association's *The WoodBook*. This data is presented as a curve in Figure 6-2.

If you make your spanning grate as strong as plywood, the graph indicates the recommended thickness for a plywood subfloor at various distances spanned. Increase the thickness for the desired factor of safety.

For safety's sake, three-quarter-inch square "S2S" teak stock (1-inch stock dressed) is the minimum you would want to use for stringers, considering both aesthetics and load. If you want the grate to bridge an engine well or other large openings, with no support in the center, you almost certainly will have to increase the dimensions of these scantlings, especially the thickness.

Lumber is commonly milled from 1-inch nominal stock to 3/4-inch finished or dressed thickness, so begin designing around this dimension. If 3/4-inch square stock is likely to be too scant for the span, find a yard that still believes in surfacing hardwood from rough 4/4-, 5/4-, 6/4-inch boards as they did in days of old, giving you dressed wood that is a full inch thick, or more. There must be adequate clearance around the frame for handling; sometimes this is achieved by making the grate in sections. Interestingly, this enhances the appearance, too.

Measure the area to determine its overall size, noting angles and installation clearances needed, then decide on the frame width and proportions of the interior gridwork.

To visualize the pattern, arrange a few scrap pieces cut square to the planned cross section. Select width and spacing that best match the proportions of the surrounding area. There's no law against expanding or compressing grid spacing; however, too little space between stringers might give the appearance of a pop-up waffle, and too much space can be a real toe-catcher. Spaces and stringers of equal widths seem to be most practical for function, construction, and appearance. Try to select boards of uniform or similar grain pattern, if you can. This also will enhance the appearance of the grate.

The frame of the grate will be wider than the stringers. To determine the width of the frame, a good rule would be to start with double the stringer width. The larger the overall area of the grate, the heftier the frame must be. A cockpit binnacle, wheel post, gear levers, or pump handles protruding through the grate will play a part in determining the grate's final width. A wide frame can be tapered on the outside to parallel the converging sides of a cockpit well, while leaving the central area rectangular. This simplifies the project. A good objective is to keep all intersecting pieces at right angles. Most of these points are illustrated in Figure 6-3.

Joinery

Where the grate rests on the cockpit sole, stringers may be mortised in shallow dadoes around the frame and glued. Or, if the frame is narrow, butt joints may be used—glued and screwed through the frame. However, if support is at the frame only (as in spanning a covered access to the bilge, engine, or cargo bay, for example), all of the stringers, or at least every other one, should be rabbeted well into the frame. Figure 6-1 is a close-up of the alternate rabbets and mortises. The number of rabbets is determined by the thickness and spacing of the stringers, and by the distance the load spans.

Stringers should be set into the frame by a distance equal to at least half the width of the stringers themselves, whether for mortising or rabbeting. The overall length of the stringers will be the same regardless of the type of joint you use.

Corner joinery should suit the appearance, structural requirements, and frame width of the grate. Corners may be lap-joined (*scarfed*), butt-joined with spline or dowel pins, or mitered with or without spline, or with mortise and tenon. Where thickness and width are moderate, a glued butt joint fastened with wood screws through the edge and into the ends of the frame pieces will be adequate. A pair of grates may flank a wheel pedestal, rudder stock, mizzen mast, or whatever is in the way, as shown in Figure 6-4. Rectangular grates used this way create an effective and attractive appearance.

If you are in the mood for a more complex project, you might surround a major protrusion with a rectangle whose wide frame is cut out or shaped to follow the contour, as in Figures 6-4b and 6-4c. This calls for a frame member wide enough to allow for the cutout plus the normal width of the frame inside the gridwork, so that both lateral and longitudinal stringers may be set into solid wood. Whether the notch for the protrusion is cut into the solid wood of a wide frame member (Figure 6-4c), or into a portion of the frame that has been built up for the purpose (Figure 6-4b), make that part of the frame wide enough so that the spaces around it are only half as wide as the other spaces. This will leave plenty of wood to let in the stringers without weakening the structure. Plan to dado the stringers to interlock crosswise, forming lap joints. Making distances between stringers equal to the width of the stringers will expedite the project; the pieces making up the grid will be interchangeable both fore-and-aft and athwartship.

Construction

There are two different ways to make stringers, starting in either case with pieces that are comfortably longer than the net length required, to allow for defects in the ends. If practical, use lengths that will yield multiple stringers; that is, two or more parallel pieces, or one fore-and-aft and one athwartship piece, from each ripped length.

Cut before you dado. Cut the milled, square pieces to final length, and then dado or rout each one, spacing the cuts exactly the same. To accomplish this, cut each stringer so that it is slightly longer than the net length required and finish square. Then dado each piece individually. This calls for a large number of cuts, but individual stringers are easier to handle than wide boards. Use a spacing jig or auxiliary fence to keep the spacing of the dadoes constant (Photo 6-1a). Set the width of the dado blade exactly to the width of the stringer by placing spacers between the cutters, or by adjusting the wobble-blade setting to the width of the stringers. Set the height of the blade to one-half their thickness, and don't be stingy here—a full one-half, plus a tad, will allow a flush fit.

Figure 6-1. *Alternating housing joints (mortises) and lap or rabbet joints combines ease of fabrication with strength. The width and length of the joints are equal to the thickness of the frame; the depth of the rabbet is one-half of these.*

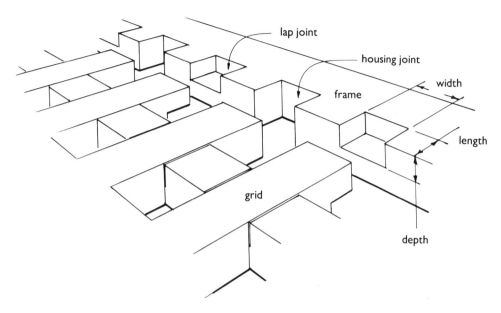

lap joint

housing joint

width

frame

length

grid

depth

Figure 6-2. *The strength of a simple beam can be calculated when the breadth (b), depth (d), and length (ℓ) are known (P = force). This becomes more complex when considering the shared support from adjacent beams (both parallel and perpendicular). Using strength calculations for a plywood subfloor will provide a guideline to factor required scantlings of a grate.*

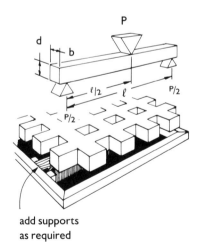

P

d

b

ℓ/2   ℓ   P/2

P/2

add supports
as required

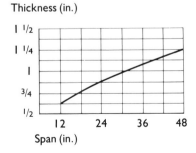

the American Plywood
Association's recommended
thicknesses for
spanning between supports

Thickness (in.)

1 1/2

1 1/4

1

3/4

1/2

12   24   36   48

Span (in.)

Figure 6-3. *Determining grid spacing and selecting frame width are integral parts of grate construction. Dado and rabbet to a minimum depth of ½ stringer width. Wide frames can be tapered to parallel converging cockpit-well sides.*

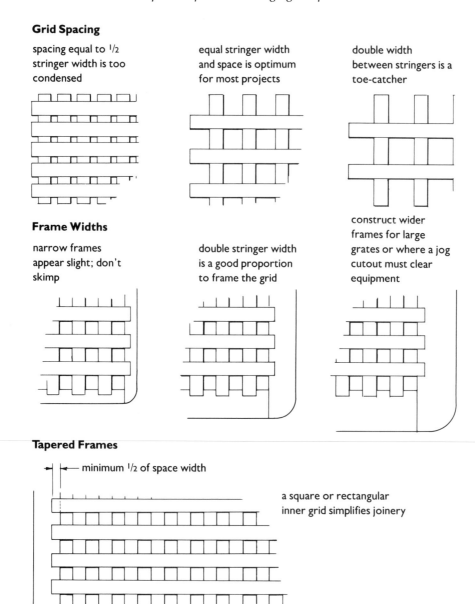

Grid Spacing

spacing equal to ½ stringer width is too condensed

equal stringer width and space is optimum for most projects

double width between stringers is a toe-catcher

Frame Widths

narrow frames appear slight; don't skimp

double stringer width is a good proportion to frame the grid

construct wider frames for large grates or where a jog cutout must clear equipment

Tapered Frames

minimum ½ of space width

a square or rectangular inner grid simplifies joinery

Figure 6-4. *Grates designed to fit around obstacles. The spaces around the cutouts are only one-half the standard width, leaving extra-wide wood for the let-in stringers.*

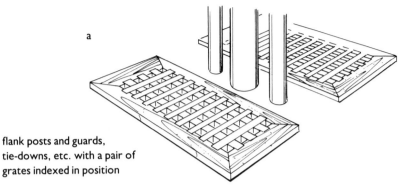

a

flank posts and guards,
tie-downs, etc. with a pair of
grates indexed in position

b

frame buildups conforming to
cockpit equipment should offset
grid by one-half space so that
mating stringers mortise into
solid wood

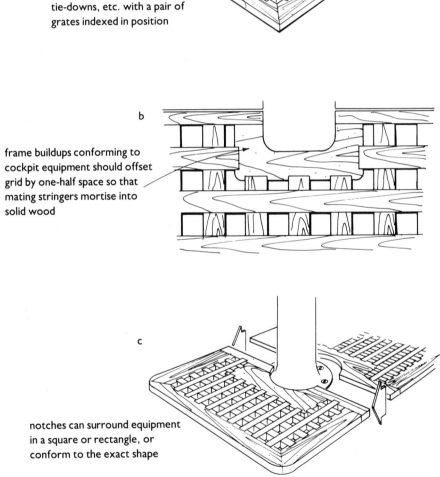

c

notches can surround equipment
in a square or rectangle, or
conform to the exact shape

Figure 6-5. *A warped board is cupped crosswise. If it is twisted lengthwise, though flat at each end, it has wind. Either makes the board useless.*

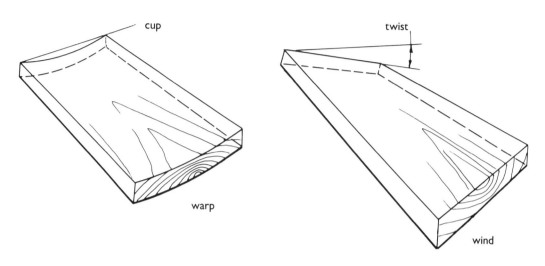

If the dado is too shallow or too deep, the difference in thickness is doubled when the top and bottom are joined. You'll have to sand this to create an even surface.

Dado before you cut. Dado or rout grooves across the face of a wide board, pre-milled to the correct thickness, and then rip it into lengths to form the stringers. Initially, the stringers should be wider than their finished dimensions to allow for a couple of passes through the thickness planer or jointer/planer. Mill the cut sides to the finished width. As mentioned, if you rip with a very sharp hollow-ground planer blade, you may not have to mill to get the finish on the sides. In this case, rip to the final dimensions.

While the method you finally choose is up to you, it's easier to handle individual stringers than wide boards. Also, although a small jointer/planer will surface the sides of individual stringers, planing such narrow pieces would put your hands precariously close to the cutting blades, even if you use all recommended guards, pushers, and guides. Your lumberyard will be happy to provide S2S (surfaced two sides) stock milled to your specification, or even happier to provide S4S stringers ready to dado.

On the other hand, if you have confidence in the finish that your hollow-ground blade will produce, and the board is not too wide, you may find it faster and less expensive to dado before you cut. Just be certain that you start with a good, flat board, having neither warp nor wind and at least one good straight edge. (For those who don't quite know what wind is, Figure 6-5 should help.)

If the grate will be viewed only from above and strength isn't critical, one might use an alternative to the full cross-lap joint (above)—the half-lap joint. This employs thin

Figure 6-6. *Optional indexing systems for use with saw or router on wide boards. Include a spacing slat in your router-guide frame to ensure correct spacing. Make guide edges straight and allow for dado width. Allow for router guide you may be using around router bit,* or *allow for full diameter of router base* plus *dado width if you are guiding on the edges of the base.*

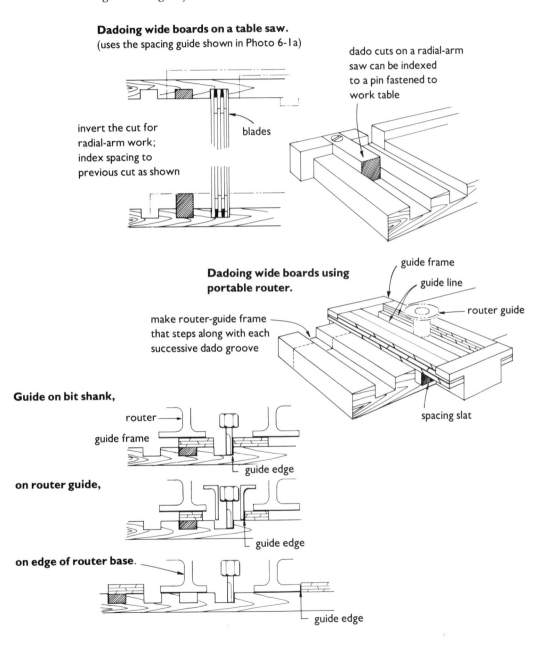

Dadoing wide boards on a table saw.
(uses the spacing guide shown in Photo 6-1a)

dado cuts on a radial-arm saw can be indexed to a pin fastened to work table

invert the cut for radial-arm work; index spacing to previous cut as shown

blades

Dadoing wide boards using portable router.

guide frame

guide line

router guide

make router-guide frame that steps along with each successive dado groove

spacing slat

Guide on bit shank,

router

guide frame

guide edge

on router guide,

guide edge

on edge of router base.

guide edge

Figure 6-7. *Details of grate construction and corner options. Rabbet as many joints as required for loads and distance spanned. Break, chamfer, or round edges. Note: Assemble and glue grid first, then trim and frame.*

Corner Options

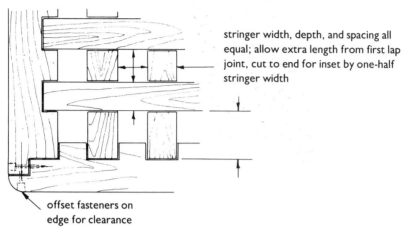

stringer width, depth, and spacing all equal; allow extra length from first lap joint, cut to end for inset by one-half stringer width

offset fasteners on edge for clearance

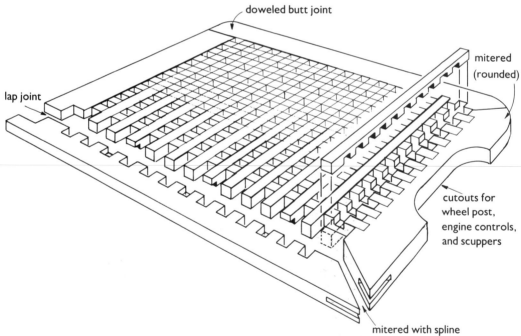

doweled butt joint

mitered (rounded)

lap joint

cutouts for wheel post, engine controls, and scuppers

mitered with spline

96
YACHT CRAFTSMAN'S HANDBOOK

a

Photo 6-1.
Constructing a rectangular grate.
(a) Clamp an auxiliary fence to the miter guide to index cuts; dado stringers to one-half depth and equally spaced. (b) Dado blades (wobble or expandable) may require some cleanup before gluing; edges should be eased slightly before assembly. (c) Dry fit all pieces to verify fit and length; carefully apply glue using a water-resistant product such as URAC or epoxy; trim slats to length and mortise/rabbet to frame. *(Series continues on page 98.)*

b

c

d

(d) Sand to an even surface; ease or chamfer edges using rasps and sanding strips; mill around outer edge with a quarter-round bit. (e) The finished rectangular grate.

e

stringers (half-thickness) across the top. The square, lower stringers only are dadoed to receive the thinner pieces.

To make the spacing jig mentioned above, start with a straight, true piece of scrap wood to use with your miter guide, like an auxiliary fence. Set the dado to the depth of the cut and the miter guide square to the blade. Make an initial dado cut through the jig. Verify dado width, depth, and angle. Once satisfied with the settings, shift the jig along by a distance equal to the desired space and make the next cut.

Fit an indexing pin in the first cut, standing proud of the guide face. Clamp the spacing jig to the miter gauge so that the second cut is aligned with the dado blade. If necessary, remove the indexing pin and make the first cut in the stringer, starting far enough away from the end to allow for the space and depth of the joint with the frame. Replace the indexing pin. Place the first cut in the stringer on the pin and cut the next dado. Keep stepping the work along, always indexing to the previous cut until the full length of the stringer has been grooved, shy of a long end to be let into the opposite frame. At this point you will no doubt think: One down, 99 to go! . . .

Interlock the first few stringers to test spacing, widths, and depths. If the grid is evenly spaced, all pieces should be interchangeable and fit when oriented in either direction. The slightest tolerance buildup in spacing will make assembly difficult.

If you elect to use the second method, which is generally employed for router and radial-saw work (but sometimes for table saws as well), you will still need a spacing jig. This jig will be a little different.

The work will be face-up if you are using either a router or a radial-arm saw; therefore, the guide, with the indexing pin, is clamped above the work with the pin projecting into the upper surface. The same step-and-repeat process ensures consistent spacing.

When indexing for portable routerwork, you may set your guides for either the diameter of the router base or the router guide (surrounding the cutter) to control width. Construct a frame that limits the travel of the bit as it forms the walls of the grooves. An indexing pin can be fastened into this router-guide frame to provide the same step-and-repeat process as described above. Spacing is controlled by moving the frame along the workpiece, or by moving the workpiece under the frame. Figure 6-6 shows several arrangements of indexing guides and router frames that will enable you to do the dadoing with a table saw, radial-arm saw, or a router.

Some handwork may be required to maximize the gluing surface. A wobble blade may leave a slight arc at the top of the cut. The expandable-type blades cut squarely, but even these may require some finish work. A fine-toothed rasp and/or sanding block will smooth these surfaces nicely, and a plane will ease the edges slightly as in Photo 6-1b.

Dry fit the assembly to ensure that no glitches will occur after you begin gluing (Photo 6-1c). Verify that the correct lengths are in their appointed locations. Stringers can be cut to length at this point, but it is better to postpone any cutting until the grid has been assembled and glued. If only a few stringers are marked for rabbeting, these could be dry fitted in place for later removal, gang-cutting, and final assembly.

Waterproof glues, such as resorcinol types, tend to be dark and possibly too messy for our purpose, so use a water-resistant one or, better still, one of the epoxy glues, at the junctions.

Square and trim the glued-up grid, allowing for the additional stringer length needed for the space next to the frame and for the inset along the frame edge. That's what we'll turn to now—cutting grooves into the edges of the frame in the same way as lap joints are dadoed in the stringers.

Cut the frame members to the lengths required, according to the method you selected for making the corners. Mark the beginning locations of the first stringers and indicate which will be rabbeted and which will be mortised. You may use the same spacing jig throughout, but remember to reset the cutting depth of the dado blade—the distance by which the stringer is let into the frame will then be equal. Where stringers are mortised, make a through-cut. Where stringers are rabbeted, cut into the edge only, no farther than one-half the stringer thickness. This cut will locate the mating stringer. Finish the joint by routing or chiseling the remainder of the rabbet, then dado the mating stringer on the underside to fit.

Where the assembly will rest flat on a cockpit sole, the grate may be set on small risers, blocks, or built-up stringers. If full-length risers are used to elevate the grate, cut limber holes in them so that water can find its way out.

From here on final assembly is obvious, but you should decide on and install the screws that improve the strength of the glued mortises and possibly the corner joints as well. Screws fastening the stringers to the frame have to enter the end grain of the stringers. To make sure that the wood will not split, drill pilot holes for the screws. These screws should be a good half-inch longer than you might be accustomed to when fastening across the grain. It's suggested that you use nothing smaller than #10 screws.

For a truly craftsmanlike grate, assemble the frame with corner splines, as in Figure 6-7, but if this is a little showy for your taste, use any one of the other methods shown. They are all strong and durable. Finish by rounding over the outer edges and then sanding the whole piece as shown in Photo 6-1d.

We'll take up triangular grates next, remembering that they require odd-angled cuts and are best reserved for special situations, and usually for smaller projects. Triangular grates require a bit more figuring, but the resulting patterns are pleasing to the eye. You just have to keep your head about complementary angles, mirror images, and the like.

TRIANGULAR GRATES AND GRIDS

The design and joinery of triangular structures are so intimately bound together, depending on their shape and angle, that there is no standard operating procedure for constructing triangular grates.

Grates or grids in bowsprit and boomkin planks are more intricate; they may be of any shape, even trapezoidal. More important, they may be closely related to the engineering characteristics of deck or associated structures, so the methods of attachment become significant. We'll take up these special grates separately.

Two standard triangles—the right triangle and the equilateral triangle—should cover most needs, except for some odd and sometimes weird parallelograms, generally divided into two triangles or a rectangle and a triangle.

Isosceles Right Triangles

Grates shaped like isosceles right triangles will accommodate the square grid pattern used for constructing rectangular grates. The ends of the stringers enter the two equal sides at a 45° angle, and the hypotenuse (the long side, for those of us who hated geometry) at the standard 90° angle. They are then mortised or rabbeted as usual (Figure 6-8b).

If the stringers are to continue past the hypotenuse into a rectangular portion of the grate, there's no problem. They are merely lapped as usual where they cross; then they continue, filling in the rectangle (Figure 6-8a). If they stop at the hypotenuse, this becomes the wide frame member, and again, the stringers are mortised or rabbeted.

Lap joints in stringers are cut in the same manner as described earlier. Mortises and rabbets in the short sides of the triangle will come in at 45° (Figures 6-8b, 6-8c, and 6-8d). Rabbeting these triangular inserts can reduce the thickness at the lap joints by one-half. For adequate strength, the frame should be 1½ to 2 times the thickness of the stringers to allow setting the full thickness of the lapped stringers into a solid rabbet (Figure 6-8c). The size of the grid and the expected load will determine the need for setting the stringers farther into the frame.

Equilateral Triangles

Stringers parallel all three sides of an equilateral triangular frame and converge along the centerline, where they are butt-joined, making a series of V's or chevrons (Figure 6-8e). Each chevron is lap-joined diagonally into crosspieces set parallel to the base of the triangle, as shown in the figure.

To cut the angled lap joints, set the miter gauge at 30° and plan on some handwork at the centers where three parts converge. To make the cuts where the stringers meet the frame, set the table or arbor to the angle, and cut the frame piece against the miter gauge in the usual way. Don't forget that the angles on one side are mirror images of those on the other.

You might not have the latitude to choose a conventional pattern when fitting a grate into an existing frame or depression. Angles of 30°/60° or 45°/90° are not magic. A triangular grid can be made in any shape. Begin by laying out the triangular frame, then design the interior grid to fit the space, and the joints to fit into the frame at matching angles. For the stringers parallel to the sides, the depth of a rabbet or mortise in the frame

Figure 6-8. *Details of triangular structures.*

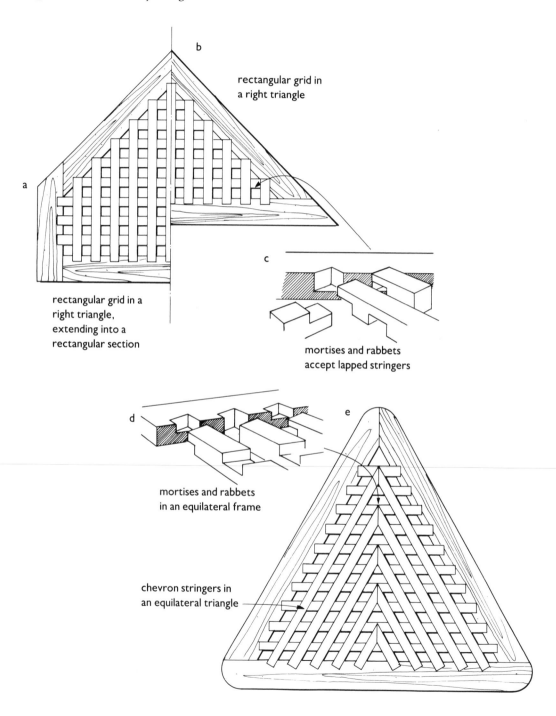

b
rectangular grid in
a right triangle

a

rectangular grid in a
right triangle,
extending into a
rectangular section

c
mortises and rabbets
accept lapped stringers

d
mortises and rabbets
in an equilateral frame

e

chevron stringers in
an equilateral triangle

has no special limits, though not cut at 90° (Figure 6-8d), except when a right-angled grid is placed inside a triangle, as mentioned.

Planks

As nautical as cross-lap grates may be, it bothers me to see the pattern applied to tabletops or seats. Grates were created to keep sailors out of holds or keep feet dry, not to be dined or sat upon. An exception to this might be a bow plank, which is actually a specially shaped grate, or perhaps a grid atop a bowsprit or filling a boomkin frame, or covering any open well at the forepeak or below decks; yet these planks are for feet, too!

Planks that extend over the bow or on top of a bowsprit or boomkin can be made of either cross-lapped grids or spaced slats. Both belong in the nautical world.

Straight stock, with nicely rounded edges, can be fabricated easily into a sturdy bow plank or boomkin plank (Figure 6-9). Separate spacers (from stock of the same thickness), placed in line between stringers, form a pleasing and functional pattern (Figure 6-9c). The ends of the plank may be square or round or shaped to accommodate hardware to tie down an anchor or house a bow roller. Slatted planks can be configured to a variety of shapes to form a base for a windlass, a bitt, a bait tank, or pillow blocks for a dinghy or survival canister, or just to spread attachment points (Figure 6-9c).

Spacers should fill the ends of the array, and there should be one or two shorter ones suitably placed along the structure for rigidity and to take additional through-bolts if required. Concentrate spacers or lengthen selected spacers in lieu of mounting brackets for stanchion bases or pulpit frame.

The slatted assembly should be glued (it goes without saying that the glue should be the best waterproof kind available) and generously clamped while drying. Once the glue has set, drill holes for the through-bolts (or clean out predrilled holes), countersink and/or counterbore for nut and washer, then through-bolt and add bungs. The distance a bow plank may be allowed to cantilever out beyond the bow or stern is based on its tie-in to the structure. The fulcrum should be well forward of the plank's center. If no other structural element is supporting it, two-thirds or more of the plank's length should be inboard. An existing post or bitt is probably fastened to the keel or stem. You could flank or surround the post and tie in the plank for maximum strength. Don't rely on the deck, deck beams, or frame timbers alone to hold the inboard end of the plank down if there is to be any significant weight on it forward of the fulcrum.

Framed planks with interlocking grids are more symmetrical by nature and are more convenient to construct (Figure 6-9b). Grids can be effectively tapered by slightly tapering the frames. Slats are more suitable if there are to be major variations in width. To spread attachment points for a relatively narrow plank, a through-bolted clamp can be included in your plank design (Figure 6-9d). This can be of metal or wood, and used to supplement multiple deck and stem fasteners. Bolting into and through wooden cleats

Figure 6-9. *Details of a heavy-duty-grid bow plank.*

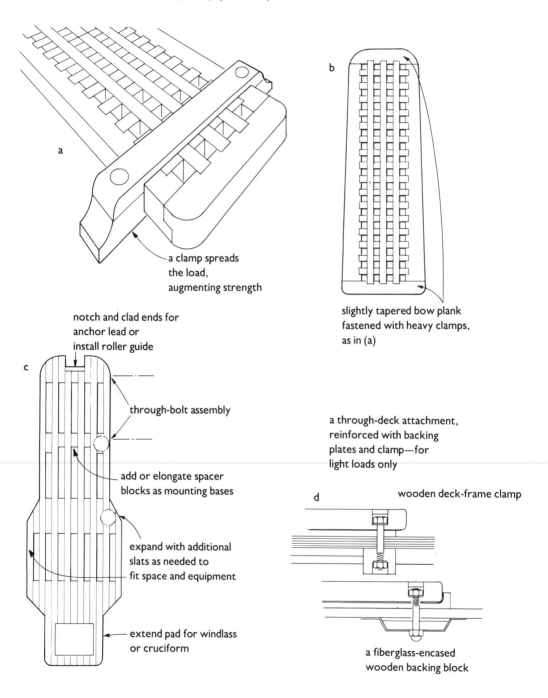

a

a clamp spreads
the load,
augmenting strength

b

slightly tapered bow plank
fastened with heavy clamps,
as in (a)

c

notch and clad ends for
anchor lead or
install roller guide

through-bolt assembly

add or elongate spacer
blocks as mounting bases

expand with additional
slats as needed to
fit space and equipment

extend pad for windlass
or cruciform

a through-deck attachment,
reinforced with backing
plates and clamp—for
light loads only

d

wooden deck-frame clamp

a fiberglass-encased
wooden backing block

below decks spreads the load. Also, wooden clamps around deck beams will increase strength.

In a fiberglass hull, the cleats and backing plates may be glassed in place, offering some additional reinforcement to each attachment (Figure 6-9d). But remember, don't rely on the deck to have any resistance to upward pull, such as would be experienced when a plank supports a weight overhanging the bow or stern.

Bow-plank strength is critical. It is expected to hold up while a crewmember stands at the end of a cantilevered plank, or to stay together when your boat surges at anchor with the rode leading through an integral roller guide. On more classic boats, strength duties may be shared if a nosepole supports a bow plank, relying at least partially on the forestay, bobstay, and cranse-iron to contribute to supporting the load. Consider the beam as being fixed at one end and loaded at the other. All fastenings migrate to solid structure, not simply decks or deck beams. Countersunk fasteners reduce the strength of materials at their locations, and stresses are concentrated at the fulcrum of the overhang. Consult a marine architect on any project where safety is critical.

Cabin Soles and Hatches

A bright, new cabin sole (not a floor; a marine floor is a structural member, something entirely different) can do more for your boat's interior than any single refurbishing project or addition. Its expanse is sizable and the location dominant, so that the elegance of the design and craftsmanship reflected in it are on display.

Teak and holly go together like bread and butter, ham and eggs, Ozzie and Harriet. Tested over years of use, this combination for cabin soles has held up admirably, and if it is compatible with the rest of the interior design, it's hard to go wrong adopting it.

Unfortunately, some boat designs prohibit laying an auxiliary sole immediately on top of the old one, because the addition reduces headroom or interferes with openings. Strips laminated to the existing sole are just as functional, and not too susceptible to scuffing and marring. However, our discussion will focus on replacement soles and hatches.

Materials

Using quarter-sawn, vertical-grain, or edge-cut stock (they're all the same) maximizes surface-wear qualities. On such stock the annual rings appear as parallel lines along the surface, interspersed with softer wood, over the whole width of the board. This cut was illustrated in Figure 1-1. Woods should match or complement the boat's interior. Whatever woods prevail, in either trim or structure, may be used for the sole. Teak and holly, or mahogany and holly (or ash, alder, or birch for the lighter shade) all go together nicely. Shy away from porous woods, such as red oak, and woods prone to splintering, such as one of my least-favorite, Douglas fir.

With time, the heat and ultraviolet light of the sun will affect the color of wood. Darker woods will bleach and the light woods will darken. What may appear as high contrast initially will mellow to a warm combination as time goes on. Varnishes containing additives that shield ultraviolet rays will slow the change, but some change is inevitable. The task of protecting the wood from light and, even more, from scuffing, falls on the varnish, so it is included here as part of crafting a sole.

In days of old, varnish hardness was graded as a function of the *length* of oil used to make the varnish. Length was expressed as the number of gallons of oil per 100 pounds of resin:

Type of Varnish	Oil (gal.)	Application
Short	5 to 15	Accommodation
Medium	15 to 20	Sole
Long	35 to 50	Spar

With the introduction of synthetic resins and oils, the nomenclature persisted. A higher proportion of oil will produce more elastic, more durable, more waterproof, but softer varnish. The higher proportion of resin will produce a harder, faster-drying varnish. It might be wise to check with the supplier—or better still, with an expert—as to which particular varnish is best for the cabin sole. It's likely to be one of the polyurethanes.

Design

Removable sections (bilge hatches) of a cabin sole can be replaced without concern for structural effect. However, if the project extends to the replacement of essentially permanent sole members, special care must be taken.

Hulls made of fiberglass, metal, or ferrocement are in a category called *monocoque* construction, which has no hefty frames to keep it in shape. Although bulkheads and floor beams augment strength and do help to maintain the lines of the hull, they are not as integral to the structure as are similar components in a wooden hull.

Boat designs rely in part on the structural contributions of permanent sole members. Therefore, in replacing a sole, it's advisable to do a little at a time, alternating sides, and in a forward-to-aft sequence. Whether the work is done with the boat in a cradle or in the water, the removal of too many contiguous members all at once could alter the shape of the hull. Attaching the new sole members to this slightly distorted hull could permanently change the form with which it has become comfortable over the years.

A cabin sole unites the sides of the hull, any frames or ribs there may be, and the floor timbers into a unified structure, which may show up on the sole as a combination of horizontal and sloping planes. If the designer has not taken full advantage of this structural pattern in some area, you may be able to remedy the oversight when upgrading your cabin sole. Just remember that if you try this remedy, you are performing surgery on the fundamentals of the boat.

Locker and bunk faces define major cabin areas within the hull's contour. As seen from above in a drawing, their outlines appear merely as straight lines where they meet the sole, but the actual edges may be far from straight and square. Inclined sections of the sole may require compound-beveled edges to fit flush against the vertical sides of bunks or bulkheads, but square-cut edges where they meet adjacent sections at the floors. Chapter 8 shows how compound angles are cut.

Figure 6-10d shows a combination of various sole elements, including horizontal and sloping parts. Note how the principal flat of the sole frames a simple cut-out opening for a hatch, using the floor timbers as supports.

More complex framing is sometimes used; for example, a hatch or companionway access might be framed in lighter-colored wood. However, too much of this can create a very busy appearance. On the other hand, anything that breaks the sweep of a large sole, such as a slope or a step, could add design interest, just as does a well-designed king plank or covering board on deck. It's a judgment call. Follow the boat's interior layout. Levels are dictated by clearance constraints. The interior contours, whether atop floors, or measured on the inner surface of a monocoque hull, will limit the width and length of cabin-sole sections. These have been worked out in the initial design, and there is probably little you can (or should) do to alter them. Pattern replacements after the old sections to facilitate design and ensure fit.

The fore-and-aft pattern of the sole should be continuous, even when the sole itself is interrupted by framed sections or changes in the height of floor timbers.

Designing an interesting treatment around a companionway, access to the bridge, or a fair transition from the sole to a centerboard trunk acknowledges the prominence of these parts in the scheme of things, but shouldn't be overdone.

Joinery

As with other projects in this book, if you have little interest in milling a great many pieces from rough-sawn lumber, take your specifications to the lumberyard or planing mill—and gently but firmly make sure they follow them! Your own task then would be the fun part: to cut to length, glue, clamp, bevel, trim, and finish.

Boards with planed edges, butt-joined with quality epoxy or water-resistant glue, all screwed (bronze or stainless steel) into or through cleats underneath make a lasting as-

Figure 6-10. *Details of cabin-sole construction.*

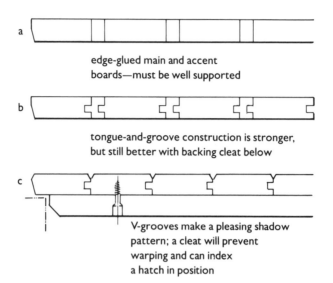

a

edge-glued main and accent
boards—must be well supported

b

tongue-and-groove construction is stronger,
but still better with backing cleat below

c

V-grooves make a pleasing shadow
pattern; a cleat will prevent
warping and can index
a hatch in position

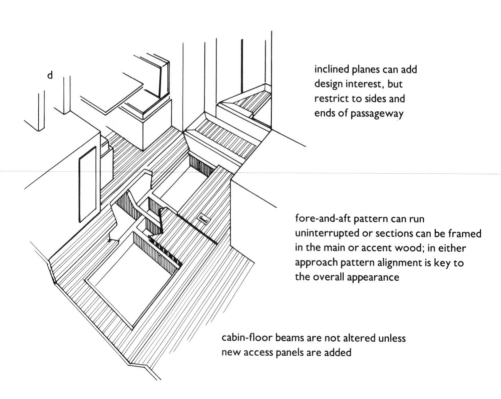

d

inclined planes can add
design interest, but
restrict to sides and
ends of passageway

fore-and-aft pattern can run
uninterrupted or sections can be framed
in the main or accent wood; in either
approach pattern alignment is key to
the overall appearance

cabin-floor beams are not altered unless
new access panels are added

Figure 6-11. *Ornamental and practical details of a cabin sole.*

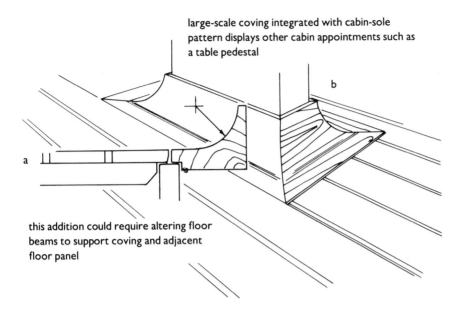

large-scale coving integrated with cabin-sole pattern displays other cabin appointments such as a table pedestal

b

a

this addition could require altering floor beams to support coving and adjacent floor panel

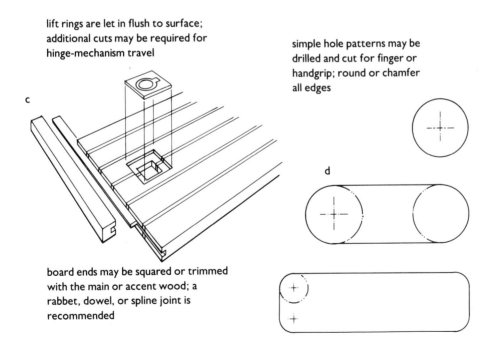

lift rings are let in flush to surface; additional cuts may be required for hinge-mechanism travel

simple hole patterns may be drilled and cut for finger or handgrip; round or chamfer all edges

c

d

board ends may be squared or trimmed with the main or accent wood; a rabbet, dowel, or spline joint is recommended

sembly. Underside cleats can be placed to index the hatch cover firmly in position. They also prevent warping and stiffen the assembly both in place and while being handled.

If you are at all doubtful about the success of butt joints, you can have the boards milled with finger joints, or tongue-and-grooved. Either method increases the gluing area and interlocks the members (Figure 6-10). Wide expanses of removable sections may warrant this extra step (Figure 6-10c).

If you are considering expansive projects whose size leads to warping problems (bilge hatches), the sole sections can be through-bolted from side to side, augmenting the strength of the cleats. The through-bolts probably will have to be comprised of threaded stainless rod, unless you can have some plain rod correctly threaded at the ends only. This would provide the greatest strength. (There are few applications where threaded stock is acceptable in boat construction, but this is one of them). Be sure to seal all surfaces, top and bottom.

Design details, such as gentle transitions to the vertical elements—bulkheads, lockers, and cabin accommodations in general—add a smooth touch of individuality while emphasizing the best features of the interior layout.

Rather than bring the sole right up to the edge of a vertical member, consider adding a large coved molding around a table pedestal, centerboard trunk, or ladder to the bridge (Figure 6-11a). Be wary of a design that requires a change in the floor beams.

Coving of 3- to 4-inch width can be made by cutting a series of kerfs crosswise into a board, knocking out the wood between the cuts, and finishing by hand with gouges, scrapers, sanders, or whatever one is used to. The radius of the cove is limited by the radius of the saw available.

Another method of coving with a circular-saw blade, running the stock very slowly at an angle across the blade, is best reserved for smaller stock; a 3-inch cove cut this way would expose a great deal of blade. Whatever the size, it's essential to make a succession of very shallow cuts. Moreover, although this method of coving has for years been used on the table saw, the radial-arm saw is far better and safer, especially for the beginner. If you try it, do use a radial-arm saw, and clamp the stock very firmly as you make the progressively deeper cuts.

Hatches in the sole demand some kind of lifting arrangements. Purists usually prefer cutouts or holes for hand- or finger grips, sometimes even wooden pulls (Figure 6-11c). These may be purer in design, but less practical than lifting rings. Holes, no matter what size, invite small things into the bilge. And spending the time to mill wooden pulls, or to insert commercial wooden drawer-pulls, only invites more work later when they fall prey to continued use, and break, leaving rough edges to annoy the hands.

Polished bronze lifting rings, chromed or plain, look nautical and are probably the most practical kind of handhold. Hinged rings are flush with the surface when idle, but provide a firm finger or handgrip for removing or handling sections. Quality products (no junk) should last forever if kept clean and polished. Cast-bronze hardware falls into this class. Brass is not quite as good. If you can find forged bronze, it would be best of all, but it's not easy.

The cutouts (*gains* in the trade) for the pulls (Figure 6-11b) can be routed out and chiseled, but it may actually be faster to do the whole job by hand. The specially shaped relief underneath the mechanism, which allows it to open freely, would have to be made by hand anyway.

There is one more small item to take note of: Though I'm not meticulous about dirt, I don't like to refinish more often than necessary, so I pay attention to dirt and sand accumulating in the wells of these pulls. They have a tendency to jump out sooner or later and grind into the varnish.

If you are averse to highly visible lifting-ring plates, you could bore hand or finger holes (Figure 6-11), but remember what could happen to a contact lens or a precious earring. 'Nuff said.

Nonskid Surfaces

Your use of the main saloon will determine the nonskid protection required. In boats that are truly "yachty," a spacious area of high-gloss surface may be a candidate for nonskid treatment. Where the sole is used actively, you might consider a V-groove between strips for better traction. You can V-groove the sole for traction whether it's built up of boards or made of a single piece of wood, and whether or not you are actually changing the sole from one construction to the other.

Evenly spaced V-grooves routed into your existing solid sole can provide the needed tread while suggesting the look of a sole built up of edge-glued boards, and emphasizing the longitudinal characteristics of the boat's interior.

Since you may groove the entire sole, or just the permanent part, decide on which it will be. Then choose the pattern and spacing of the grooves. Try to space them as real boards would be spaced—with some 2 inches between grooves. It is probably best to lay the pattern out on paper, remembering that the grooves must be aligned with the centerline of the boat, even if the fore-and-aft passageway is offset from the center, as it may be. Because removable parts are easy to work on, start with a hatch cover.

Decide on the pattern and whether both permanent and removable sections will be grooved. With a plan for the interior arrangement in mind or on paper, select the portion to be grooved first, and proceed as follows.

Find a flat, unhindered space and lay the work on it. Mark off the desired spacing (let's say 1½ inches on narrower pieces, to 2 inches on wider ones), centered in the section. Set a pair of dividers to this dimension and walk its legs across the width. Adjust the setting as necessary to produce equal spacing over the full width. This becomes your pattern for other V-grooves in the vicinity. If you started with a hatch cover, use the same groove spacing and depth for permanent sections, and align the grooves with the ones on the cover.

On the removable pieces, rout the first groove to the desired depth. Then clamp or tack a batten in place, at the proper distance from the first, allowing for the width of the router base or the guide—if you are using one—and rout the next. Repeat until the job has been finished. (A reminder: A V-groove bit is centered on the groove line, not offset to accommodate the tool's radius). Put the hatch cover in place and extend its groove lines forward and aft. This is best done by using a batten to ensure straight, parallel grooves.

Much of the grooving may be accomplished using a portable router and V-groove cutter, although in tight spaces some handwork will be required. If you're V-grooving removable sections only, clamp or, if necessary, tack a batten (straight and true) parallel to and spaced away from the first groove by the width of the guide. Set the router depth to the desired width. Make the cut keeping the router base or guide hard against the batten. Reposition the batten, working from either side, for the next cut.

Where the travel of the router is hindered, you will have to mark out and continue the grooving by hand, using small V-gouges—a job calling for real patience. This effort can be minimized by taking care in the design stage. As much as possible, concentrate on the accessible surfaces for grooving.

Insulation and Noise Abatement

Long-distance motoring is made more pleasant by the addition of sound insulation. This will not reduce the overall vibration of the hull and the rest of the permanent structure, but it can significantly lower the sound levels, especially noise coming from movable sections.

Vibrations transmitted from the engine(s) or generator by ill-fitting or loose sections may be controlled to some extent by indexing the removable sections of cabin soles so that they lie centered tightly in their allotted spaces.

In addition to preventing their inherent vibration, you can insulate these panels to reduce noise, especially in the vicinity of the engine room, by applying a sound-insulating layer.

Typical sound-insulating material consists of a lead sheet between layers of foam. Your marine supplier or engine shop ought to have specifications on such products. Some soundproof materials may be glued and taped in place, but a few good-size washers with round-head or pan-head stainless steel woodscrews, placed at the corners and in between as needed, will ensure that the sheet stays put.

Thoroughly seal the undersides of the new panels before applying insulation, which may not suppress moisture as well it does sound. A few coats of a polyurethene varnish or paint containing a wood preservative may prevent future problems. (Follow the manufacturer's cautions and directions for handling preservatives.)

7.

RACKS AND SHELVES

Black-Box Racks • **Chart Racks** • **Binocular Racks** • **Bookshelves**

Signal-Flag Racks • **Dish and Utensil Racks** • **Spice Racks and Jars**

Towel and Paper Racks • **Bottle and Wine Racks** • **Line Stowage**

Opinions may differ on when a rack is a holder, or a holder a rack. In this chapter we aren't going to make hair-splitting distinctions in arrangement, based on the design or appearance of the project. Instead, we'll let the function prevail.

For instance, galley items are grouped in one section, while projects associated with navigation are discussed in another section. Black boxes and books are grouped with the projects for navigational equipment, as are some entertainment items, which are often physically similar to navigational electronics and are stowed and restrained in the same way. This is also true for books; books not related to navigation fit in nicely with the essential ones. Flags are listed here also, since their basic purpose is for signalling, whether you use them that way or not.

When the urge to build comes over you, keep in mind that some bulkheads should be free of obstructions; you just may have to lean against them. However, there are many spaces, even in the smallest of cruisers, that can be used to provide additional, organized stowage, convenience, and decor.

BLACK-BOX RACKS

Not all nautical black boxes—mainly electronic devices of one kind or another—should be mounted permanently. Some should be stowed snugly in a rack, yet they also should be removable for use in some other location, or for maintenance or winterizing.

Radio direction finders (RDFs) of an unconventional design (something other than the compass-rose-on-top variety) may be shaped like a single-deck or stereo tape player. Most of the time our own RDF is used as the entertainment center on our rather simple boat. But when used for its intended purpose—taking bearings on a radio beacon, or as a pelorus—it is temporarily relocated parallel to the centerline. Here, it is free of obstructions and gives us room to swing the antenna full circle. At other times the unit fits snugly in its bulkhead rack.

Installation of a more traditional RDF could include a sliding base using either drawer slides or perhaps a pivot arrangement if this suits your accommodations better (Figure 7-1 and Photo 7-1).

Design your rack to fit and hold the component firmly. For example, the dials of a multiband radio/RDF are made accessible through a cutout at the right. A molded protrusion in the case at left mates with a corresponding shape routed into the adjacent support. A rack of this design keeps the unit in place under most conditions (except when turning turtle or pitch-poling, which I don't even want to think about), yet allows easy vertical removal.

Other black boxes that might be mounted similarly, although they are not navigation devices, include CD players, tape decks, and VCRs for the anti-Spartan, creature-comfort yachtsman who revels in sybaritic luxury.

Figure 7-1. *Possible design approaches for black-box racks.*

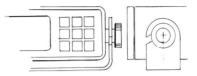

navigational equipment comes in many forms, styles, and sizes; allow for accessibility, clearance, and ventilation

mounting brackets, included with many electronic components, simplify installation

a single-purpose rack can be designed to fit one case or chassis design

flush-mounted indicators with waterproof bezels can be set into a shelf; a remote-to-readout black box can occupy another shelf in a multipurpose rack

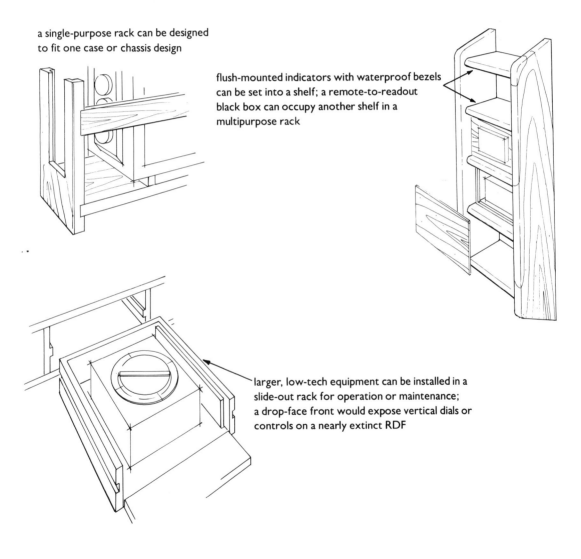

larger, low-tech equipment can be installed in a slide-out rack for operation or maintenance; a drop-face front would expose vertical dials or controls on a nearly extinct RDF

Photo 7-1.
A finished black-box rack.

CHART RACKS

The scope of this project depends on boat size, layout, and present or planned accommodations. If you have a navigation station but no handy place to keep your charts, you might want a bulkhead-mounted rack nearby. Rolled charts and folded ones call for different kinds of racks. Let's start with rolled ones.

Rolled-Chart Racks

Horizontal or vertical compartments in a shallow box will hold rolled charts neatly and conveniently. On a vertical rack, the nearer side can house a protractor, a set of parallels, dividers, and writing instruments. The space given to charts and your complement of navigational instruments depends on the size and cruising range of your vessel.

If your "official nav station" is the saloon table or a bunk, you might want to add a tilt-out work surface hinged along the top, shown in Figure 7-2. Where the rack can be mounted fairly high (allowing for clearance above to remove the rolled charts), supporting struts are cut from the edge of the work surface. These pivot on screw and washer, and drop into position at an angle convenient for use when standing. It might be possible to mount the rack lower down, so that it would be suitable for use when seated on a facing bunk or chair. The struts are held in place in the folded position by the angled cuts at the free ends.

To make a more horizontal work surface, hinge a gusset or a pair of gussets cut from the rack's face panel just below the continuous hinge line. The angle of the work surface will be determined by the slant of the top of the gusset when it it has been swung out 90°. Dual gussets meeting at the center would increase rigidity. To lower the work table, the gussets are folded flush into the face. Depending on the trim of the rack, it may be necessary to provide a small channel on the underside of the nav table to clear the continuous hinge that attaches the gusset. Add a pencil ledge or fiddle along the lower edge to keep your work in place.

Folded-Chart Racks

From my experience, a rack for folded charts can be built most easily if you install two nicely finished battens across a pair of overhead deck beams to keep the charts up and out of the way.

For the more ambitious, the acrylic-and-wood rack shown in Figure 7-3 is a handy addition to hold folded charts of the world. Obviously strips of plywood or slats of solid wood can be used instead of acrylic panels if their appearance blends better with your boat's interior.

Before designing the specific size, gather your charts together, or at least know the range of sizes, to give you the dimensions of the the rack that will fit your needs and your charts. Small-craft chart folios fold to about 9 × 17³/₄ inches; single small-craft charts fold into panels about 7³/₄ × 15 inches.

Bins of clear, smoke, or colored acrylic in ³/₁₆- to ¹/₄-inch thickness should hold a reasonable supply of twice-folded, full-size charts across a 16-inch front in two tiers. Tiers can be added and the width increased if room and need exist. If you make them wider, increase the thickness of the acrylic or wood panels and/or fasten wedges on center between the angled panels and the back. Be sure that sufficient compartment width is available on both sides for the folded charts.

Rout facing slots at 15° in the inboard face of each side panel. (Remember left and right!). Continue for the length of the panel, toward but short of the front. All slots must come equally close to the front edge. Round the top edge of the acrylic using woodworking tools and fine sandpaper. Finally, polish the edge with pumice on a cloth wheel, powered by your bench or hand-held grinder.

Insert acrylic panels from the back. Wedge a stop in each slot below the panel to hold it hard against the top of the groove. Fasten the back panel into grooves rabbeted along the side and bottom pieces. The bottom shelf and vertical retainer may be mortised or butt-joined into the sides.

The edges of the rack may be chamfered, rounded, or bull-nosed. You can add a fairly deep open tray across the bottom, or enclose it to form a small locker with a lid. You could even fit it with sliding panels to make a neat compartment for your navigational tools.

Figure 7-2. *A rack for rolled charts can accommodate a small table and provide stowage for navigational tools.*

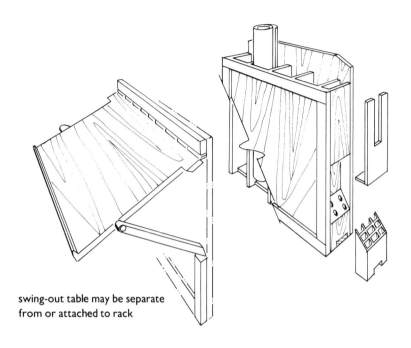

swing-out table may be separate
from or attached to rack

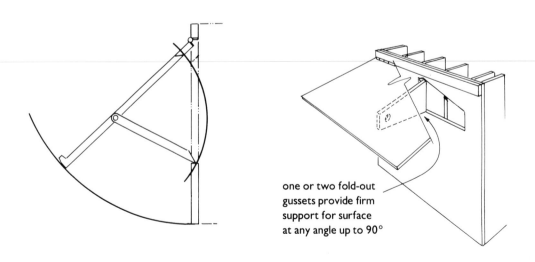

one or two fold-out
gussets provide firm
support for surface
at any angle up to 90°

Figure 7-3. *Rack for folded charts, with acrylic bins and wooden frame.*

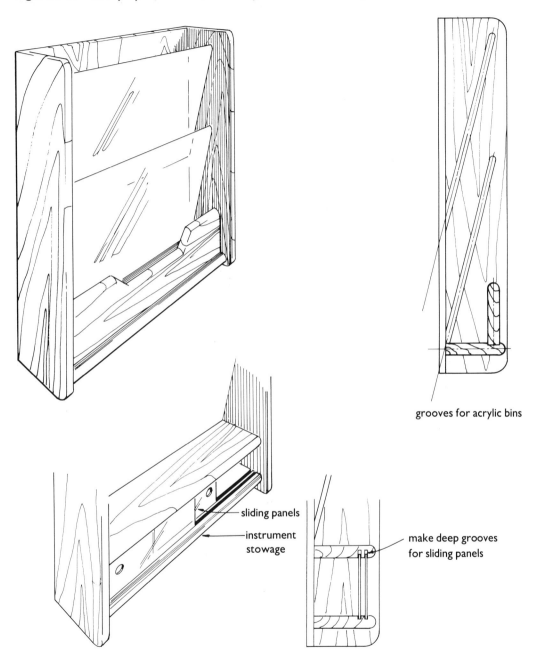

grooves for acrylic bins

sliding panels

instrument
stowage

make deep grooves
for sliding panels

Binocular Racks

Good binoculars deserve good racks; racks that hold them snugly and won't let them fall out, but let the user remove them as easily as possible. Yet good racks don't need to be complex. They need only be effective.

The traditional open rack shown in Figure 7-4a is effective and easy to make. It's obvious that your own rack should fit your own binoculars; design it accordingly.

If you want a truly vertical rack on a cabin side with a tumblehome, you will want to make it deeper than usual so that you can remove and replace the glass freely. It must be a little deeper overall, and the base must be deeper still.

The easiest way to establish the angle that you'll need to make the rack plumb is to use a carpenter's bevel square. Set one blade against the sloping bulkhead and level the other. Tighten the wingnut to set the angle, and transfer the angle to your pattern.

Another method is to measure the angle from the vertical using a level and protractor. For this method, a steady hand that comes from not smoking, drinking, or messing around is required.

A variation on this rack (Figure 7-4b) consists of a full housing that protects the optics from dust, grime, and, to some extent, moisture. This enclosure will allow you to add a desiccant bag to further control the humidity if necessary. Finger-lap joints add some design interest; here, too, is a place to show off your dovetailing expertise. More details on these corner treatments are described in Chapter 3.

A small, bronze hook-and-eye latch could be installed, or a (Velcro) patch could be glued to the inside lid and to the rabbeted surface. An exposed cloth loop or tab would make opening the box easier. Don't overdo the Velcro, or the box may have to be pried open. The breakaway front, piano-hinged at mid-height, provides a permanent panel to hold the binoculars in place when the cover is open.

Bookshelves

Your nautical library of reference books and favorite tales should be displayed out in the open if possible, yet it should be protected against movement while your boat is underway or at anchor in a rolly cove. Books tend to soften up on board ship; a good, solid retainer—a super bookend—will help prevent this. Bookends also provide another chance to show off what you can do with wood.

Luckily, most of us don't carry extensive libraries; maybe all of your books will fit on a small shelf or rack. You could designate locker space as your local library, but it is far better to add a rack against a bulkhead or along a cabinet top. Any corner space, well above the heads of seated guests, is a possible spot for a bookshelf. With two sides cleated into a corner, a cantilevered shelf can be supported by a turned post suspended

Figure 7-4. *Open and covered binocular racks.*

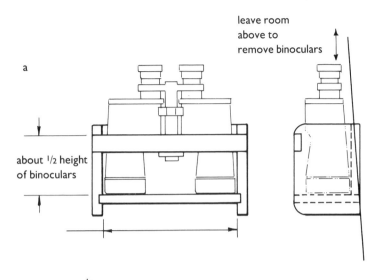

a

leave room
above to
remove binoculars

about 1/2 height
of binoculars

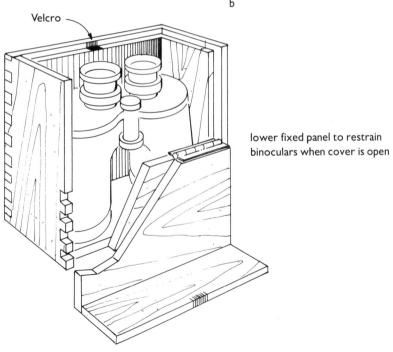

b

Velcro

lower fixed panel to restrain
binoculars when cover is open

from an overhead beam. The spindle should be turned to match the profiles of any other turned fiddles or posts aboard. A fiddle around the exposed sides, as described in Chapter 5, would improve the looks of the corner.

If you do choose simply any flat surface as your library, just add a pair of substantial bookends. These could be dowel-pinned directly into the surface (Figure 7-5c). A method that would be less traumatic to the surface entails including a base in the design. In this case, the whole assembly would be attached to the surface with cleats or small fasteners. Your library may expand and contract as time goes on, so you would do well to make it adjustable. Drill sets of paired holes along the the base to accept the ends in a number of places.

A pair of ends (only one if the other consists of a bulkhead) and a restraining bar comprise the assembly. Because a bookshelf occupies a place of prominence, your woodworking will stand out. The end(s) can be carved, routed, or simply left plain, but whatever design you choose, finish it well. A typical design is shown in Figure 7-5b.

The restraining bar across the face should be fairly hefty, and it should be designed to be removed easily but not by any movement that the ship is likely to make. The up-and-over configuration shown in the example fits this criterion. The bar can be set into the ends or it can stand proud. Another method is to rout facing grooves so that you can drop the crossbar in place.

The rosette in Figure 7-5b is a classic design for bookends but rare in the hands of the amateur craftsman. Still, it would be suitable in most surroundings. Beyond that it gives you a chance to do some truly fancy routerwork. Figure 7-6 and the explanation that follows will show you how.

Use a protractor and compass to loft the design onto the workpiece (or draw it on paper and glue it to the work). The illustrated example divides a circle into 12 sections of 30° each. The design may be hand-carved, but the precision produced by using a power router, with the help of a jig, adds to the crispness of the design.

This routing job is rather different from most; it involves an angle-routing jig—a sloping bed—and some elementary trigonometry.

The length of the routed petal, or *radial*, is a function of the slope angle and the depth of the cut at the end of the run; we can select the values we want. If we know three dimensions in the triangle, one being the length of any side, we can calculate all of the others. (See the section on louvers in Chapter 8 for a discussion of right triangles and trig tables.)

First, we know the depth of the V-groove we want at the terminus or length of the petal; it forms the short side of the triangle. Second, we know the radial or length of the groove on the surface of the work. Figure 7-6a is a sectional view of the setup, with sample dimensions.

The bed guides the router's deepening cut as it progresses into the work. As the router travels outward from the inner circle, the slope allows it to cut more and more

Figure 7-5. *Detail of ends and restraining bar on a bookshelf. See also Figure 7-6.*

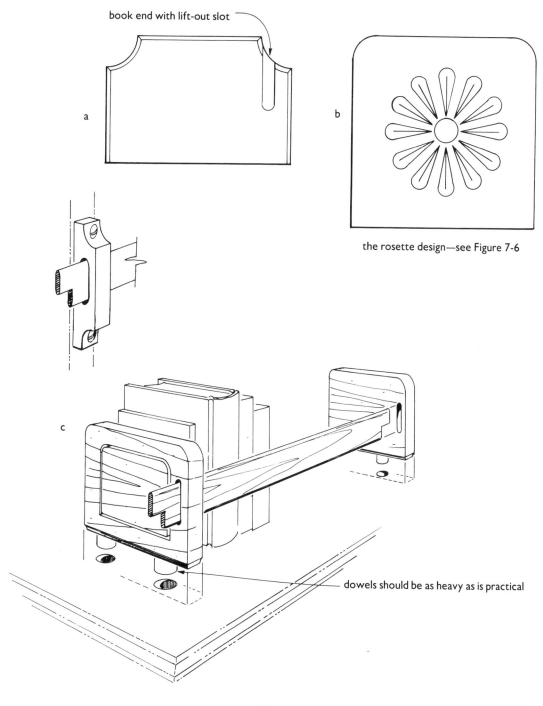

book end with lift-out slot

a

b

the rosette design—see Figure 7-6

c

dowels should be as heavy as is practical

Figure 7-6. *Layout and jig for routing a rosette.*

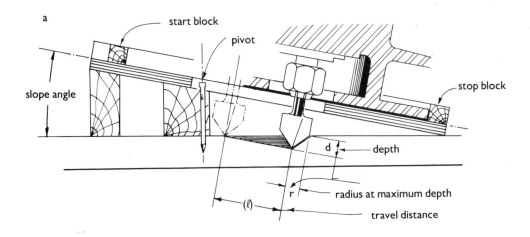

a

start block

pivot

stop block

slope angle

d ↕ — depth

r — radius at maximum depth

(ℓ)

travel distance

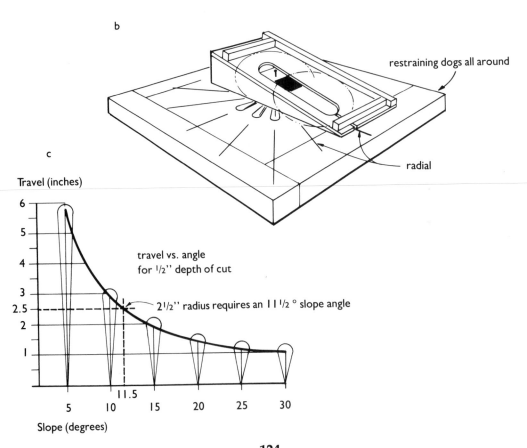

b

restraining dogs all around

c

radial

Travel (inches)

travel vs. angle
for ½" depth of cut

2½" radius requires an 11 ½ ° slope angle

6
5
4
3
2.5
2
1

11.5

5   10   15   20   25   30

Slope (degrees)

Figure 7-7. *Layout of the scallop design. Routing is stopped by eye because there are so many different radial lengths.*

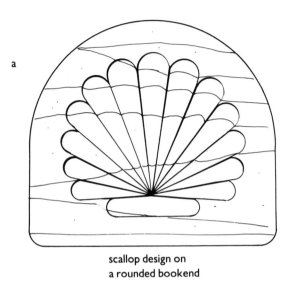

a

scallop design on
a rounded bookend

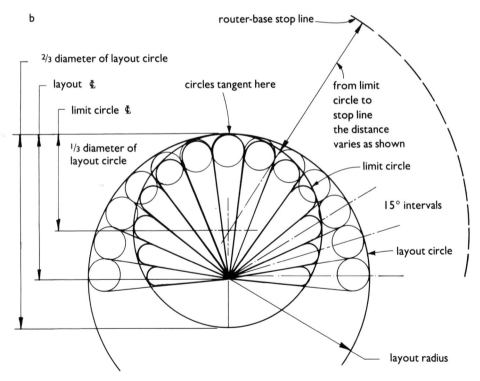

b

router-base stop line

²/₃ diameter of layout circle

layout ₵

limit circle ₵

circles tangent here

from limit
circle to
stop line
the distance
varies as shown

¹/₃ diameter of
layout circle

limit circle

15° intervals

layout circle

layout radius

Photo 7-2.
Routing a scallop design for a book-shelf.

deeply, from just touching to maximum depth at the end of the radial cut. At the same time, the width of the groove increases from zero at the circumference of the inner circle to maximum at the outer end or terminus. The cut retains its V shape all the way.

With a given length (r) of petal—i.e, the radial measured from the inner circle to the outer end—and the depth at the end (d), it's easy to calculate the slope angle (D) for the bed.

Similarly, given the angle, it's easy to figure out the length of the petal. Both equations and sample calculations are given below. In both cases assume a depth of 0.5 inch.

To determine the slope angle, select: (1) the outer or major radius of the finished design; (2) the inner radius that defines the circle where the router bit will first touch the surface of the work; and (3) the depth required to yield the desired width of the V-groove at the end of each petal.

Subtract the inner radius from the outer to find the length of the radial cut (r). Let it be 2.5 inches, and let the maximum depth (d) be 0.5 inch as specified above. Then use the following equation:

r = radius of petal, from center to limit (2.5 inches)

ℓ = length of groove centerline, or travel of the router

d = depth of cut (0.5 inch)

D = angle of bed (10°)

$\sin D = d/r = 0.5/2.5 = 0.2000$

$D = 11.5°$ (rounded off in plain English)

The router travel (ℓ) will be 0.25 inch less than the length of the groove because of the radius of the bit. So, for the travel subtract the radius of the bit and set the stop accordingly. Study Figure 7-6a and it will all become clear.

If you want to know the length of the petal at the surface of the work, for a given bed angle, use this equation:

$$r = d/\sin D$$

where the values are the same as those above.

I have calculated the results for three representative angles to give you a feel for the numbers involved, as shown below.

For a 10° slope: $r = 0.5/\sin 10 = 0.5/0.17365 = 2.879$ inches.

For a 15° slope: $r = 0.5/\sin 15 = 0.5/0.25882 = 1.932$ inches.

For a 20° slope: $r = 0.5/\sin 20 = 0.5/0.34202 = 1.462$ inches.

These figures are too fussy for most woodworking practice; you might prefer to use the graph in Figure 7-6c. Choose the length you want on the horizontal scale and move up to the curve. From the intersection move over to the vertical scale and read the angle off directly. This will give you the angle, near enough. Obviously, the smaller the angle, the longer the cut.

Back to the fun part. Cut a slot in the jig for the router bit and chuck. Attach a wooden fence along one side to guide the router base, and a stop-block at the radius to terminate the cut. Mark the centerline of the jig; it will be used later to align the cut with the radii marked on the work. Pivot the jig around on a small nail driven through the jig's centerline and into the center of the workpiece. The nail hole can be filled or covered later with a wooden button. The block holding the pivot pin should clear the bit where the cut begins.

In order to support the router, the jig may have to be much larger than the workpiece; therefore, the work must be firmly dogged in place with pieces of scrap wood of the same thickness. It will probably be necessary to extend the radial lines onto these pieces so that you can follow them, as in Figure 7-6b. Mark each radius on the work. Center the pin in the workpiece and rotate the jig around this as a pivot; align it with the first radius. Clamp the jig securely to the work and rout the groove. Step the fixture around to each radius in turn to complete the design.

A scallop-shell design would be an attractive nautical alternative to the rosette. A router is used in much the same way, except that a veining bit is employed instead of a V-grooving bit to cut the design (Photo 7-2).

The layout shape remains a circle, with the segments radiating from its center, but they terminate at the circumference of an inner circle as shown in Figure 7-7b.

The outer circle is for layout only. It determines the length of the longest scallop. Only the central cut will extend to the full radius of this circle. The inner circle, tangent at the top, defines the lengths of the remaining scallops. The stop limits are from the inner radius and extend over the distance from the edge of the veining bit to the router base. A wooden stop block is not practical here because of the varying lengths of the cuts, so a limit line is used instead, and the router is guided by eye. Travel stops when that line is reached.

There are many other router designs, which don't need detailing. One variation includes tracing the perimeter of the block with a veining bit a half-inch or so in from the edge, all around.

Signal-Flag Racks

Purists are quick to point out when flag etiquette is violated by the display of the wrong colors at the wrong time, in the wrong place, on the wrong day. It is a frightening thought: The Etiquette Authority has jurisdiction over how you stow your ship's flags and colors below!

Traditional flag racks provide 40 spaces; 26 for the alphabet, one for the code/answering pennant, 10 spaces for numerals, and one each for three repeaters. All other flags, pennants, and burgees remain furled on their staffs, hidden in drawers or lockers.

A flag rack is the neatest way to stow signal flags and colors (Figure 7-8). A shallow design is sufficient for this unit, because the flags can be folded in any reasonable way to conserve space.

A flag rack isn't for every boat; it's too large for some, too pretentious perhaps for some skippers. But in the right setting, possibly on the bridge of a large trawler, it can be a focal point, occupying a place of prominence. In another vessel it might be purely utilitarian, built in somewhere between frames or other structural members.

Skippers carrying less than the full complement of flags may wish to pare down the project to fit their own ideas of "dressing ship," while preserving a little tradition in the design. Rules of colors, based on ensign size (1 inch on the fly for each foot of LOA), should help you size the spaces in the flag rack.

Arrange the flags in proportions suited to the location. In a horizontal space, the 40 pigeon holes might be divided 5-high × 8-wide, 4 × 10, or 2 × 20. Reverse this arrangement where available space is vertical.

If you include a place for your national colors or yacht ensign (furled and capped on the staff), courtesy ensigns, owner's pennant, club burgee, and other flags and pennants—on or off pig sticks—drawers may be included above, below, or around the pigeonholes. Flanking lockers could house ensign staffs or pig sticks, if height allows. Openings should provide easy access, yet have enough fiddle to hold the flags in place.

Signal flags are sometimes strung with brummel hooks or, more often, with rope-and-toggle fastenings. Space must be provided in each compartment to stow the flag with its rope and toggle.

DISH AND UTENSIL RACKS

Whether galley dishes are to be stowed inside a locker, cupboard, or an open bay, the most functional design is the one that divides the area into accessible, protective compartments. Vertical dividers faced with slotted panels will hold tableware nicely. Figure 7-9 illustrates some racks and drawers for crockery, glassware, and flatware. Glasses (Figure 7-9a) and plates and cups (Figure 7-9b) can be stacked behind restrainers, spaced for easy retrieval. A drawer for flatware is shown in Figure 7-9c. Although any design must provide overhead clearance so that the dishes can be removed, almost anything goes, so long as it's practical and looks good. Stackable dishes (for example, Heller-type) are most efficiently stowed nested in columns, under restraint.

You're probably not expecting dinner parties for 30, so the space for your dishes can be fairly small, maybe from six to eight place settings. Look very critically at what you have (or want) to stow, and divvy up the space accordingly.

Stemmed glassware may be stowed in overhead slots forming T-shaped spaces.

Figure 7-8.   *A flag locker. Its size may be kept within limits if flags are carefully folded. Etiquette codes prescribe exactly 40 pigeonholes for signal flags. It can be constructed to accommodate flags on short staffs.*

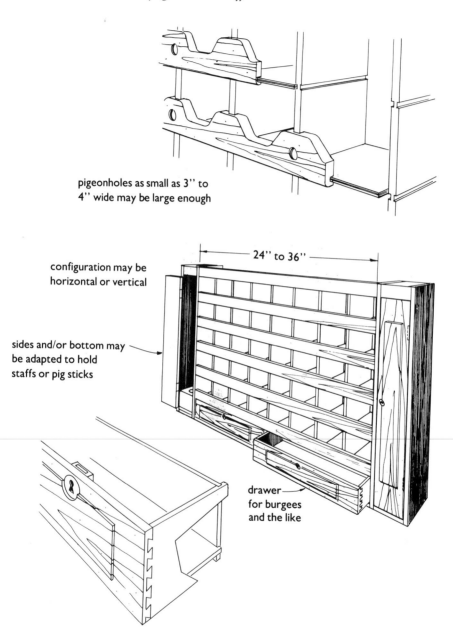

pigeonholes as small as 3'' to 4'' wide may be large enough

configuration may be horizontal or vertical

24'' to 36''

sides and/or bottom may be adapted to hold staffs or pig sticks

drawer for burgees and the like

Figure 7-9. *Stowage for glasses and dishes.*

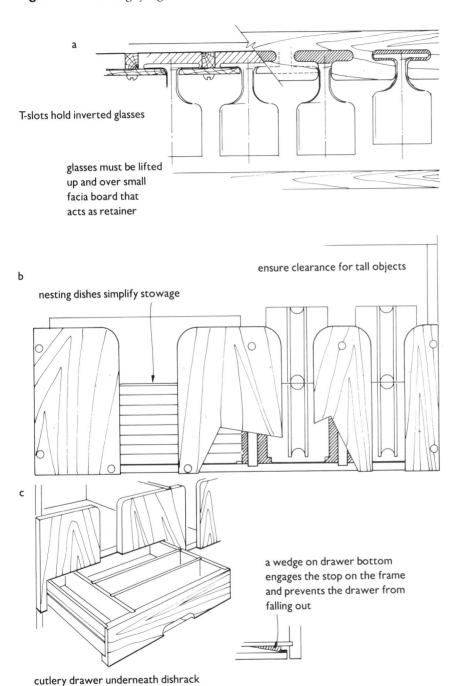

a

T-slots hold inverted glasses

glasses must be lifted
up and over small
facia board that
acts as retainer

ensure clearance for tall objects

b

nesting dishes simplify stowage

c

a wedge on drawer bottom
engages the stop on the frame
and prevents the drawer from
falling out

cutlery drawer underneath dishrack

Figure 7-10. *Various utensils can be stowed flat against a bulkhead. Make frames for restraining canned goods, and add corner stowage for pots and pans.*

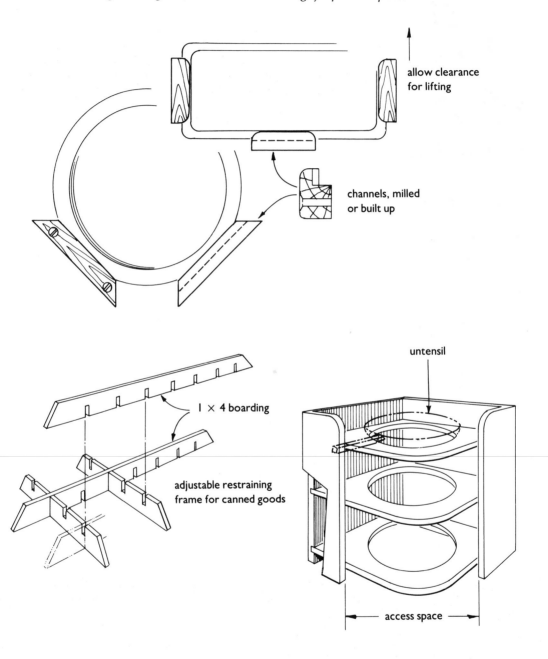

allow clearance
for lifting

channels, milled
or built up

1 × 4 boarding

adjustable restraining
frame for canned goods

untensil

access space

Shape the mating surfaces of the slots to match the radius and angle of the bases of your wine glasses where they meet the slats. Figure 7-9a shows a variety of possibilities for the T-slot. The row of T-slots can be finished with a facia panel, which is a little larger than the slot face but allows clearance through the facia. Glasses can be lifted out, although the oversize facia holds glasses queued behind it. If possible, stemmed glasses should have bases wider than their bowls to maintain spacing and separation.

Flatware stowage can be integrated with the unit that holds the glassware and crockery; you can build in drawers or suspend them below. One option is shown in Figure 7-9c.

I had planned to include a knife rack for this section, but after some thought, I felt that knives should be well protected in a drawer to prevent a reenactment of the *Attack of the Black Ninja* under rough conditions. It would be a good idea to add a safety lip to the front of the drawer, so that it must be lifted up before it can be drawn out. The bluewater sailor might like to add a hinged or removable cover over the edged tools in this drawer, so that nothing short of a major disaster could throw them out.

The designated cook wants easy access to the tools, whereas the skipper wants to secure the stuff when no one is eating or cooking—a seldom occurrence on a boat.

Lengths of wooden angle will hold lipped pans and bowls securely in place against a bulkhead, behind a locker door, or along the ceiling inside the locker. These lengths should be placed to retain three sides of a rectangular shape, or form a wedge-shaped space where the weight and shape of a round mixing bowl (for example) will make it hunker down in place. Mill the retaining angle a little wider and deeper to allow space for self-adhesive strips of padding to cushion the grip. These details are shown in Figure 7-10.

Skillets, other pots with handles, and pans also can be stacked in a three-sided rack as shown, or the locker base can be fitted with an adjustable comb and fence to keep the cookware in place (Figure 7-10).

In a large class of smallish boats, lack of stowage space presents a problem. Most likely, supplies will be stowed in the bilge, between frames, or perhaps in any old locker(s). Creating space for orderly stowage sparks a good deal of ingenuity among boat owners. Small, seemingly useless spaces quite often can be modified to accommodate a good supply of food.

SPICE RACKS AND JARS

Any shelf located within reach of the ship's cook can be made into a bonafide spice rack. Likewise, any small container can become a spice jar.

But if you haven't seen commercial jars that suit you, a convenient option is to make your own from acrylic tubing. The scale of the rack and jars can be large or small, depending on the amount of space you want to devote to this addition and on the variety of spices you'll need to fulfill your culinary ambitions. The truly novel part of this spicy project lies in the design and construction of a personal and unique set of jars, such as those illustrated in Figure 7-11.

They are made from lengths of acrylic tubing, fitted with teak lids and bottoms. Acrylic tubing is available in diameters of up to 2¾ inches—clear, colored, or opaque. Spice jars need to be sealed against moisture; O-rings provide a proper seal. They come in all sizes, and since this is hardly a critical application, close enough is good enough. Select an O-ring that measures slightly less than the inside diameter of the cylinder.

With the acrylic tubing and O-rings at hand (or knowing the dimensions), you can design the caps and bottoms. The bottoms are turned with an inner groove matching the inside diameter and wall thickness of the cylinder. The bottom of the cylinder will sit in this groove, cemented in place with clear epoxy. The outside diameter should be a bit larger than the cylinder's outside diameter, matching the outside diameter of the cap.

The top could be similar, but of course not cemented in. The difference between top and bottom is that the top needs a seal. Thus the design requires that the top be turned with an integral plug to fit into the tube. The O-ring groove is cut into the wall of the plug. This groove should be wide enough to hold the ring, and just deep enough to allow a slight compression of the O-ring when pressed inside the cylinder. This construction is shown in Figure 7-11a.

I suggest using a lathe for this project, although a set of tops and bottoms could be cut with a bandsaw and undercut with the aid of a jig. It's best, however, to regard these turnings as small bowls, mounted on the face plate of a wood-turning lathe. Depending on the size of the jars, you might use a hobby lathe instead.

Each piece is rough-cut and glued to a piece of pine or another bit of good, flat, dressed scrap for fastening to the face plate. Before gluing, insert a piece of newspaper between the workpiece and the scrap. The assembly will hold firmly while being turned but will come apart easily when a sharp knife blade is gently inserted between the pieces.

Lay out the plug design in profile and measure both longitudinally and with calipers across the diameter, to match the desired design. An adjustable profile gauge (needle bar), or cardboard profile template might be helpful in duplicating a set of lids and bases.

The diameter of the turned lid can be the same as that of the cylinder. However, if you want the O-ring seal to be a bit on the tight side, a firmer grip may be needed. Turn the lid to a slightly enlarged diameter; this will provide a better finger grip. Check the fit to the cylinder while the lid is still on the lathe. Remember to allow for the undercut that will enable you the press-fit the O-ring inside the cylinder. Don't remove the workpiece from the lathe until you're all done; once any turning has been removed from a lathe, it is difficult, if not impossible, to recenter it.

Work the blade around the glue joint beginning with slight pressure, especially when cutting parallel with the grain of the finished piece. You can press a little harder when working perpendicular to the grain.

Figure 7-11. *Spice jars and racks to fit them.*

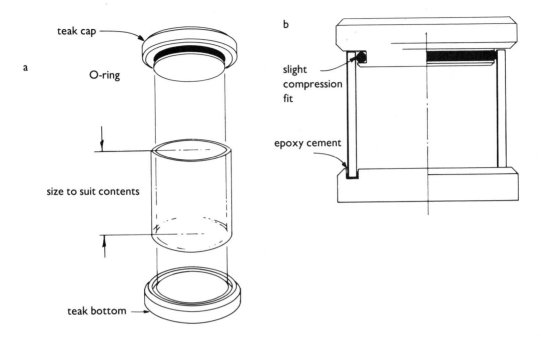

a

teak cap

O-ring

size to suit contents

teak bottom

b

slight compression fit

epoxy cement

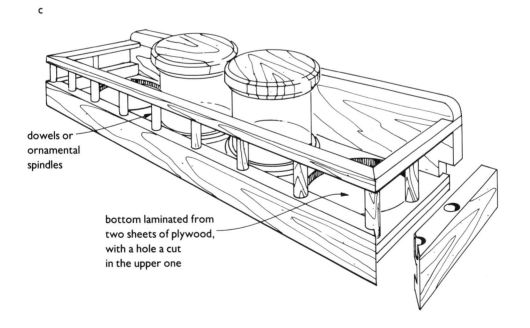

c

dowels or ornamental spindles

bottom laminated from two sheets of plywood, with a hole a cut in the upper one

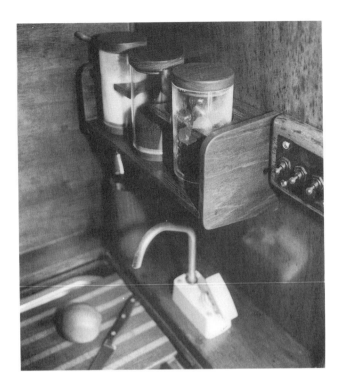

Photo 7-3.
A finished spice rack.

Wood-turners are probably asking: "Why not cut this piece off with the parting tool?" Why not, indeed, if you can afford to cut away so much of a thick stock! Remember that the scrap is attached to the face plate with wood screws, and the lid glued to it probably started as surfaced 1-inch wood (net 3/4-inch or less). But either way—paper split or parting tool—the top must be thick enough for the plug that holds the O-ring seal.

Spice jars, whether made or bought, must ride securely. Yet they also must be within easy reach (Photo 7-3). A double-ply base would allow you to use a hole saw to cut locating holes through the upper thickness, which would then be laminated to the solid piece below. Or this could be done by routing out circles, perhaps by placing adjustable separators between containers—all to keep the cylinders from knocking around. An example of a simple spice rack is shown in Figure 7-11.

Figure 7-11c shows a rack in which the jars are held in place by means of a series of holes in a mid-height restraining plate. Construction is fairly obvious. If the base itself is used to separate and hold the jars, as in Figure 7-11c, a hefty fiddle across the front is suggested.

It is fairly easy to keep a fully stocked galley. As supplies are depleted, spaces open up in which items can mix but rarely match, visit each other for a time, or simply roll around. The adjustable separator fence mentioned above works very well in the ship's locker. It can corral food and drink over a weekend or a year-long cruise.

Racks are, in fact, many and varied. Here are a few more—for purposes as far from the galley as one could expect.

Towel and Paper Racks

No cruising boat can operate without "head paper." You won't find it—the real seagoing McCoy—in the supermarket directory under that name. Never mind. Whatever the name, it's all the same; naturally, one dimension fits all.

Also few boats can operate without paper towels. I know trees are being sacrificed on this humble altar, but being a woodworker, I subscribe to the "renewable resource" point of view. Replant, reforest, renew. Plastic towel holders, handy as they may be, can be a real eyesore. We moved our own holder from between the main cabin ports to a convenient space under the sink. If yours must be in plain view, make a custom wooden holder that will invite proper respect.

Following extensive research, I found that both paper towels and tissue are rolled on 1½-inch cores, and measure 5 inches in diameter when new. If the products you buy are different, adjust the holder dimensions to fit.

A common design for the end pieces will fit either type of roll. Both use lengths of 1-inch dowel inserted in facing slots. The assembly is comprised of a stretcher and the two ends spaced to hold the dowel that holds the roll. Install the holder with wood screws fastened through the stretcher. Figure 7-12 shows some variations on a few basic designs.

The dowel track is angled for two reasons—easier loading and to provide security in any sea. (It's hard to imagine a sea that would first drop the boat vertically and immediately afterwards angle it 30°!) It may be "gilding the lily"; the tracks could be routed straight with no dire consequences. The angle is just a little insurance that the paper roll will stay in its holder.

A hinged cover (Figure 7-12b) can be added to either rack. In the example the height of the stretcher was increased to accommodate a continuous hinge. Decorative ends are always an option, but a little, plain, well-finished panel, sans embellishment, is totally suitable.

A couple of alternative approaches include a dowel extending through holes in a pair of gussets and secured with tapered pins, as in Figure 7-12c, or a simple cleat holding a bail bent from brass, bronze, or stainless steel rod, as in Figure 7-12d. Even brazing rod will do.

Figure 7-12. *Roll holders. The diameters are the same for paper towels and tissue; only the length of the roll varies.*

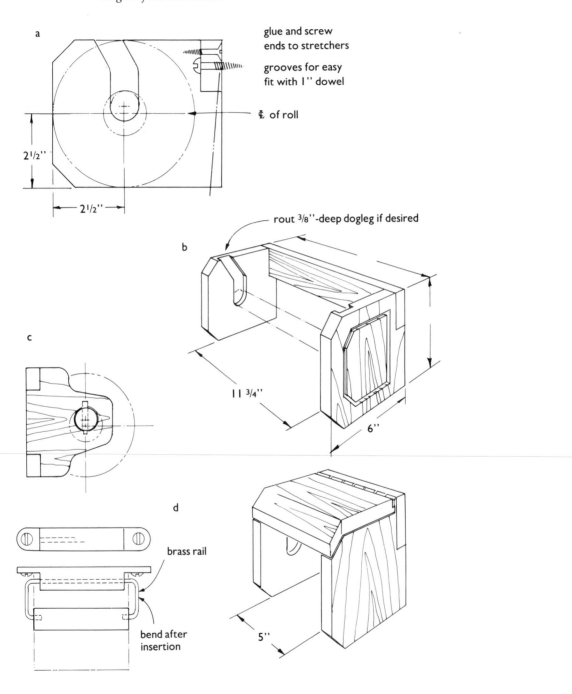

a

glue and screw
ends to stretchers

grooves for easy
fit with 1″ dowel

₵ of roll

2½″

2½″

rout ³⁄₈″-deep dogleg if desired

b

c

11 ³⁄₄″

6″

d

brass rail

bend after
insertion

5″

Bottle and Wine Racks

A fitting end to a good day on the water may be a cool gin and tonic when the hook is down in your favorite cove; think, too, of a warming Irish coffee back at the mooring to cut the chill of a brisk fishing trip. Think of a bar—on board, not under the keel.

A bar is a great invention on land or sea, but the precious bottles need to be restrained to prevent messy mishaps; not to mention the ultimate catastrophe—the loss of that special bottle of brandy. Whether you are the "raise the cocktail flag" type who likes to contemplate a display of your favorite libations, or one who occasionally gropes for a bottle stashed in the far reaches of a locker, you could find a rack both decorative and useful on board.

If a large-scale project better suits your layout, look at one of the discussions in Chapter 4; it may hold something that will help you.

Bottle Racks

The rack shown in Figure 7-13 will display your bottles and your skills too. Made of birds-eye maple, it will look as though it might have come from the original *Queen Mary*.

You might design your project around a set of decanters, perhaps "captain's decanters," with wide bases and short necks. Decanters may be round or square, but whatever the shape, the upper holder should be located a little over half the height of the container's belly. Its overall length will be a function of the available space and the number of house brands you are proud to pour. The hole pattern, and therefore the physical dimensions, can be varied to fit the space and the number of bottles—okay, decanters—four within a square, two rows of three, or whatever. . . .

A shallow drawer can be installed in lieu of the tray, but this would require changing the lower support from the single lengthwise span to individual supports below each bottle, spaced across the width to clear room for the sides of the drawer.

Mortise the front and sides into large squares, then round the outside corners—make sure to cut to a full radius using a bandsaw. Corners can be cut from a cylinder turned on a lathe, then quartered and rabbeted into the straight side pieces, but this process is better suited for shallower, four-cornered projects such as the helm-station accessory described in Chapter 4 in the section on holders.

The overall height may be increased to accommodate a pull-out tray below, which can be used as a little table or removed altogether for serving. The tray is particularly neat if it has been made with an integral fiddle, as shown. The sides of the fiddle are wider than the front to accommodate the slider rabbet underneath. Forget this fiddle if you expect the rack to receive a whack or two; stay with the solid design and narrow the ledge extending above the rabbet. If the rack will be in a protected area, away from traffic, you can make it a little fancier.

Figure 7-13. *A ready-to-use bottle rack. Dimensions vary, depending on the items to be held.*

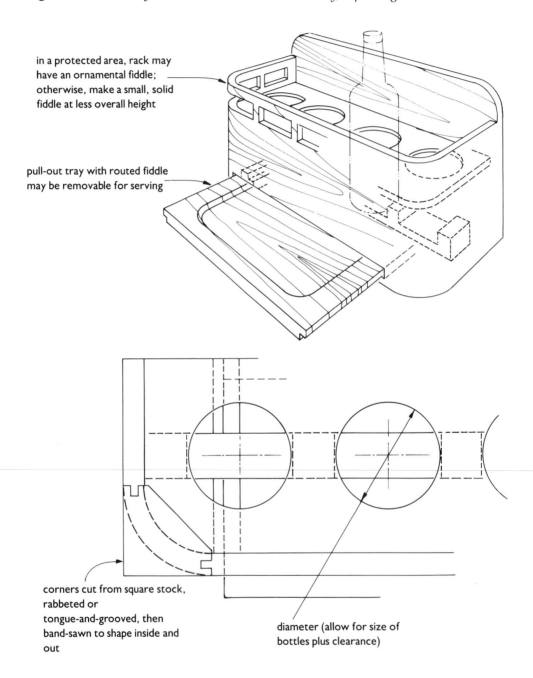

in a protected area, rack may have an ornamental fiddle; otherwise, make a small, solid fiddle at less overall height

pull-out tray with routed fiddle may be removable for serving

corners cut from square stock, rabbeted or tongue-and-grooved, then band-sawn to shape inside and out

diameter (allow for size of bottles plus clearance)

The dimensions of either of these projects depend on the size of the bottles. Whites (usually in longer-necked bottles) will be on ice in the fridge or the ice chest. Reds, and the whites that are waiting for chilling space, will be kept in your nice new rack.

Wine Cellars

After many sketches I came up with nothing more imaginative than the box shown in Figure 7-14 for stowing wine. The dividers constitute the rack. Because it will be in a locker and, we hope, the bottles will lie flat in it to keep the corks wet, it seemed the most practical device.

These boxes can be made of pine (pine shim stock comes in $1/2$-inch thickness), teak, cedar, or redwood, milled to the proper thickness. Each compartment holds one bottle. If you are going on a long voyage, or, as is more likely, planning a long party, you might have the otherwise flush bottom protrude to nest into the box below.

If space constraints dictate that you must—with the greatest reluctance—stow bottles upright, you can use the same basic design. Just add a front panel, about one-third the height of a bottle, and a removable restrainer, located at about two-thirds the height (Figure 7-14b). For vertical stowage fasten the box to a bulkhead or into the corner of a locker.

A top-loading locker could be your wine cellar. In this case you might try a simple cradle (Figure 7-14c). Bottles can rest in cradles if the compartment sides enclose both ends, or the bottle bottoms can be backed up in the cradle by laminating a solid piece behind the scalloped cradle. A Velcro strip would restrain the bottles against the motion of the boat.

LINE STOWAGE

You can make a rope locker that hides heaped lines more orderly by installing a pin rack or toggle rack on a bulkhead and/or across frames.

Hanging up your boat's lines is far kinder than laying them down haphazardly; this applies to both braided and twisted ropes. Hanging them promotes good air circulation, keeping lines dry and controlling mildew. Besides, you can get to that heaving line faster if you don't have to sort through a can of damp worms first.

Both designs (Figure 7-15) assume that the holder will be installed high enough off the bilge (or whatever) to accommodate the fall of the coiled rope. Rope and toggles will hold lines that have been coiled, wrapped, or looped in a reasonably seamanlike way.

The top of Figure 7-15 shows a straight cleat with vertical holes that have been threaded with $5/16$-inch or $3/8$-inch rope, with an eye splice at one end. Once through the cleat, the line is set in position by a figure-eight knot at the top (or top and bottom if preferred). Buy or turn some wooden toggles to slide on the line and secure with another figure-eight knot.

Figure 7-14. *Racks for a wine cellar. Wine is best kept horizontal.*

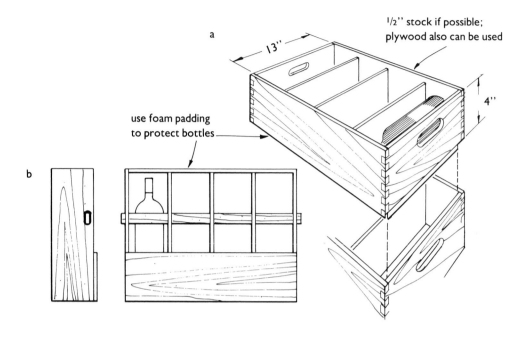

a

13"

¹/₂" stock if possible; plywood also can be used

4"

use foam padding to protect bottles

b

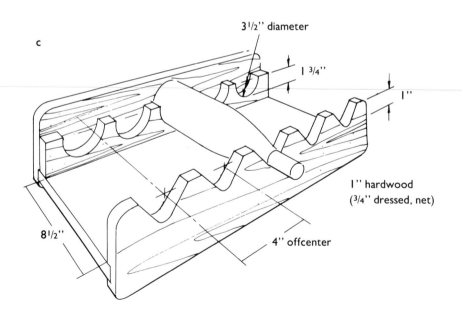

c

3¹/₂" diameter

1 ³/₄"

1"

1" hardwood
(³/₄" dressed, net)

8¹/₂"

4" offcenter

Figure 7-15. *Two methods of hanging coiled lines. Pins may be fixed or removable.*

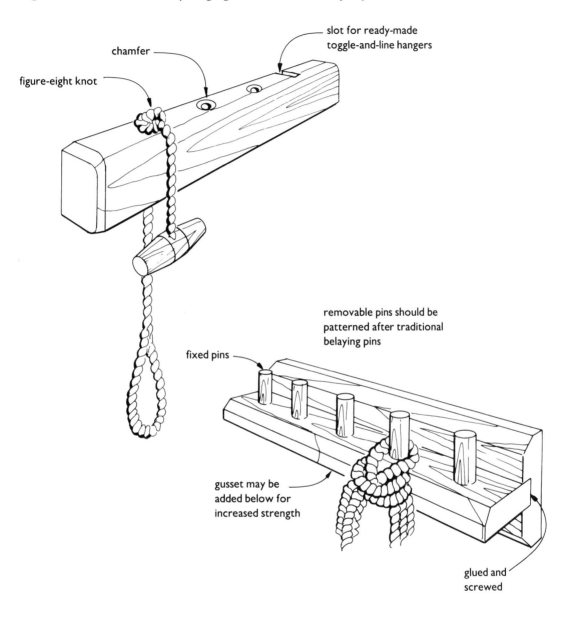

slot for ready-made
toggle-and-line hangers

chamfer

figure-eight knot

removable pins should be
patterned after traditional
belaying pins

fixed pins

gusset may be
added below for
increased strength

glued and
screwed

If commercial or preassembled toggles seem better, dado slots in the back of the cleats instead of drilling holes. This makes the equivalent of holes along the solid bulkhead; run the small lines through the slots and the arrangement will work in exactly the same way as the other.

The other approach shown adapts a pinrail design (with fixed pins) for use in a locker. Size the pinrail to fit your needs. Gauge the proportions by the number of pins, spacing, and the weight of the lines stowed. The horizontal member or shelf set into the dado at the cleat will provide good strength. If considerable weight is anticipated, add a gusset to support the shelf. The size and placement of the pins depend on the size and quantity of line stowed, and on your method of coiling. Hanging the rope from a single loop requires only minimal clearance behind the pin, whereas if multiple coils will be looped over the pins, allow for extra clearance behind and between the pins.

Hidden away in the bowels of the boat, these racks can be as Spartan or as fancy as you like. You can make the pins from commercial doweling, turn your own, or you can turn small removable belaying pins, just like the ones in the big old boats. Then you'd have an honest-to-goodness bluewater pinrail.

8.

VENTILATING PANELS

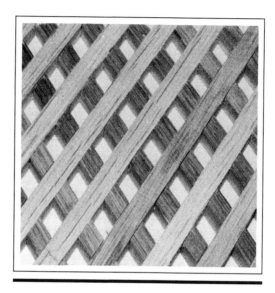

GENERAL DESIGN

A shipwright acquaintance once related a rule about designing boat interiors: Always make a path for water to flow. The same is true for air. Good circulation reduces problems ranging from stale air to more troublesome struggles with mildew and rot.

Liberal intake and exhaust paths promote good ventilation in boats secured against weather and intruders. Cowl, clamshell, and mushroom vents, open portholes, and any spaces between hatch covers and their coamings will exhaust the warmer air that rises by convection. This air is replaced by fresh air entering through lower vents in companion-way doors or dropboards, or through open portholes.

The sizes of exterior vents are determined by the local climate. To compensate for seasonal changes, the flow can be regulated by sliding doors behind the vents. An alternative might be a set of summer and winter dropboards. Bronze screening behind outside openings will control flying pests.

But this is not all. Lockers and compartments need their own internal circulation, which can be achieved by inserting upper and lower vent panels in existing doors and bulkheads. The same steps apply in fabricating either louvered doors or inserted panels to improve appearance and air flow. Louvered doors for cabin lockers may require heftier frames than do panels inserted into existing doors; the rigidity of panels is derived from the rigid structures that surround them. Figure 8-1 shows typical details of construction. Rectangular louvered structures are at an intermediate level of difficulty; to be sure, they call for care in design, layout, and control of dimensions in the joinery.

Angled grids or lattices—not louvers—present the next higher grade of difficulty, but unless they are very large, they are still ordinary weekend projects for the reasonably experienced boat owner.

Louvers with nonparallel sides, as with many dropboards, are a real challenge because they involve compound angles. If you derive satisfaction from self-inflicted punishment, try making a louvered panel that will be set into a tapered dropboard or, better still, the whole board. A good bit of extra planning is required for this type of trapezoidal panel or door.

Whether your vessel is a Swedish Sleek, a Taiwan Teak, or a Backyard Birch, the design of the louvers should conform to its existing characteristics. Unless you plan a completely new interior, strive to duplicate or complement the boat's joinery, shapes, and proportions—its look.

The *set* of the louvers (that is, their angle and lap) as well as their overall proportions—throughout the interior—should be the same, or at least bear a family resemblance. To arrive at a design format, consider the practical aspects as well as the aesthetics of the project.

In addition to appearance and physical size, another consideration is protection from damage. If heavy gear will be transferred in the vicinity of vulnerable slats, they should be on the hefty side, made flush or inset in the frame for added protection. The horizontal members of the frames (*rails*) protect the panel, just as the boat's rubrail protects the hull. The *stiles*, or vertical members, are milled to match the rails. The two sets combined form the frame.

Select design characteristics that best fit the purpose of the project. Figure 8-2 will give you some guidance on design and application.

Louvers should overlap when viewed from adjacent seats or bunks, but not excessively. Seen from the bowels of the bilge, overlap is not as important—your reason for being in the bilge will outweigh the revelation that you're able to see the sky through a louvered vent. With these general characteristics in mind—heavy or slight, rounded or squared edges, wide or narrow frames—begin to design.

Figure 8-1. *Louvered doors (a), whether hinged or sliding, must be stout enough to keep their shape and alignment in spite of stresses at sea. Louvered panels (b) set into doors or bulkheads may be lighter, since they are supported by the surrounding structure.*

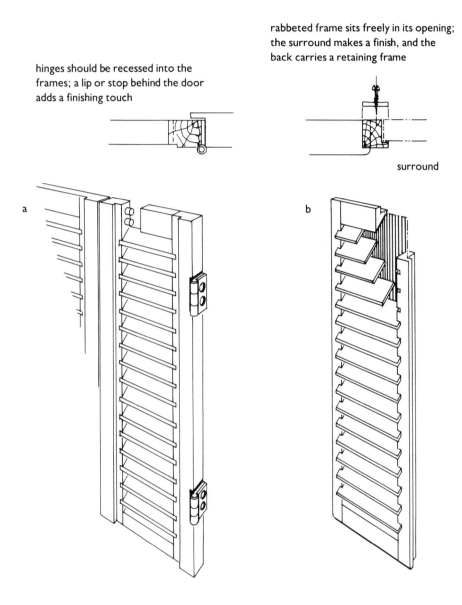

rabbeted frame sits freely in its opening; the surround makes a finish, and the back carries a retaining frame

hinges should be recessed into the frames; a lip or stop behind the door adds a finishing touch

surround

a

b

VENTILATING PANELS

Figure 8-2. *The angle and spacing of louvers should be such that you cannot see through the panel. Upper louvers may be inverted. Though lower positions may require fewer louvers, the spacing and angle in all panels match (a). The assembly is shown in (b) and the design details in (c).*

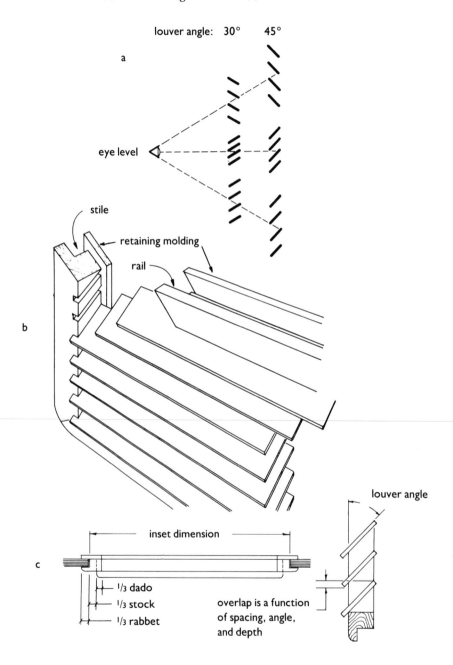

louver angle: 30° 45°

a

eye level

stile

retaining molding

rail

b

louver angle

inset dimension

c

¹/₃ dado
¹/₃ stock
¹/₃ rabbet

overlap is a function
of spacing, angle,
and depth

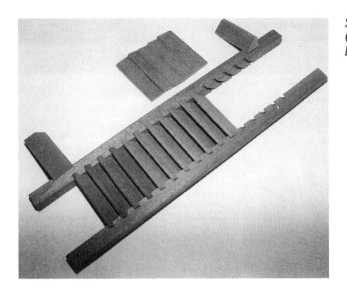

Stiles (dado-slotted), rails (cut to louver angle), and louvers ready for assembly.

TOOLS AND JIGS

"Measure twice, cut once" is good advice for any woodworker, but it is especially appropriate for projects such as those in this chapter, which involve multiple, matching cuts. Available tools and your level of confidence will influence your ambitions and designs.

The examples shown here were cut on a table saw, but obviously a radial-arm, circular, or even a handsaw would get the job done. Also, a high-speed router is a versatile tool for routing grooves as well as for shaping the frame (*molding*), and for other joinery tasks.

Louver slots may be cut by hand, but power tools make the job easy and, with the aid of a miter guide and auxiliary spacing jig, ensure consistently true results. A miter gauge, set to the louver angle, is a must—both for making a jig to guide the cutting of multiple parts and for making the parts themselves. Jigs will be treated separately as we come to each project, since the project itself determines the makeup of the jig.

LOUVERED RECTANGULAR PANELS

Methods of assembling the slats to the frame include butt-gluing them to the stiles (not too substantial), doweling them (lots of holes), using mortise-and-tenon joints (more work than necessary), or, as described here, inserting the slats into angled dadoes or grooves in the stiles.

Both stiles and rails are rabbeted on the back so that they will fit the opening cut into the door to receive the finished panel. The full-width panel forms an outside molding, giving a finished appearance.

Since we will be dealing with slats and slots, and their dimensions, here are a few simple definitions:

- *Slat thickness.* This is a matter of convenience, dictated by the shape of the cutting tool used; i.e., the diameter of the router bit or width of the dado blade.

- *Slat width.* The width of the slat is the sum of the slant length of the groove in the stile, plus the distance that the finished louver stands proud of the frame, including allowances for any bevels on the edges of the slats.

- *Slat length.* The length of the slat is equal to the width of the opening in the frame (i.e., stile-to-stile), plus the depth of the groove in the stile.

- *Panel height.* The height of the panel is its overall measurement, including the facia molding on the front. The vent height is the dimension of the slat-and-space area from inner edge to inner edge of the rails. The inset height is the panel height minus the total width of the two rabbets that enable the panel to be set into the door.

- *Rails.* Both the top and bottom rails must be cut from stock that is (1) wide enough to accept a bevel duplicating the angle of the adjacent louver slats and (2) long enough to complete the corner joints.

- *Stiles.* Left and right stiles extend beyond the total height of the vent, including the widths of the rails and the frame; thus, the stiles are long enough to form the corners of the frame.

Ventilating panels must be well proportioned and well placed; that is, balanced in the door in much the same way as a picture is balanced in its frame. A panel must match or complement adjacent structures or features. To give a basic example: If two adjacent matching doors both have ventilating panels, these should match each other in size, placement, and proportions to the doors. Cutouts should be planned and marked at the desired locations, but not actually cut until the vents have been constructed. This will permit adjustment of the cutouts to fit the louvered panels.

With the cutout dimensions established, select the frame width that will be exposed at the face. For stiles, this dimension should allow for a third of their width to overlap the hole in the door as molding. The inside edge, where the slat grooves will be dadoed, takes up the second one-third. The remaining one-third in the center is solid wood, between the rabbet or inset and the angled grooves. The thickness of the rail should be measured from the outside face of the molding (this is called a *facia* molding) to the inside face of the door into which the panel is inserted.

When louvers are flush, the dado method described here will expose the ends of the slots in the stiles. Where louvers stand proud of the face, these slots are not apparent. If visible slots are objectionable (I don't object to them), the joints could be either doweled or mortised and tenoned, although these processes are fairly demanding. The added trouble may not justify the effort. An alternative would be to narrow the ends of the slats, let them into the stiles, and trim the area where the slats insert with a strip of thin veneer.

Rail lengths must span the opening, plus twice the one-third stile overlap, to allow stock for the corner joints. The thickness and facia molding are the same as for the stiles, but their height will be greater if the inner edges of the rails duplicate the angle and spacing of the louvers.

The length of the slat should be either the net length desired, or net plus the lengths seated in the grooves—depending on the method of assembly chosen. The width should equal the slant angled across the stiles, plus any protrusion. Allow for beveling if the louvers are to be flush with the panel, face, and rear. The number of slats is determined by the angle, overlap, and spacing within the opening in the panel. Generally, the overlap may be minimal; you might want slightly more for private areas. Again, the overall design must be consistent.

Rabbets to fit the panel into the door will be your final milling task on the frame. By making this the last step, you preserve maximum surface area, which allows you to control the workpiece while dadoing the grooves in the stiles and beveling the inner surfaces of the rails. Chamfer or mill the edges, and cut and fit the corners. Rabbeting for the inset can be left until the panel has been assembled, if desired.

This brings us back to the first step—making a jig for the cuts in the rails that will accept the slats.

Making the Jig

To make the jig for the stiles, set the miter gauge to 45° (or whatever angle your plans call for). Set the depth of cut and saw a groove in a piece of straight and true scrap wood—which will eventually be clamped to the miter gauge as your spacing jig. Set a pair of dividers to the desired spacing and step off the locations for the successive grooves. Adjust if the total space (slats plus their individual spacings) falls short of or exceeds the desired height.

Measure and mark this spacing on the spacing jig, which already has one cut in it. Make the next cut. If the groove width and depth are right on, and the two cuts are the proper distance apart, clamp the wood to the miter guide and align your second cut with the dado blade. Cut the groove. You now have two slots.

Fit a pin (called an *indexing pin*) into the first slot, just long enough to extend beyond the face of the jig. This will register the work for subsequent cuts.

Remove the indexing pin and dado the initial groove in the stile (Photo 8-1a). Remember to start the grooves far enough away from the ends to leave you enough wood to complete the corner joints with the rails. Mitered corner joints are good for interior work, but where joints will be exposed to the weather, lap joints, with the rails extending the full width of the frame, are preferred.

Reinsert the indexing pin. Place the first groove over it and make the second cut. Move the workpiece along in this manner, registering each cut groove and, voilà!, the spacing is even (Photo 8-1a).

To make opposite grooves, the miter setting must be changed for cuts in the opposite stile. Even when one is using a 45° angle, it's the opposite 45°, and no amount of twisting or turning of the second, similar side will mirror the angle of the grooves on the first. Reset the guide to this opposite 45° and make two new indexing grooves, duplicating both the angle and the spacing exactly.

The greater the number of louvers comprising the panel section, the more critical the spacing becomes. Any buildup of mismatched tolerances over a tall louver panel will almost surely result in obvious canting at one end of the stile.

Assembly

Cut the miter or lap-joint corners. Cut the length of the slats so that they enter neatly into the grooves in the stiles, if this has not been done already. Then bevel the inside edges of the slats flush with the frame. Edges on the face may be beveled to the angle they form with the stile, whether flush, inset, or protruding. Chamfer or round the edges with a plane or cabinet scraper.

Carefully apply glue to the mating parts and assemble the stiles and slats. It's handy to work against a carpenter's square to keep the assembly true. If the backside rabbet has yet to be cut (and that's okay), square and glue the top and bottom rails to the stiles. You now have a completed unit, ready to be fitted into its door (Photo 8-1b).

Fitting Frames

After the glue has set, shape the facia molding and rabbet the back. If you used miter joints, you can strengthen them now with small brads through the rabbet. Measure the let-in on the back to conform to the size of the receiving hole, adding a little clearance for an easy fit. The louver panel should sit flush with the back of the door when the integral, or facia, molding is snug against the front. Cut the pieces for the inside, or retaining, molding to match the thickness and width of the facia molding; miter them at the corners and screw them to the inside of the louver frame. (Oval-head screws with finishing washers give a good appearance here.) If the louver panel is under thickness, the back

a

b

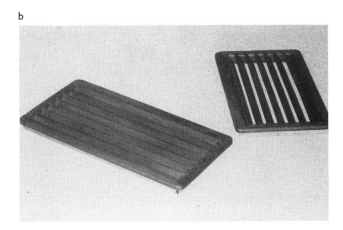

c

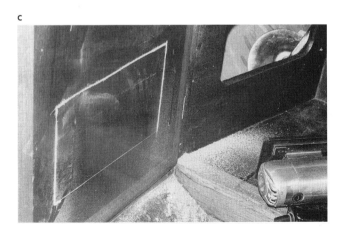

Photo 8-1.
Constructing and installing a louvered rectangular panel. (a) Set the miter guide to the louver angle, insert the indexing pin, and dado the stile to the desired angle and spacing, ensuring consistency. (b) Rabbet and set the prefinished panels into the door. (c) Cut a matching hole to accept the rabbeted panel; raw edges will be hidden by the wide face on frames. (Series continues on page 154.)

d

(d) Make a matching retaining frame for the back of the panel; if the panel is thinner than the door, rabbet the frame to fit flat and fasten with oval-head screws and finishing washers.

a

Figure 8-3.
Details of a ventilated dropboard.

if there is a tumblehome, design angle, spacing, and overhang of slats to make sure water stays out; bevel edges outward

b

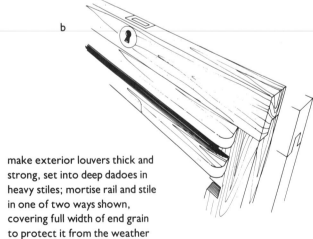

make exterior louvers thick and strong, set into deep dadoes in heavy stiles; mortise rail and stile in one of two ways shown, covering full width of end grain to protect it from the weather

molding may need to be inset to hold the assembly in place. Photo 8-1c shows the receiving hole, laid out and ready for cutting, while Photo 8-1d shows the louver panel in place, its molding covering the hole.

Exterior Louvers

Special considerations for exterior louvers include the use of waterproof glues or epoxies (instead of the water-resistant varieties used in the interior) and a generous overhang on the outside, especially if the location has any degree of tumblehome, as shown in Figure 8-3a. Use mortised joints, of either type shown in Figure 8-3b, to protect the end grain of the stiles from the weather.

Exterior louvers can be made integral with companionway dropboards, Lewis doors (horizontally hinged), or conventional doors hinged at the sides; or they can be made up as panels and inserted, as described above.

For outdoor use there are not many alternatives to the louvered ventilator. Still, the complexities of louvered construction sometimes can be avoided altogether simply by milling a series of horizontal slots in the boards, making sure that the cuts are well angled to shed water. This method does, however, expose the inside surfaces of the cuts to the weather to some degree. Therefore, it should be used only on solid wood, not plywood.

DROPBOARDS (TRAPEZOIDAL FRAMES)

Because dropboards are often trapezoidal rather than rectangular—the bottoms narrower than the tops—the next project describes how louvers are set into trapezoidal frames. Our project will consist of a trapezoidal dropboard with a central mullion (Figure 8-4). It calls for laying out and cutting compound angles, which is considerably more difficult than what we have just gone through.

The angle and spacing of the louvers are measured from the vertical (Figure 8-4). The louvers are at right angles to that vertical—i.e., they are horizontal but will meet the side at the very same angle at which the side meets the vertical—as seen in Figure 8-4a.

Whatever the angle of the stile from the vertical—the angle of divergence (D)—the groove to accept the horizontal slats will match it. Thus, for a 15° angle of divergence, the groove will be 15° off the horizontal, as in Figure 8-4a.

In a trapezoidal structure, we are dealing with both a compound angle and increased spacing between slats on the angled side. With a little trigonometry, the angle and increased spacing can be calculated using the equations shown in Figure 8-4b. One alternative would be to loft a section of the frame, project the spacing at right angles to the vertical, and mark where these lines intersect the angled side. Then you can measure the spacing along the angled side as well as the increasing slat lengths required to fill the widening space in the panel.

Figure 8-4. *Layout and saw settings for trapezoidal louvered vents.*

a

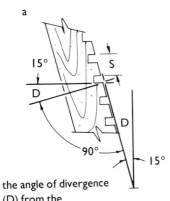

the angle of divergence (D) from the perpendicular gives the angle of the dadoed groove; the spacing (S) is measured along the slanted edge

c

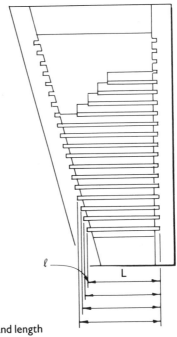

b

calculating space (S) and length increments (ℓ) of slats:

in the right triangle, (s) and (D) are known; (S) and (ℓ) are calculated using these equations:

$$S = \frac{s}{\cos D}; \quad \ell = s \times \tan D$$

each slat is longer than the one below by the increment (ℓ), which can be calculated from the equation shown

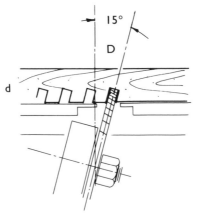

set miter gauge at louver angle; tilt arbor to angle (D)

Let's take the trig approach first. According to my trusty *Machinery's Handbook*, we can solve for the unknown lengths by considering the right triangle formed by the central mullion, the slats, and the angle (D).

For example, assume that the vertical spacing is 1 inch, the side is diverging at 15°, and the starting (narrowest) width between stiles is 3 inches. Using the *Machinery's Handbook* (or any other trig tables you may have), if you know one side and one angle of a right triangle, you can solve for the unknown side's length.

In this case we know that one leg (s) is 1 inch long, and we know the angle (D) is 15°. To find the distance between the slots—length (S) on the slanted side, using the following formula:

$$S = \frac{s}{\cos D} = \frac{1.000}{\cos 15°} = \frac{1.000}{0.96593} = 1.035 \text{ inches.}$$

To calculate the increase in length (ℓ) of successive slats spaced 1 inch apart:

$$\ell = s \times \tan D = 1.00 \times \tan 15° = 1.00 \times .26795, \text{ or } 0.27 \text{ inch.}$$

Translating this to the table saw, each 1-inch space on the vertical member will call for a 1.035-inch space along the 15° angled stile, and each slat will be 0.27 inch longer than the slat below. Woodworkers don't generally deal in 35-thousandths of an inch, so rather than put full faith and credit in these calculations, one might try the layout or lofting approach.

First, cut correctly spaced grooves in the mullion—the vertical member—and lay up the other parts of the frame at the position and angle desired. Then measure the lengths for the slats and the spacing between slats on the angled stile. Test this spacing with dividers to ensure that the top and bottom slats will remain parallel and horizontal when assembled.

After determining the spacing on the diverging side, cut the spacing jig accordingly. The louver angle remains constant regardless of divergence, so set the miter gauge at that angle (30°, for example). Tilt the saw arbor or table (depending on the type of saw you have) to the angle at which the slats will enter the diverging frame; in this case 15° (Figure 8-4d). Cut the compound angle at these settings.

The rest of the construction is essentially the same as that for rectangular shapes, with due regard to the corners, which generally do better lapped than mitered.

A point to remember: If your design has no center mullion but only two diverging sides, you must increase the lengths of successive slats by 2ℓ. The total length of a slat will be L + 2ℓ, where L is the length of the slat below.

ALTERNATIVES TO LOUVERS

Ornamental Cutouts

In places where some air circulation is needed, but large vents are unnecessary, cutouts designed to nautical themes such as the club burgee, the owner's emblem, or a

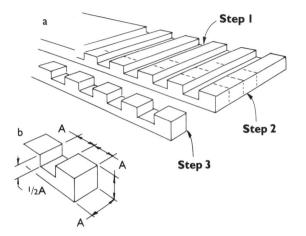

a

Step 1

Step 2

Step 3

b

A

A

A

A

½A

c

the grid may be set square to
the frame, as shown, or angled,
usually at 45°

Figure 8-5.
*Constructional details for a square
grid. To make angled grid strips
from wide boards, follow these
steps:* **Step 1:** *Dado grooves across
grain to a depth equal to one-half
thickness of board, spaced exactly to
its thickness (a). Drawing (b)
shows the relationships between
cuts and lands. Dimension A is the
thickness of the board.* **Step 2:** *Set
rip fence to yield finished width
that is equal to the thickness. A
good, sharp, hollow-ground planer
blade yields the best finish.* **Step 3:**
*Cut the pieces to length, invert the
crossmembers, and assemble. See
photo series at right.*

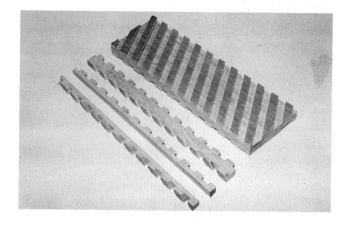

Figure 8-6. *For a diamond grid, cut the dadoes in the board at 30°. When assembled, the effect is a diamond with a 60° angle. With cuts at a 45° angle, the same method creates a different diamond pattern.*

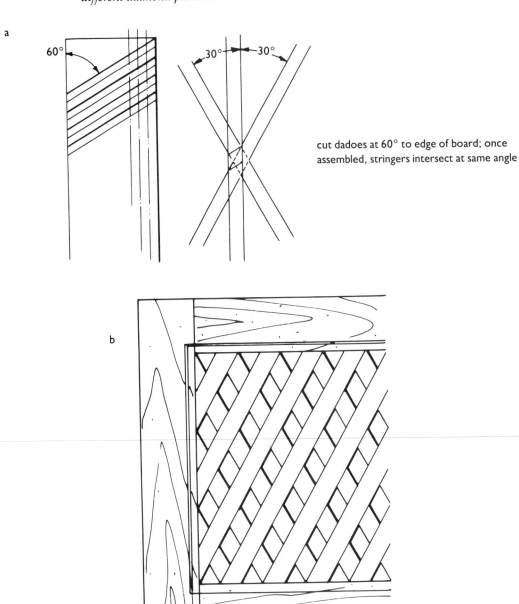

a

60°

30° 30°

cut dadoes at 60° to edge of board; once assembled, stringers intersect at same angle

b

the assembled panel

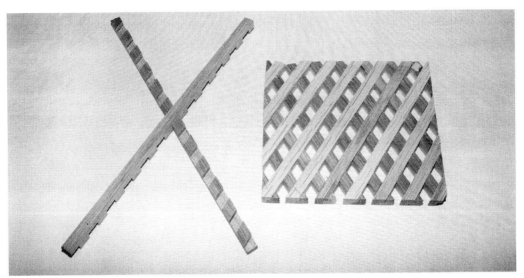

See description at left.

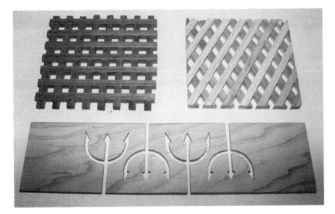

Photo 8-2.
Several alternatives to louvers.

trident, anchor, and so on, can form effective and decorative openings, easily designed and cut (Photo 8-2).

For example, you might make a pattern of a trident and lay it out repeatedly to suit the application, making sure that the placement on each door or panel is the same. Cut the vent—generally with a scroll saw—only when you are satisfied with the proportions and placement. The cutout shape would look good on a hung door or on the sliding door of a small locker. It could also be cut into existing panels.

Grilles

Grilles can serve as good, small vents. Applying the technique used for construction of double lap-joint grates (Chapter 7), a mortised grid of 3/8-inch lattice is a good approach. The same bench-saw setup used to cut louver grooves is used here. All dimensions of the latticework—groove width, space between grooves, and cross-section dimensions—are equal (Figure 8-5b). The dadoes are cut to one-half the thickness of the stock, which is then ripped to widths equal to the thickness (Figure 8-5a). Half of the pieces are inverted and interlocked with the other half to form a grille.

Diamond Pattern

If the miter gauge is set at 30°, and the pieces are laid at an additional 30° to each other, they will mesh to form a diamond pattern. In the example shown in Figure 8-6a, enough stock was cut from one original wide board to provide stringers from the both top and bottom of the single piece. The panel appears as in Figure 8-6b. A diamond pattern also results when a right-angled grid (Figure 8-5) is canted at 45°.

For either grid pattern, stock should be cut to the finished lengths, or to multiples of them.

9.

LADDERS

ONBOARD LADDERS

In nautical nomenclature "ladder" includes any flight of treads that takes you from one level to the next. The tight quarters of interior layouts may require you to build a hybrid—something between a typical ladder and typical stairs. Whatever . . . the result is a ladder.

There are a few specific terms you'll need to know before you begin this project: *rise, flight, run, tread, landing, riser, nosing, carriage, open string,* and *closed string.* You'll find a brief definition of each in the glossary at the back of this book (Maybe you can impress your friends at your next get-together!)

If your tastes lean toward grandeur, you might begin with an an open-flight ladder and transcend to a spiral ladder to the bridge, or to a staircase—complete with balustrades—leading from the saloon to the cockpit! My preference leans toward the simple, but at either extreme the companionway is usually of sizable proportion and forms a natural focal point when viewed from the interior.

A ladder, as you surely know, is a structure that invites accident; so, in the interest of safety, I'll repeat a few truisms.

Safety considerations are all the more important when steps become wet and slippery, especially if they're pitching and rolling in a rough sea. The slope angle should be a tradeoff that takes both the climber and clearances into consideration. Make the run long enough to clear whatever is located behind the ladder, but avoid overhead obstructions. A stout rail or a series of handholes is required where the run is short and the ladder therefore nearly vertical. Here, descenders should face the ladder; handrails installed close by or cut into the sloping sides will remind them to do so.

There should be enough exposed tread to plant your feet firmly, with sufficient depth to prevent stubbing your toes (or, perhaps more importantly, to prevent scuffing the varnished bulkhead or case panel at the back!). Figure 9-1 shows calculations and details of ladder design.

Where the run is longer, more like that of stairs than of ladders, increase the tread to provide wider footing. For stairs, a comfortable riser height is about 8 inches, but ladder rungs should be spaced farther apart, say 10 to 12 inches, for a comfortable climb.

However, the riser height itself is not as important as constancy of height. For any rise, especially longer ones leading to the depths of the saloon or engine room, or up to the lofty heights of a flying bridge, it's important to remember that: The scantlings should be strong, the tread level and the riser height constant—from origin to the first tread and from the last tread to the destination level. The body quickly perceives and intuitively expects repetition. The slightest change in riser height experienced over the first few steps can throw off a first-time climber. You yourself know that the top step is a little higher than the rest, and you automatically compensate for it. Your new guests have yet to learn that fact. Keep them in mind.

Calculate the number of spaces between treads, including the destination level, in the total rise to determine riser height. If you are designing a ladder to rise 4 feet, divide the rise (48 inches) into five equal spaces, giving a riser height of 9.6 inches. The number of steps or rungs would be four, the fifth being the destination level.

To calculate the spacing on the slope, we again reach back to our days in geometry class.

Your ladder forms a right triangle with the lower deck and the vertical rise. Its slope is the hypotenuse. The hypotenuse of a triangle is equal to the square root of the sum of the squares of the two sides; in this case the run and the rise. If c is the slope length, b the run, and a the rise, then

$$c = \sqrt{a^2 + b^2}$$

$$c = \sqrt{9.6^2 + 9.6^2}$$

$$c = \sqrt{92.16 + 92.16}$$

$$c = \sqrt{184.32}$$

$$c = 13.58 \text{ inches.}$$

If you know the slope angle and the height of rise, you can use trig to solve for the hypotenuse using the following equation:

$$c = \frac{b}{\sin B}$$

$$c = \frac{9.6}{\sin 45°}$$

$$c = \frac{9.6}{0.70711}$$

$$c = 13.576 \text{ inches.}$$

Where you are designing to an existing but not precalculated riser dimension, you can divide the carriage or sloping side evenly, as follows:

Suppose you want five spaces for four treads. On a large sheet of paper draw a right triangle, with the base proportional to the run and the height proportional to the rise. The hypotenuse, representing the length of the carriage, will be proportional too.

Place a rule with "0" at the top of the rise. Pick five equidistant marks on the rule and swing the rule so that it intersects the run, somewhere. You can extend the run if necessary to contrive the intersection. Obviously the marks have to be far enough apart to reach that far. From the point where the lowest mark reaches the run, draw a line to the top of the rise. Mark the line at each of the chosen points.

Now draw a series of lines through each of these points and the hypotenuse, parallel to the run—i.e., the base of the triangle. Where each one crosses the hypotenuse, make a mark. This will give you equal intervals along the slope (Figure 9-2).

If the intervals are about 9 inches each, they're about right. If they're much greater, or less, try a greater or lesser number of intervals. This sounds involved, but it doesn't take much longer to do it than to describe it, and it will give you a reliable layout for your ladder.

Ladder Rails

Where the run is nearly vertical, handholds can be cut into wide, sloping sides, in line with the climbing figure. As the run dimension increases and the slope is reduced, the rails should be raised to a convenient grip height. Handrails can be attached to the steps or the sloping sides, or onto adjacent bulkheads or cabinets. Rails may not be needed where there is a long run with a short rise, provided one exposes a good expanse of tread. There should be a generous 8 inches of tread beyond the nosing of the tread

Figure 9-1. *Angles and details in ladder design.*

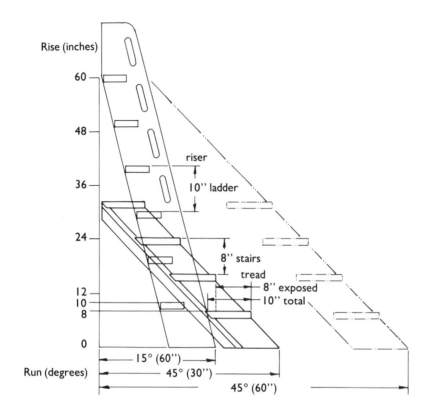

Rise (inches)

60 —

48 —

riser

36 — 10" ladder

24 —

8" stairs
tread

8" exposed
12 — 10" total
10 —
8 —

0 —

15° (60")

Run (degrees) 45° (30")

45° (60")

Joining Tread to Closing Sides

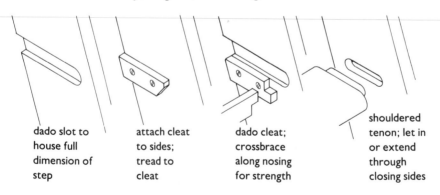

dado slot to
house full
dimension of
step

attach cleat
to sides;
tread to
cleat

dado cleat;
crossbrace
along nosing
for strength

shouldered
tenon; let in
or extend
through
closing sides

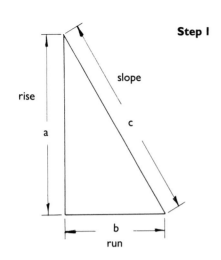

Step 1

slope

rise

a

c

b

run

Figure 9-2.
Geometry in ladder design. Step 1 gives the slope length; step 2 shows how to divide it for equally spaced treads.

use this equation to solve for slope length when rise and run are known:

$$c = \sqrt{a^2 + b^2}$$

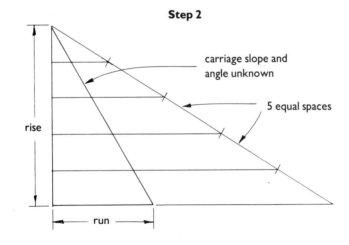

Step 2

carriage slope and angle unknown

5 equal spaces

rise

run

Figure 9-3. *Designing ladders for safety. Nonskid sheets (right) may be glued to finished treads, but must be watched for curling. Note: Compensate for any reduction in material thickness where tread is reduced by grooving or drilling; add risers or short crossmembers as required.*

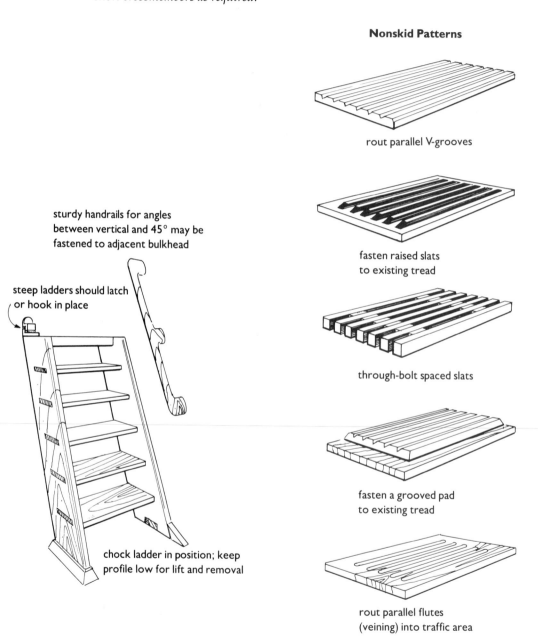

Nonskid Patterns

rout parallel V-grooves

fasten raised slats
to existing tread

through-bolt spaced slats

fasten a grooved pad
to existing tread

rout parallel flutes
(veining) into traffic area

sturdy handrails for angles
between vertical and 45° may be
fastened to adjacent bulkhead

steep ladders should latch
or hook in place

chock ladder in position; keep
profile low for lift and removal

Figure 9-4. *Various design approaches can be taken to provide equal strength by building up the area of section: (1) A = bd = 8 × 3 = 24 sq. in.; (2) A = bs + ht = 8 × 2.0625 + 2.75 × 2.75 = 16.5 + 7.5 = 24 sq. in.; (3) A = bs + ht = 8 × 2 + 4 × 2 = 16 + 8 = 24 sq. in.*

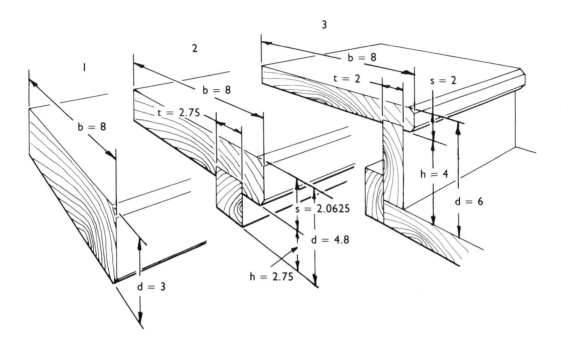

above. A short 45° slope shouldn't need rails if there are sturdy cabinet tops or racks within reach for support.

Ladders can be open or encased at the back. Where encased, the ladder can double as an access cover for the engine compartment, icebox, or battery box, isolating that space. An enclosed flight may be insulated to muffle engine noise, or thermally insulated if the assembly covers an icebox.

Removable ladders should sit firmly in place, held by cleats and/or fastening hardware. Excess weight isn't normally a problem, but be sure that any removable ladder is light enough to handle. Don't exceed 30 to 35 pounds, or 25 pounds if the ladder isn't very accessible.

Nonskid Treads

Slats go with boats—water won't pool in a slatted tread. Slatted treads provide fair traction; just leave the edges on each slat fairly square, with just a slight break or sharp chamfer. Scantlings should be increased to ensure the required strength (Figure 9-3).

For solid steps, a few practical nonskid tread designs include (1) applied strips of commercial material, (2) parallel grooves routed in line with the nose, (3) added raised pads, similarly grooved, or (4) fastened individual slats to provide added traction.

Don't skimp on these nonskid areas. Provide plenty of slats or routed grooves over most of the tread. A traversing shoe should make firm contact with a nonskid area, extending well beyond the normal footprint—even a size 14. A small pad of nonskid, especially if raised, might present rather than prevent a hazard.

Construction. In all designs, whether a ladder or an elaborate staircase, treads must be firmly attached to their carriage or to sloping planks. Riser height must be consistent throughout, and the tread must be horizontal when the ladder is in place.

Tread can be let into opposing dadoes in the sloping sides. For a more decorative result, a shouldered tenon can butt the inside surface of the closing board and extend through a mating mortise to be finished flush with the outside.

Wood should be strong and clear. On interior ladders plywood veneer can be used to construct a back panel, or it can be used along the sloping sides, but avoid plywood for treads. Any hardwood edging will be in the area of greatest stress; beyond that, ply treads preclude routing nonskid grooves. It is better to use solid boards, edge-joined with dowels or with tongue-and-groove glue joints if necessary.

Hardwood edging on plywood can be wide enough to accommodate handholes. Staunchly fasten these structural members with a deep tongue and groove, or liberally glue and screw to guarantee strength. Countersink and bung screw heads along the outer edges.

Stresses. In the interest of weight conservation, most amenities on board smaller vessels are built on the slight side. Nevertheless, we must not sacrifice safety for the sake of weight or appearance.

Force applied to a step or rung concentrates at the attaching joint. Although the joint may be strong, rolling-shear stresses can cause the wood to fail, regardless of the fine joinery. You might be reasoning from earlier remarks that vertical grain would be best for treads, because these surfaces will be walked upon. Au contraire! Here, flat-grain stock is preferred; it presents a stronger network of longitudinal fibers to the areas of stress along the nosing and at the closed string support, whereas vertical grain could *break in shear*—split—more readily where fiber concentration is more or less aligned with the lines of stress. The normal orientation of the grain on a rung or step should be in its strongest direction—that is with the grain perpendicular to the supporting dado, mortise-and-tenon, or cleat. If the grain were to run in the same direction as the line of support, the wood might break very easily in rolling shear. It is in this orientation that wood fibers can roll over each other and fail.

Figure 9-4 depicts three ways to build a ladder of required strength. Thickness (or depth) is selected based on the load and span. Secondly, a thinner plank can be augmented by a brace to net the same strength, and lastly, if you are building an enclosed ladder, the full risers add additional strength to common-milled thicknesses. In these examples it is assumed that the ends are let in and captured into sloping sides or fastened to cleats in turn fastened on the sloping sides.

Standard "1-by" stock (3/4-inch dressed) may be adequate for narrow treads, well fastened and well supported by riser boards. But for open construction, I suggest full 4/4 or thicker material. You can add strength by increasing the thickness or by supporting the tread with a wooden brace, apron, or full riser panel below.

Bronze or stainless steel hardware is available to hook removable companionway ladders in place or to swing them away. Specialty hardware also is available for folding swim ladders, so you can make a small, storable unit as described below.

OVERBOARD LADDERS

While folding aluminum ladders do reduce storage problems, they sometimes can sacrifice rigidity, and (regrettably) they may come with a fully illustrated owner's manual for opening and closing the assembly!

Larger vessels, especially powerboats, may have a swim platform from which a permanently installed swim ladder can be swung into the water. We who occasionally climb out of the water, up the freeboard, and over the rail need a little help in performing this feat. In a pinch, a boatswain's chair or trapeze swung from a halyard or a deck fitting is helpful. However, occasional swimmers deserve a bonafide ladder as in Figure 9-5.

A rope-and-rung, or Jacob's, ladder might suffice. It stows easily and yet is not too difficult to use—after a bit of acrobatics on the lowest (submerged) rung. These ladders have a tendency to swing and may not be too kind to the hull. Any swinging ladder should provide sufficient depth to keep toes away from the hull and include bumper material (available in extruded lengths) let in and epoxied to each rung where it contacts the hull under a swimmer's weight. Hemispherical rubber buttons also provide protection. The stringing pattern for a rope-and-rung ladder is as follows: Start down one side and then up again, leaving enough length to attach to a winch or other substantial fitting on deck; then start back down and up the other side, which will be tied off. While stringing, tie a figure-eight knot under each rung at the correct spacing. (If you want to do a truly elegant job, don't tie off the two ends; splice them with a neat, tapered splice.)

A larger overboard ladder may be lashed or hooked on deck when not in use. However, on-deck stowage can get in the way, obstructing visibility, or it may become a hazard to crew scrambling on deck. If you can design a folding ladder that can be stowed below, all the better.

Despite any stowage inconvenience the conventional design is classic. Polished bronze or chromium hardware is readily available from purveyors of specialty items, as mentioned in Chapter 1. Hinge, hasp, and hook configurations dictate the ladder's pro-

Figure 9-5. *Designs for overboard ladders. Hardware for hook-over ladders is available in sets; standard marine-quality hardware can be used for installed swim ladders.*

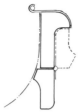

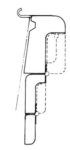

integral pads with bumpers will snug against a rounded hull to steady a climb

a high freeboard may necessitate a double-drop ladder

a mounted step ladder must overhang platform for extension to clear the step edge

thread rungs on 3/8'' braided or twisted line and tie knots under each pad corner; tie together at top, with enough line to loop over a cleat, winch, or other suitable fitting

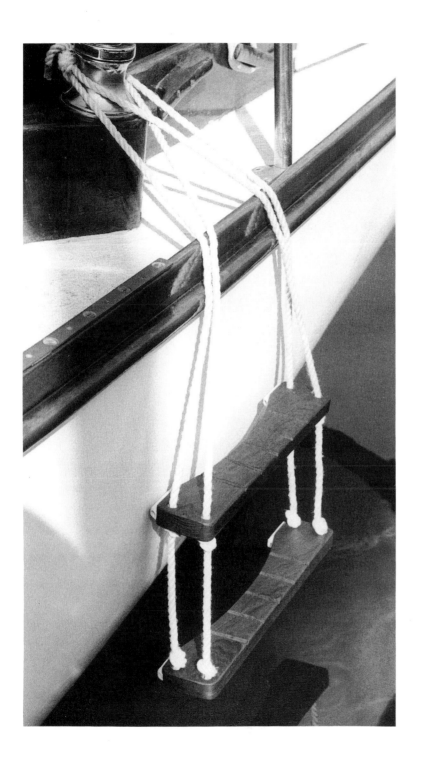

file, but at the same time leave plenty of opportunity to show the elegance and skill of your workmanship.

If you are selecting individual items of hardware (rather than using a ladder kit) remember that hinges should not work against their fasteners. Forces should be in shear with respect to the fasteners, not aligned with them. Remember to let in the hinges to reduce the gap and to get maximum usable width in the folding parts.

Constant exposure to the elements would indicate teak as the wood of choice. The same joinery precepts discussed previously hold true here, but do remember to use waterproof glue.

10.

TABLES

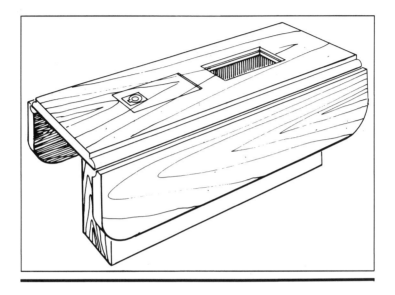

Cabin Tables • **Saloon Tables** • **Cockpit Tables**

BUILDING TABLES

As with the other projects in this book, individual tables should be proportioned to the size of the vessel—there's no need for 10 places at the table if the accommodations and physical space limit the capacity to fewer bodies. Regardless of its size, a cabin table or settee is a place for meals; it doubles as a chart table, a game table, or just a place to sit and read. Massiveness doesn't imply elegance—a small table can be inviting to the solo skipper or captain and mate.

Your boat already may include a settee or nook, and simply replacing its chrome and plastic top with natural wood might be improvement enough. But a custom table will display your joinery skills prominently. In addition to the detail of the tabletop, the base also can be attractive, mounted on the boat's centerboard trunk rather than on four legs or a pedestal. You could mount it on a mid-cabin locker that you've designed and built for the purpose.

Tables may be temporary structures, stowed or swung back into a bulkhead, or they can encircle a keel-stepped mast or whatever odd shapes there may be on your vessel. An area that accommodates several activities can benefit from a table that folds away when not in use. Most typical is the drop-leaf table, which should be fastened securely when folded. Adjustable arrangements that make up the "double" in double bunks are peculiar to your interior arrangement, bunk height, and, if you use the back as a mattress extension, even the thickness of your cushions.

Stand-alone tables for "le grand salon" (to us simple sailors, the "saloon") don't differ much from shoreside tables, except for some hold-down provision for the table and what's on it. Ships' tables should include fiddles to keep place settings in place. In a sailing cruiser, where a long tack is common, the table can be on gimbals fore-and-aft to maintain a fairly level surface, with a provision for locking it in position according to the heeling angle.

Design and Layout

Slat and grate tops are not too practical for permanently installed tables. Solid surfaces serve you better and prevent your having to pick spilled food from numerous holes or slots. Some choices are shown in Figure 10-1.

Simpler tabletop shapes include squares, circles, and rectangles; in suitable surroundings any one of these can be pleasing. One or both ends of an essentially rectangular table can be laid out as a semicircle; or the corners can be rounded off with quarter-circles, with a smaller radius tangent to the right-angled edges. In Figure 10-1 a three-panel table is shown as a drop leaf—the leaves are finished with a quarter-round edge, although any radius could be used.

An elliptical table, which also can be made with drop leaves, requires a slightly more complex design. Perhaps the most mysterious part of the elliptical design is the layout of the ellipse. You can use either a beam compass or the old pencil-and-string trick for the job. Figure 10-2 illustrates the beam-compass method.

The final example in Figure 10-1 is a planked tabletop with clampboards at each end. This design would fit right in on the classic boat.

Materials and Joinery

The easiest way to construct a sizable tabletop is to use marine plywood with a face veneer that matches whatever wood may be nearby. A top surfaced with Formica or other impervious material is a pleasing combination; for example, matte white Formica trimmed with teak. Finishing the edges of any laminate presents a good opportunity to

Figure 10-1.   *Design and joinerwork in tables for the cabin.*

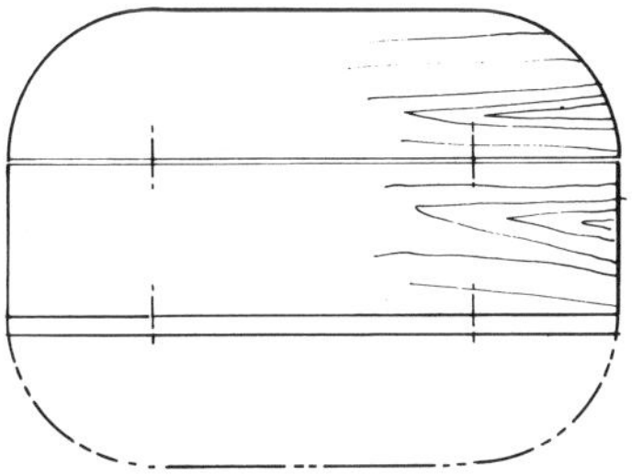

Tabletop Cross Sections

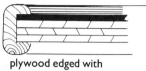

plywood edged with rapped fiddle

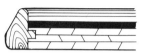

edged with beveled fiddle

tongue-and-groove flush with plywood

solid boards dowel-pinned and glued

solid boards with spline or biscuits

drop-leaf edge; tongue-and-groove joint

tongue-and-groove with bevel

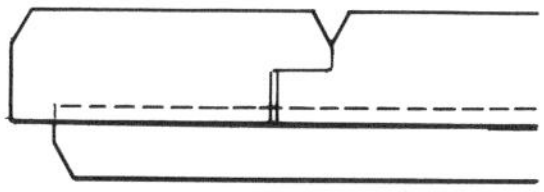

shiplap with or without bevel; underside cleats flush or inset

a drop leaf for narrow spaces

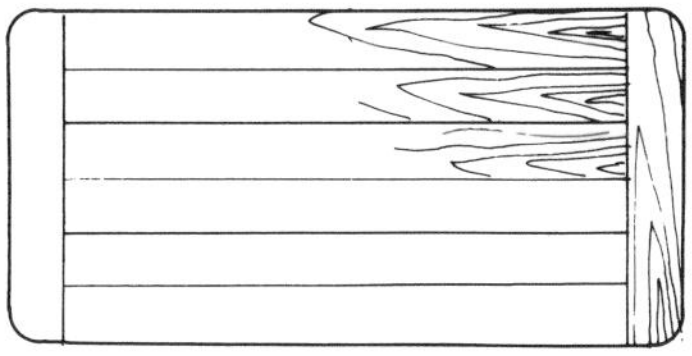

plank top with tongue-and-groove end clamps

177

Figure 10-2. *The layout of an ellipse. It is best to draw it full-size on kraft paper, following these steps. Step 1: Draw two intersecting centerlines at right angles, ab for the length and wx for the width. The center where they cross is o. Step 2: With w and x as centers and radius wx, draw two arcs that intersect at the ab centerline. (If the arcs are correct, both the arcs and the centerline will meet at the two points just beyond a and b.) Step 3: Divide oa and ob in half and mark the centers c and d. Step 4: At c and d, draw circles tangent to the two arcs first drawn. These arcs will be nearly semicircles in your ellipse.*

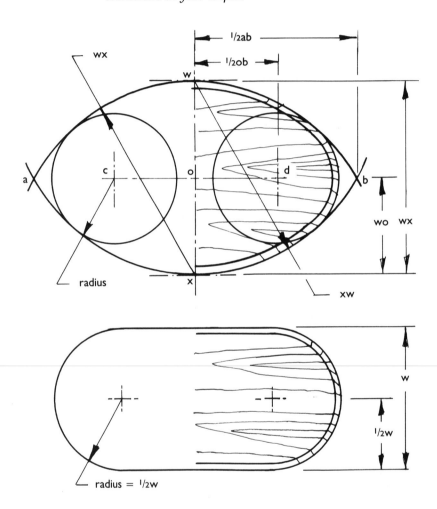

Figure 10-3. *Narrow passageways may require folding tables. Hinging should be planned carefully. Construct a folding tabletop using continuous hinge or sewing machine hinges, the latter let in flush; add fiddles to underside for exposure when folded. To construct a drop-leaf table, rout or shape the drop-leaf joint using a drop-leaf bead-and-cove cuttter. Butt hinges and sturdy support arms prevent sag.*

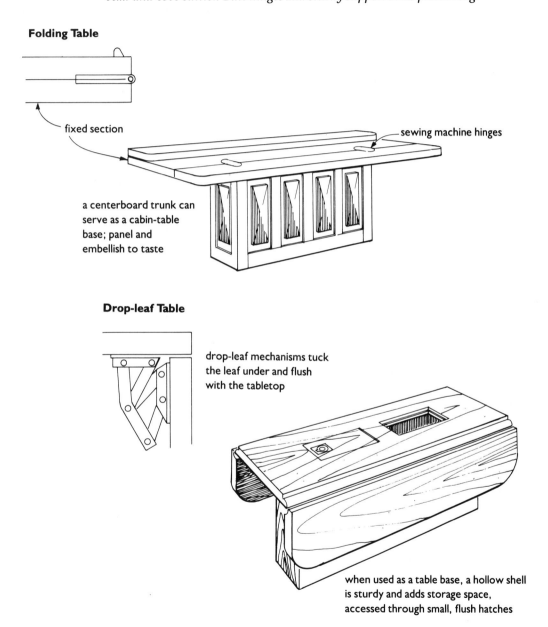

Folding Table

fixed section

sewing machine hinges

a centerboard trunk can serve as a cabin-table base; panel and embellish to taste

Drop-leaf Table

drop-leaf mechanisms tuck the leaf under and flush with the tabletop

when used as a table base, a hollow shell is sturdy and adds storage space, accessed through small, flush hatches

179

incoporate fine joinerwork, ranging from a simple edge to an integral fiddle. If the drop leaf is made of plywood, all exposed edges must be framed with solid wood.

Solid wood is the time-honored material of choice for tabletops, and it is especially practical where the length of the table far exceeds the width. The glued edge-joints between the boards must be strong; rout the edges to form tongue-and-groove or glue joints. Or you might prefer to dowel-pin or spline. Dovetail keys are even more effective. Splines may be hidden or exposed. You can produce an attractive end-grain detail by dressing and finishing the splines at the ends. This is especially pleasing if you use a dovetail key to join the boards.

Remember to alternate grain direction when edge-joining flat-grain boards. If you choose to dowel these pieces, it would be handy if you had a horizontal drill, such as a Shopsmith. Simply lower the drill-press head to the horizontal position and set the table to one-half the thickness of the boards being joined. With this setup, a drill in the Jacobs chuck can be fed into the center of the planed edge of the board. If you don't have a Shopsmith, you can use a set of dowel-pin centering plugs instead. In this case, drill the holes in the edge of one board, insert the corresponding plugs, and press the adjoining board against the sharp marking points. The marks indicate where the mating holes must be drilled so that the two pieces will align. Take great care to drill all holes at true right angles to the edges, or the boards will not come together. Some woodworkers build an angle plate from high-grade plywood and mount it on the drill press. When the workpiece is clamped to the angle plate, the drill automatically enters the edge at right angles.

Boards joined by any of these methods may be slightly beveled at the edges, forming grooves that add some design interest and an illusion of length. The grooves are not too practical if you plan to plot a compass course over the indentations, but they won't interfere with most other activities. Whatever the edge joinery, planked tabletops can be clamped using underside cleats that double as base attachments. Another option is, once again, the clamp board let in across the ends; it makes a good finish that nicely conceals the end grain. You also can add battens underneath, either flush or let in, to make a truly interesting seagoing tabletop.

Among the basic tabletops described above, edge-joined construction is best suited for making folded-top and drop-leaf tables, although veneer plywood can be used—as I indicated earlier—provided it is framed or edged. The matching, solid edge can be plain and fairly narrow, or, if it is wide enough, it can be milled to make a drop-leaf joint.

In any design you choose, don't forget the fiddles. It's easy enough to incorporate them into the design right at the start.

Suitable hardware includes: a piano hinge along a flush butt joint, for either the folded-top or drop-leaf table, as in Figure 10-3; sewing machine hinges for the folded-top table; or the more traditional drop-leaf mechanism with hinges and a release device. Insist on substantial hardware that will not droop over time. Nobody likes a droop-leaf table, especially the builder!

Among others, The Woodworkers' Store offers various drop-leaf supports including extension arms for tables with and without aprons, and a double-action hinge that tucks the drop leaf under and flush with the vertical edge of the top, then swings it up and back hard against the edge when it is opened all the way.

For greatest comfort, design to standard heights where possible. The height of a standard table is 29 inches; that of the standard seat, 17 inches. If these heights are not practical for your arrangement, maintain a vertical chair-to-tabletop distance of 12 inches and a comfortable horizontal distance from fixed seats to fixed table edge, remembering that not everyone is as svelte as you are—or once were. Underside aprons, supports, and braces should not extend too far below the tabletop where they can encounter knees. By all means, eliminate any sharp corners that could incapacitate the galley crew at clean-up time.

Cabin Tables

Cabin tables are the workhorse tables of the average yacht. They should be outfitted with fiddles and, depending on your power/sail persuasion and cruising ambitions, gimbals. A gimballed table can be free-swinging and counterbalanced, but you should be able to pin it in position when sea conditions warrant. Figure 10-4 shows the most important features of the gimballed design, including a counterbalance to keep the table as horizontal as possible. And this brings us to the issue of supports for the table.

Only large yachts have room for the standard four-legged table. A trestle table, however, is a good design for close quarters, and especially for gimballing. The pedestal table probably causes the least interference on an active yacht; the trestle comes in a close second. Supported by a pair of braces, set in from the ends, the assembly can (and should) be bolted or angle-braced to the cabin sole. The two legs serve as good anchoring posts for the gimbal arrangement.

In the design shown, the basic trestle has been duplicated to make four pieces all alike. Two of them are shortened and inverted to hold the tabletop, and the other two form the legs. The tabletop assembly rests on in-line trunnions cradled in corresponding slots in the tops of the legs. The stretcher between the legs may be made of wood or metal.

A brass pipe weighted with sand or concrete will provide counterbalance. A swing of 15° is a comfortable angle. To design for more is to ask the crew sitting on the lee side to view their meal from under the table. Provide some form of indexing, perhaps a pin inserted through a series of holes, to set the table at a variety of suitable angles, or a track where a bolt and wingnut can be tightened at a comfortable angle for a long haul.

Figure 10-4. *A gimballed trestle table. The counterweight should be heavy and strong—it may take some abuse.*

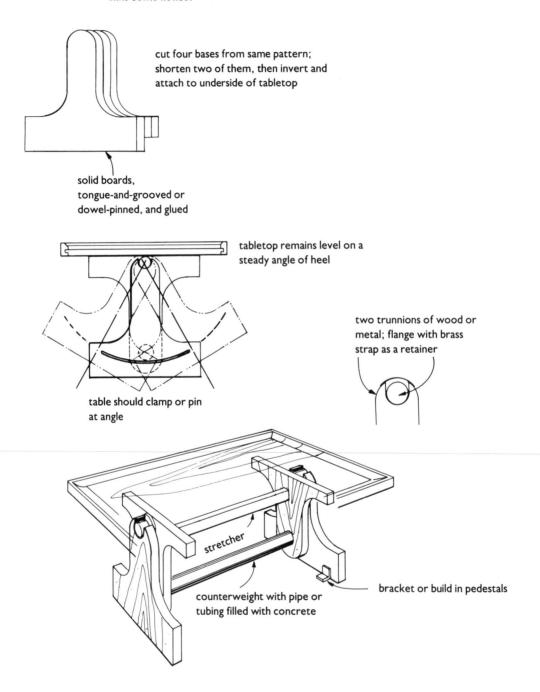

cut four bases from same pattern; shorten two of them, then invert and attach to underside of tabletop

solid boards, tongue-and-grooved or dowel-pinned, and glued

tabletop remains level on a steady angle of heel

two trunnions of wood or metal; flange with brass strap as a retainer

table should clamp or pin at angle

stretcher

counterweight with pipe or tubing filled with concrete

bracket or build in pedestals

Figure 10-5. *These 15" cubes, placed in a roomy cabin, make convenient tables, stools, and storage chests. Make them strong enough to sit on.*

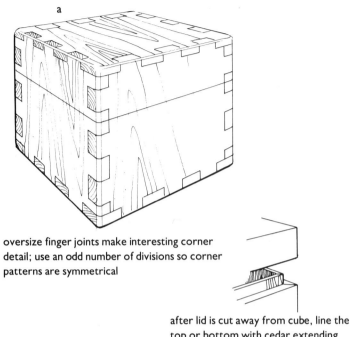

a

oversize finger joints make interesting corner detail; use an odd number of divisions so corner patterns are symmetrical

after lid is cut away from cube, line the top or bottom with cedar extending into mating piece

plywood veneer panels let into hardwood frames

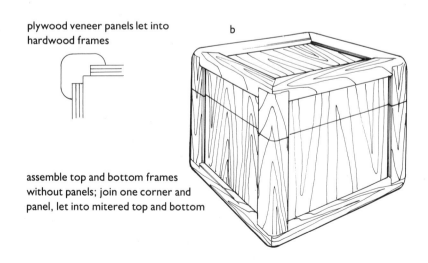

b

assemble top and bottom frames without panels; join one corner and panel, let into mitered top and bottom

Figure 10-6. *Ingenuity is called for in the design of cockpit tables. A clamp-on and a portable table are shown here.*

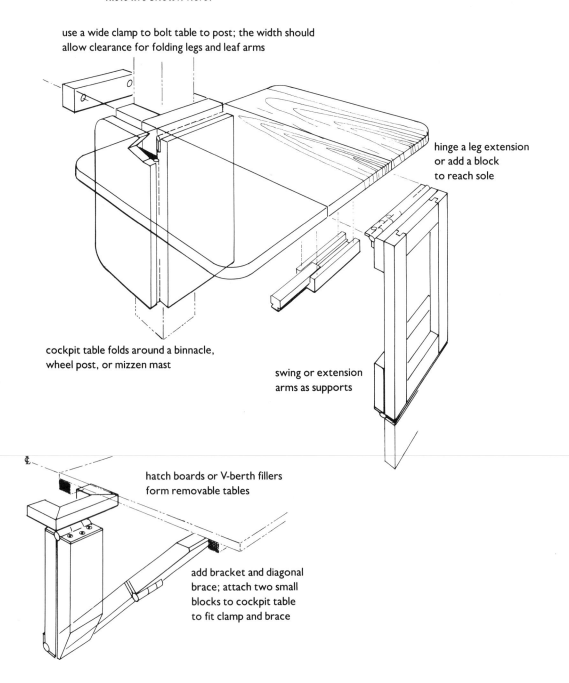

use a wide clamp to bolt table to post; the width should allow clearance for folding legs and leaf arms

hinge a leg extension or add a block to reach sole

cockpit table folds around a binnacle, wheel post, or mizzen mast

swing or extension arms as supports

hatch boards or V-berth fillers form removable tables

add bracket and diagonal brace; attach two small blocks to cockpit table to fit clamp and brace

Saloon Tables

Some yachts can absorb whole rooms full of shoreside furniture in their spacious saloons. The only modification might be a bracket or another type of fastening to keep the item in place. Traditional furnishings work well in such surroundings.

For the more typical—and affordable—vessel, any provision for multipurpose furniture is welcome. For example, small cubic chests can double as tables, lockers, and, with a handy cushion thrown on top, as additional seating. On larger yachts, a pair of wing chairs might share one such chest/locker/table, or a truly spacious interior might accommodate a table for each wing chair.

A typical box is shown in Figure 10-5a. The box has a lift-off lid that fits over an inner lining, possibly of aromatic cedar. This design can be modified to serve as a sea chest, complete with strap hinges, corner plates, an ornate hasp and clasp, and rope handles. A variation is the plywood-and-frame structure in Figure 10-5b.

At the Spartan end of the spectrum, a table might consist of a work surface covering a long drawer. Just add a 3/16- or 1/4-inch plywood insert, let in along the top of the drawer sides. Face it with a sheet of Formica. You might add a hinge to allow access to the contents below without your having to pull the drawer all the way out.

Cockpit Tables

In the cockpit, a combination drink holder and table can improve creature comfort while underway. A few of the designs presented in Chapter 4 suggest just such an addition. If the unit were intended to function more as a table and less as a drink holder, it could swing up from a pedestal stand or fit into a mating bracket in the cockpit well (Figure 10-6).

You might like the idea of a portable table, one that can be stowed or, better yet, used below for some other purpose and brought out to the cockpit for a summer meal under balmy skies. (You could get to like that. . . .)

I've had some second thoughts about using grates or slats as tabletops (Remember what I said in Chapter 6?). However, my second thoughts relate only to temporary tabletops. In the interest of efficiency and conservation of space, a triangular insert from the V-berth, or a dropboard for the companionway hatch, could serve as a handy extra table in the cockpit. Brackets, braces, and auxiliary legs can be designed to fit these somewhat irregular shapes. The only modification to the quasi tabletops would be the addition of the said brackets and braces, etc.

11.

HATCH COVERS AND SKYLIGHTS

HATCH COVERS

Hatch covers are among the most prominent features of your boat. They deserve the very best materials and joinery you can muster. Those who build hatch covers won't use them as platforms—those who don't will stand wherever they please. The message is: Design for the latter. Covers must be strong enough to withstand both normal and extremely abnormal loads. Design your hatch cover for a deckhand to jump on—*once*—there must be a limit to what the skipper will tolerate!

Design

There are two basic types of hatches: flat and curved. Obviously, the detailed design and construction of the two kinds will differ, but there are quite a few common elements that should be taken up at the outset.

In addition to strength, the most fundamental design requirements include watertightness, durability, appearance, and a general sense that the design conforms to the overall look of the boat. Covers take a beating. Constant exposure to the elements and different moisture levels, above and below the cover, can strain the best joinery. Just to torture the joinery a little more, wood swells in summer and shrinks in winter.

You'll probably fit your new cover to an existing opening, so the design will be influenced or even dictated by the coamings and attaching hardware. This is not to say that a single pair of hinges can't be changed to two opposing pairs of hinges with removable pins to provide a choice of opening direction, or that a hinged cover cannot be made into a sliding cover. However, don't go too far when making modifications around hatches; it is important to protect the boat's structural integrity. Don't modify deck beams or molded coamings.

Still, there are good and sufficient reasons to change a hatch cover. Maybe you need more light below, or better ventilation, or the old hatch cover has been damaged, or you simply want the boat to look better. Any or all of these reasons can be good excuses for retiring to the shop for a while. . . .

The crown of your deckhouse, be it a doghouse, trunkhouse, or wheelhouse, becomes more convex as the cabin sides converge forward or aft of their maximum beam. (Usually forward—only fairly large boats have separate, major hatches aft of the maximum beam.) To the eye, the crown may seem constant, but in fact it constantly changes. In profile view, the house and hatch line should converge with the deck line at the boat's stem, as shown in Figure 11-1. Avoid bumps and lumps that drastically interrupt the boat's roof line. As one looks forward or aft, parallel to the boat's centerline, the crown of a cover should follow the crown of the deck or house where it is installed. Where the thwartships vertical face of the hatch meets the deck you have two options—curve it to parallel the crown or make it straight and horizontal.

Materials for hatch covers range from molded fiberglass to various kinds of marine-grade plywood to solid wooden planking. Some covers integrate solar panels that augment the power supply. A large class uses transparent materials instead of wooden planking. These latter materials are special enough to warrant separate treatment in the section on flat hatch covers.

There are many looks and methods of construction, from a dry-seam cover, faired into a smooth arc, to distinct boards, either faired to an arc or laid in a series of flats over the crown. In planked covers, seams may be either *dry* (glued using waterproof glue or epoxy) or *caulked* (bedded and sealed with elastomer).

Figure 11-1. *On a lower-profile vessel, the lines through the coach roof and a forward hatch should meet the chord of the boat's sheer at the stem. Otherwise, the general appearance is boxy and awkward.*

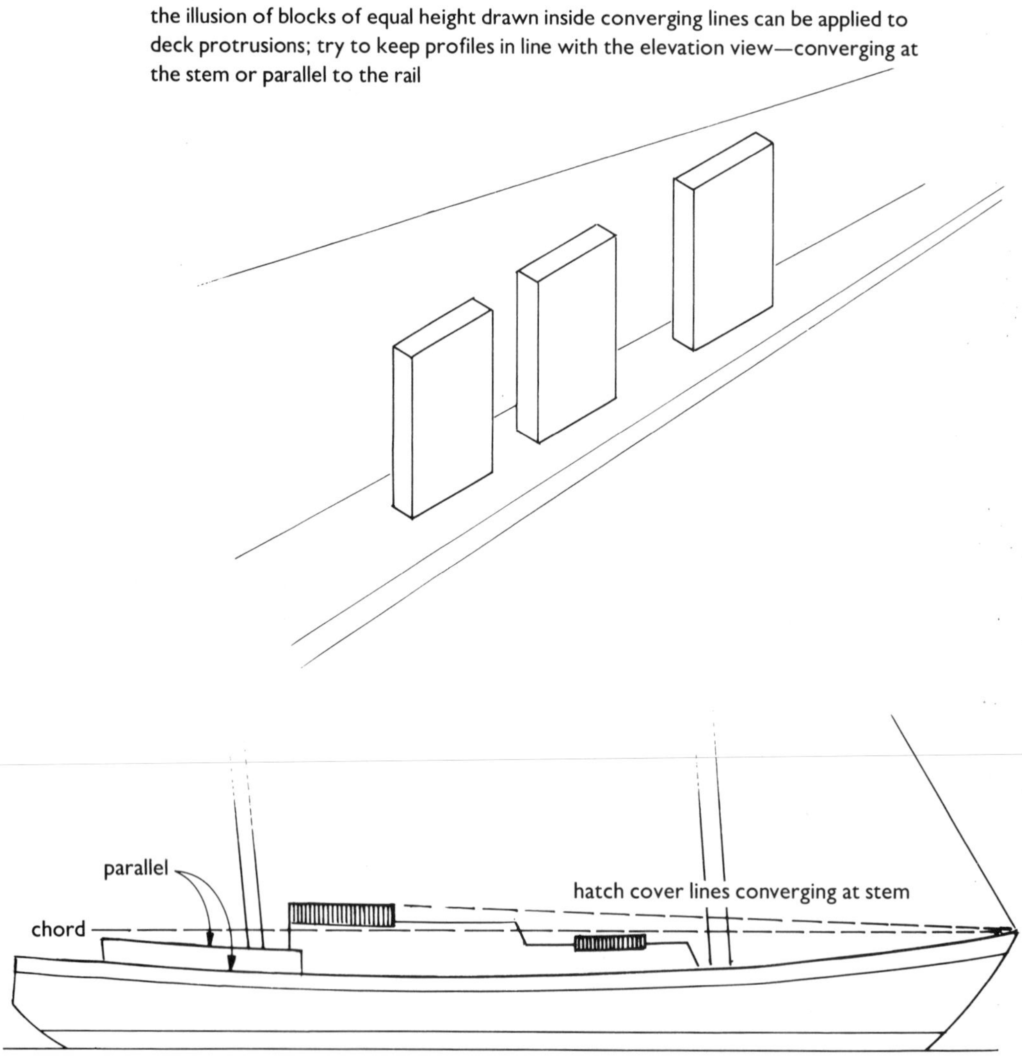

the illusion of blocks of equal height drawn inside converging lines can be applied to deck protrusions; try to keep profiles in line with the elevation view—converging at the stem or parallel to the rail

parallel

chord

hatch cover lines converging at stem

Mix or match the designs of hatch covers with the design of the rest of the boat—with respect to materials, shapes, patterns, and joinery. If there is no pattern to follow, select a style that best sets off the overall appearance of the boat.

Construction

Before getting into the details, a few words on materials.

Hatch covers demand the best; wood should be premium-grade material, nothing less. If you can get it, all hardware should be bronze—flat-head and oval-head wood screws, continuous hinges, and any brackets, braces, and hasps. *Brass is inadmissible.*

As mentioned, the crown on the cover should seem to match the crown of the nearest coach roof or deck. Some schools suggest a slight exaggeration of the crown, since it will appear flatter in its surroundings.

Crowned hatch covers have an inherent tendency to flatten when weight is applied. To resist deflection, the scantlings of the vertical members (we'll call them *frames*; the thwartships ones are *beams*, the others are *sides*) must be increased. If you ignore this requirement, your cover surely will deflect under load, which could lead to the disruption of the glue joints and might spread the frame itself. Flat covers have a still greater tendency to bow under similar loads.

A full ⁴/₄ (1-inch measured thickness) frame material should be adequate for lap-joined corners. The beams of the lap-joint structure should extend the full width of the cover beneath the planking, as in Figure 11-2. Place the undercut in the other member of the joint so that all planks are screwed into a single member, across the entire width of the cover, not straddling a joint.

Whether or not the coaming has been rebuilt, the existing hatch will dictate the dimensions of your new cover. Options in the design of the cover include matching either the thickness and cross section of the coaming and aligning the cover to the outside of the coaming, both members being rabbeted, or overlapping the coaming on the outside to form a kind of shell around it. Figure 11-2 shows both types of construction in detail.

Bluewater cruisers probably should opt for a cover and coaming that can be battened down against heavy weather, whereas a runabout or a daysailer might select the shell design, which allows some space between coaming and hatch cover. This choice helps ventilate the accommodation yet, while not quite as watertight as the first, it does fairly well against anything but a sea coming green over the bow.

When constructing a hatch cover, orient the planks so that the grain runs in the same direction in all of them. Otherwise it may be quite difficult to plane the final assembly without chipping the surface. Photo 11-1 illustrates a number of details for assembling planks and making bungs. I recommend that you make your own bungs if possible. This yields the best match in the type and grain of the wood.

I mentioned hardware earlier; make it hefty. Caulking materials are a live topic in themselves. Aside from the treatment of the edges that are to be caulked, which we will take up separately for flat and curved covers, there are a number of details to be considered.

First of all, unless the instructions of the seam-compound manufacturer say otherwise, the edges that are to be caulked should be painted first. The type of paint or varnish is not too important; it won't show. Its function is important, though, because it prevents water vapor from working into the wood under the caulking, with subsequent slow rotting. Then the cotton should be driven firmly into the seam, but not hard enough to spread or damage the edges. Use caulking cotton only. This is a loosely spun bundle that looks like an extremely poor grade of cord in a state of disrepair. A real caulking iron is best for this job, but any wide, thin blade—quite dull—will serve in the narrow seams of a yacht's hatch cover. After the cotton comes another coat of paint (again subject to the manufacturer's instructions), this time to prevent water from getting into the cotton. At the same time it prevents the seam compound, or one constituent of it, from being preferentially absorbed by the cotton, leaving an insufficient amount of the good stuff to seal the joint properly. Only after this has been done is the seam finally payed with the chosen compound.

Nowadays all the popular seam compounds are *elastomers* (which means they are rubbery); just what you want for the come-and-go of wood as the humidity varies. Typical compounds include 3M's 5200, Thiokol's two-part polysulfide, Detco, and Sikaflex. According to a study on sealants by the magazine *Practical Sailor,* silicones will seal Lexan, PVC, and acrylics, but they will not bond to wood. Polysulfide compounds, either one-part for bedding compound or two-part for seams, will stand up to fuel spills and deck cleaners, whereas polyurethane-based sealants tend to soften when attacked by some two-part deck cleaners. Read the container and specification sheet on the seam compound to determine suitability. One-part elastomer is the easier way to go, even if you give up protection against chemicals that you won't be using anyway.

Manufacturers' instructions will identify processes and characteristics, but one-part elastomers generally can be payed into grooves with a caulking gun. The material either will stand proud of the surface to compensate for shrinkage during cure, or it should be troweled flat. Tape isn't always the wisest precaution since you may wind up sanding both elastomer and gummed-up tape from the surface. A precaution that will expedite cleanup is to prefinish the planks using a few coats of whatever finish you will use on the cover. This way, wandering compound won't penetrate the grain.

Essentially, follow product instructions. If you are advised to apply elastomer to raw wood only, keep the seam grooves raw for best adhesion. Seal only the adjacent surfaces.

Preparation of seams.   Caulking cotton and seam compound have to have a place to go, so you will want the seams to be open at the top, but not lower down. This will call for some beveling. Bevel the lower third of the edges so that the planks will butt, making a tight seam and a neat appearance as seen from below. Possibly only one edge of each plank will have to be beveled, as shown in Figure 11-3, but if this bevel tends to close the top V-groove, make a second bevel cut in one edge or in both top edges to open a good caulking seam.

Fasteners. Screws should be bronze (a good second choice is stainless steel), countersunk, counterbored, and covered over with a hefty bung. It is best to drill screw holes, angled slightly toward the adjacent plank. When driven home, angled screws will tend to force the plank downward and sideways toward its neighbor. All planks should be glued with the best waterproof glue and clamped securely in place before fastening. Rely on screws to hold, not to force, the board into position.

Use a combination drill bit to suit the screw size (1¼-inch #8 or #10, for example). Some models are adjustable for screw length. Combination bits can drill a pilot hole and a shank hole and countersink and counterbore in one operation. Countersink and counterbore the screws fairly deeply, but no more than halfway through the board. The nearer the edge of the board, the deeper the screw should be set to give the depth needed for a bung that can be faired neatly into a smooth surface, whether the cover is flat or crowned. Net a bung at least ¼ inch deep when finished. Stagger plank fasteners into beams and sides to prevent creating a fracture line in the frame member (Figure 11-2).

You either can buy plugs (bungs), or make your own. Plugs may be cut on a drill press using—what else?—plug cutters. For easy trimming with a sharp chisel, plugs should be cut perpendicularly to the wood grain on the flat of the usual board. And don't show off your fine hole pattern by inserting the bung with its grain at an arbitrary angle to the grain in the planking. Align it as well as you can.

Would you believe that there's a right and a wrong way to finish off the bungs? To start with, you don't know which way the grain runs—upward toward the end of the bung or downward toward the planking. If you try to chisel off the excess material, and the grain runs into the bung below the surface of the work, you have a problem. To prevent this minor catastrophe, start with the chisel *bevel-down* and the edge high up against the bung (Figure 11-2). When the bung is cut, the grain will run up or down— rarely level. From then on, chisel away from the low to the high side. The bung can be carved off flush with no trouble. Note that the chisel is used bevel-down throughout.

FLAT HATCH COVERS

One advantage of flat covers over the crowned variety is that they may be constructed from wider planks, resulting in fewer joints. Crowned covers require narrower strips to conform to the arc. Nevertheless, your design criterion should not be the number of caulked joints but the pattern that best fits the surroundings. If the planking pattern will stand alone, and wide boards are not alien to the appearance of the boat, opt for wide boards. If you are more or less matching a seamed deck, try to conform to its appearance.

(Continued on page 197)

Figure 11-2. *Details of hatch construction.*

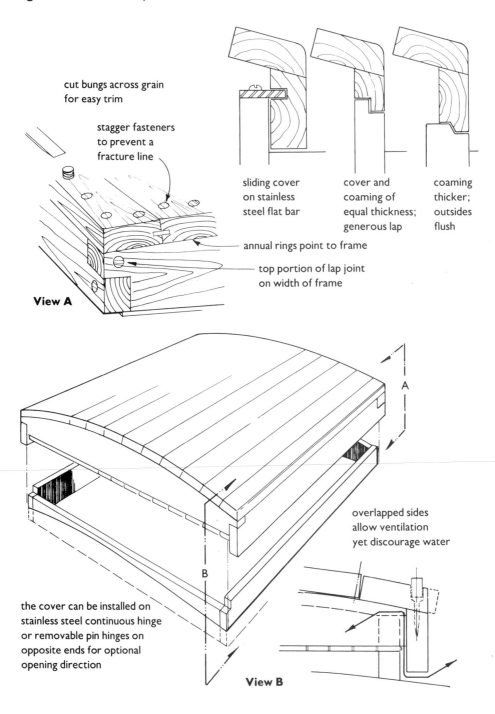

cut bungs across grain
for easy trim

stagger fasteners
to prevent a
fracture line

sliding cover
on stainless
steel flat bar

cover and
coaming of
equal thickness;
generous lap

coaming
thicker;
outsides
flush

annual rings point to frame

top portion of lap joint
on width of frame

View A

overlapped sides
allow ventilation
yet discourage water

the cover can be installed on
stainless steel continuous hinge
or removable pin hinges on
opposite ends for optional
opening direction

View B

a

Photo 11-1.

Details for assembling planks and making bungs. (a) You'll use lots of bungs. Cut them with a plug cutter through the face of the board. (b) Install beams after first few planks are attached. Let beams into sides or cut short to fit inside coaming. (c) Assemble random-length planks; square and cut off later. (Series continues on page 194.)

b

c

d

(d) Insert bungs over screw heads. If loose, coat with varnish. This seals bungs in but allows future removal. (e) Round or chamfer edges, fair planking, smooth, and sand. Use 220-grit for final sanding.

e

Figure 11-3. *A planked hatch. The beams may be let into the side frames or stopped short of the coaming to clear.*

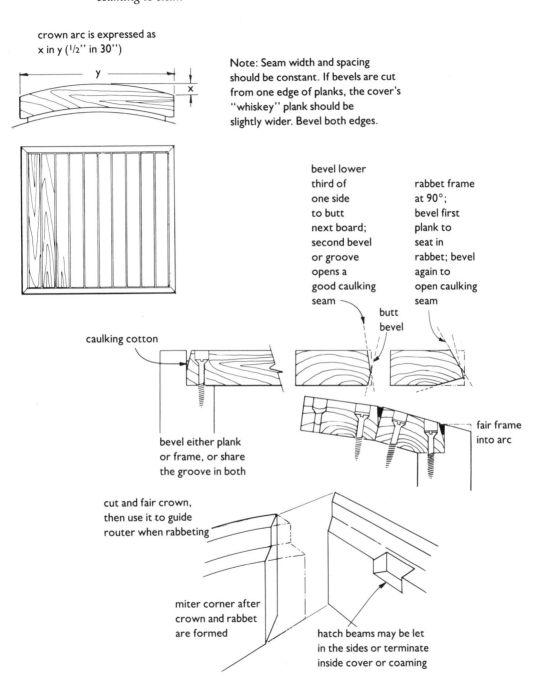

crown arc is expressed as
x in y (¹/₂'' in 30'')

y

x

Note: Seam width and spacing should be constant. If bevels are cut from one edge of planks, the cover's "whiskey" plank should be slightly wider. Bevel both edges.

bevel lower third of one side to butt next board; second bevel or groove opens a good caulking seam

rabbet frame at 90°; bevel first plank to seat in rabbet; bevel again to open caulking seam

butt bevel

caulking cotton

bevel either plank or frame, or share the groove in both

fair frame into arc

cut and fair crown, then use it to guide router when rabbeting

miter corner after crown and rabbet are formed

hatch beams may be let in the sides or terminate inside cover or coaming

Figure 11-4. *A flat, planked cover. It may be built up on beams or as a facing on a plywood or fiberglass substructure.*

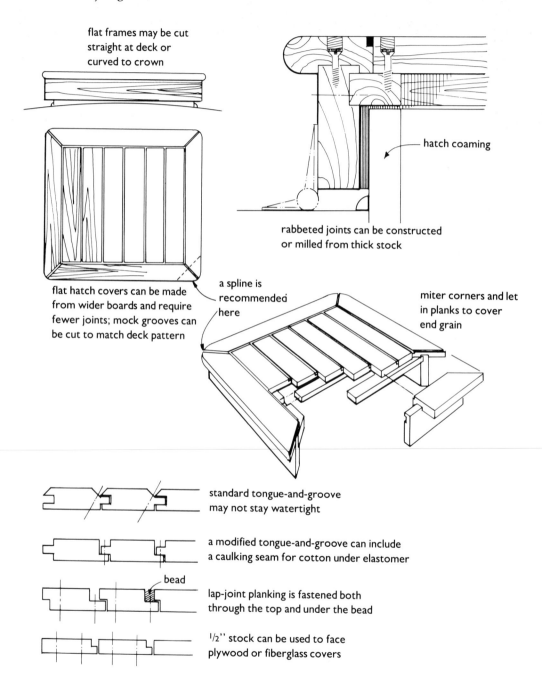

flat frames may be cut
straight at deck or
curved to crown

hatch coaming

rabbeted joints can be constructed
or milled from thick stock

flat hatch covers can be made
from wider boards and require
fewer joints; mock grooves can
be cut to match deck pattern

a spline is
recommended
here

miter corners and let
in planks to cover
end grain

standard tongue-and-groove
may not stay watertight

a modified tongue-and-groove can include
a caulking seam for cotton under elastomer

bead

lap-joint planking is fastened both
through the top and under the bead

1/2'' stock can be used to face
plywood or fiberglass covers

A lesson from the old ChrisCraft runabouts: Mock seams evenly spaced along wider boards reduce the number of real joints to be waterproofed. Parallel grooves between the actual tongue-and-groove joints are caulked for pattern only. This method makes for a strong panel and reduces the number of steps in construction. Blind fasteners through the lower members of the lapped construction—beneath the seam compound—will hold the planking in place. The upper members can be screwed down in the usual way. The main point is that however the fastening is done, the lapped or tongue-and-groove construction adds to the integrity. End grain is vulnerable where it is exposed and not thoroughly sealed with varnish or paint. This presents a problem where the wood, such as teak, is left natural or simply oiled to seal. Building to eliminate exposed end grain isn't difficult, but thicker stock may be required for the bands that surround the planking (Figure 11-4). Mitered corners in 1-inch or 1¼-inch (dressed) stock, or better, provide the required strength in the joints; the best practice is to spline the miters. The extra thickness also provides depth to let in the planks for the most effective covering of the end grain.

Prior to assembly, treat the ends with shellac or varnish, or otherwise seal them before bedding and caulking. Glued seams, however, should remain raw for best adhesion of the glue.

The flat design makes it easy to conceal end grain. As shown, the sides, front, and back members are constructed alike, with all members mitered at the corners (corners could be lapped; not shown). The frame members may be built up or milled from solid stock; rabbet or dado to fit your own design and size the frame to fit on top of the hatch coaming (may be rabbeted as in Figure 11-6), or outside the coaming altogether. Edges should not be cantilevered much beyond the vertical sides; the unsupported edges could break. Moreover, a big lip can be a real toe-catcher.

If you plan to inset a port, deadeye, or translucent/transparent panel to let in some light, a flat cover makes this addition easy. Any of these can be set in through the planking, or the entire central area can consist of an acrylic or a polycarbonate panel. Commercial portlights can be installed in hatch covers very easily. They are already well sealed into a flange. Just cut the hole, bed the flange in place, and voilà!

Wherever you use a broad expanse of plastic, add protective strips (Figure 11-5); they not only protect the surface from scratching, but they also protect the crew against slipping. Everyone aboard will appreciate that.

If your design includes a plywood substrate, or if you are veneering or facing an existing fiberglass hatch cover, you may find thinner surface material adequate. You could, for instance, use ½-inch-thick planks, premilled with one edge grooved for the seam compound. Bed them in compound and use screws to fasten them to the subsurface. If you are fastening them to fiberglass, use sheet-metal screws.

A flat, planked cover may not suit you. You could make the cover from a sheet of marine plywood or transparent material, which we'll take up later.

You might, for instance, use the best marine plywood—¾ to 1 inch thick—as the principal material and frame it with the same wood, solid. The edges of the plywood can be splined with the frame, mortised into it, or rabbeted. Just be sure to conceal the glue line well and use waterproof glue.

For added light below, either transparent or translucent panels can take the place of the solid center. You can avoid top seams by extending the transparent sheet to the outer edge of the hatch frame, so that now you have a flat hatch cover of transparent plastic. If you choose this option, refer to the separate section on transparent covers in this chapter before going any further.

If you choose to set a clear panel into a frame, there are some details of joinery to observe. To prevent moisture from collecting between the bedded panel and the surrounding frame, lay flat strips of stainless steel, well bedded with silicone, over the seam line, as shown in Figure 11-5. Fasten the panel down with closely spaced stainless steel screws. If the strips are thick enough to allow a suitable countersink, use flat- or oval-head screws. If not, pan-head screws will do nicely.

Wooden slats atop the clear panels protect against abrasion and, perhaps, the impact of a falling object. They also provide a nonskid surface in the event a crewmember didn't get the word about walking on your hatch covers.

But flat is flat—there's more pizzazz to a curve. Beyond that, your boat's design may call for curved hatch covers. We'll handle them next.

Curved Hatch Covers

Curved covers are made in two main classes: glued construction and caulked. There is a little more to contend with in caulked work, so we'll start with glued construction.

When boards are *fayed* edge to edge across an arc, a groove is formed at the top of each joint (Figure 11-2, View B). The width of the groove depends on the radius of the arc and the width and thickness of the boards.

There is also a small wedge-shaped space between the supporting member and the plank, where the flat meets the arc. It may appear that some hollowing is needed on the underside of the plank, if the parts are to fit neatly. This hollowing can be done over the entire length of the board, or it can be confined to the end rabbet joints. But this is difficult work. One school of thought is that planks should be narrow—not more than 2 inches wide—and they should be glued and screwed down upon the gentle arc of the crowned beam. Judging from my recent examination of a number of boats designed by well-known builders, the latter approach is fairly widespread.

To prepare the boards for a curved hatch cover, start by beveling *one* edge of *one* board to match the angle of the adjacent board. Cut this angle on a table saw, then plane with a jointer/planer or a smoothing or jointer plane to give a flush glue fit with the contacting edge of the next board. (You may be able to avoid the planing step if you use a sharp, hollow-ground planer blade in your saw, as mentioned earlier).

For added strength, each seam can be splined, lapped, or mortised, which would interlock the planks and increase the gluing surface. Though easy enough on a flat cover, this procedure could become tricky on a curved one. In the latter case, the cuts for the spline or tongue and groove would have to be somewhat tangent to the arc after the edges were beveled. It's best to leave well enough alone; glue and screw the boards down as close together and as accurately as possible.

Fairing comes next. Plane or shave the edges to a pleasing contour. Then fair the crown to a smooth arc using hand planes, shaves, rasps, sanders, or any combination thereof. Always work with the grain. The wood itself will soon tell you which direction that is. Stay away from heavy-duty disk or belt sanders unless you have lots of experience with them and a very light touch. Even then, put them away until you're ready for the final forming with the finest grade of abrasive. Unfortunately, your hand is likely to be quicker than your eye when surfacing with these tools.

As you work, you will be able to feel the highs and lows. Edgelighting also helps bring out the hills and valleys. Toward the final stages, long, even strokes with a sanding block will bring the shape to final form. Block sanding with successively finer grits, down to 220-grit, will prepare the cover for dusting, tacking, and varnishing.

A curved hatch cover that depends on caulked seams for watertightness starts out differently, as illustrated in Figure 11-3. Lay a ruled straightedge, or stick, marked with the centerline and width of the hatch, across the crown of the hatch. At the full width of the hatch, measure the drop to the edge at both end marks. If the distances on both sides are not equal, adjust the stick seesaw fashion until the distances are equal. Then measure again. This measurement tells you the amount of the crown. It is expressed in inches per inch of width; for example, $1/2$ inch per 30 inches of width.

String a spline—a flexible batten—bowed to the desired arc. In the example, the batten should bow $1/2$ inch at the center, above the bowstring tied to it 15 inches from center at each end, as measured along the string, not the bow.

Where the crown is severe, you can strike its radius using a string with a pencil loop at the marking end. This is essentially a trial-and-error method. The only general guidance is to lay out a cross: The short member is the width of the hatch cover, and the long member is the centerline that extends a little way above the short member and a long way below it. The center for your string-and-pencil compass is on this centerline. (You could find the equation for the crown height and use it, but not everyone is equipped to do that.)

Whatever method you use, transfer the arc to a piece of pattern stock and cut the shape. This will prevent your having to repeat the procedure when marking other members. (For the purist: Technically the arc is supposed to represent the upper surface of the finished piece. When you use it to loft and cut the frame, the arc at the surface of the planks will be a hair's breadth flatter than it should be, but I won't tell if you won't!)

To rabbet the crowned frame edges to let in the planks, first cut and fair the top arc of the frame, then follow the curved edge with a router bit set to the desired depth. The rabbet will now parallel the top.

As mentioned earlier, grooves can be cut into each piece before assembly, or routed afterward. Cutting the grooves beforehand is probably better, since this does away with fastening temporary battens to the assembled cover, especially where the crown makes it almost impossible to use a router-guide extension.

Seam compound will not seal forever, no matter how tight or well payed the seams may be. Leaks are more of a nuisance than a structural threat that you have to consider when laying down and paying deck planks, but following the procedures used for decking could extend the waterproofness of your hatch cover. This involves beveling to form a caulking groove and driving cotton into the lower part of the groove before the elastomer is payed into the upper portion of the groove (Figure 11-3).

Figure 11-4 also shows hatch beams. These crossmembers are analogous to deck beams; they hold the entire assembly in shape. Depending on the design, beams may be short—fitting inside the coaming—or they may be long enough to lie on top of the coaming and butt the sides. An alternative is to make them still longer and to let them into the side frames; this makes a very strong and neat result when viewed from below. Thus, if you are going to build a cover that will overlap the coamings, you can have the beams rest on the coamings, or stop them just inside to clear.

Beams can be cut to the inside arc or laminated from thin stock to the shape of the arc. Laminated beams can be glued up in a mold or built up in place inside the hatch cover. However, laminated beams would be easier to finish if assembled apart from the cover. There's little doubt that laminated beams are stronger than cut beams, especially with respect to impact.

TRANSPARENT HATCH COVERS

The advantage of a transparent hatch cover is obvious—it lets in light. There are disadvantages, like Peeping Toms and surface-scratchers. You make the choice.

Having made the choice, you must now implement it, using materials whose characteristics and properties are very different from those of wood. Therefore, we will start this section with some thoughts on available transparent materials and their characteristics. For full information, it would be a good idea to obtain manuals from the manufacturers.

Glass is out. Any glass will shatter—it has little impact strength. Safety glass is tempered after it is trimmed to size, which gives it its superior strength. Needless to say, this makes it expensive and subject to long lead time. It is heavy, too—not for us ordinary boatmen.

Acrylic and polycarbonate sheet are the two practical alternatives. They are available under such names as Plexiglas and Lexan, respectively. Acrylics are approximately 15 times more impact-resistant than glass of the same thickness. Hence, they withstand moderate impact, but they do lack the surface hardness of glass, so cleaning practices are critical. They should be cleaned with a soap solution, rinsed very thoroughly, dried with a soft cotton cloth, and protected with paste (no-cleaner-added) wax. Keep away all solvents, including acetone, lacquer thinner, etc. Naphtha and kerosene can be used for degreasing on some of these products. Verify before you try.

Polycarbonate has about 15 times the impact strength of acrylic but possesses less surface hardness; it is very easily scratched. Cleaning suggestions include hosing off with fresh water, drying with a clean chamois, and finishing with a soft cloth. The surface may be protected with suitable polish. If deep scratches occur, it is possible to fill these dings and scratches with some filler materials designed and formulated for the specific type and brand of polycarbonate. The filled area may be sanded and polished back to clarity.

Acrylics and polycarbonates can bend to conform to a slight crown, but if their thickness allows them to conform, they might not be strong enough for the job. Flat is better. The manufacturers of acrylics, for example, do not recommend cold-forming. However, if the material is to be formed, the radius of curvature must be at least 180 times the thickness of the sheet. For example: An 18-inch long, 1/4-inch thick sheet should not be cold-deflected more than 3/4 inch. *And that sheet is much too thin to be considered for a hatch cover.*

Moreover, when cold-bent, these thermoplastics will *craze*—develop myriad, tiny fissures due to stress. The time it will take for this to develop depends on many factors, including which cleaners and solvents the material may have been exposed to. But sooner or later . . .

Acrylic expands and contracts about 10 times as much as wood, so allowance should be made in the frame clearance, and screw holes should be drilled a little oversize. As you will see, the actual amount of clearance is not very large; simply not butting everything too close together and allowing space for bedding is likely to be enough in most cases.

Here's how to figure how much clearance is needed. The coefficient of thermal expansion of both acrylics and polycarbonates is roughly 3.75×10^5 inches per inch of length per degree Fahrenheit. If you have a hatch that is 30 inches wide, which is likely to be exposed to temperatures ranging from 50 degrees Fahrenheit at night to 130 degrees Fahrenheit in the broiling sun, here's what you do. Determine the difference in temperature range: $130°F - 50°F = 80°$. To calculate the actual expansion multiply $30 \times 80 \times 3.75 \times 10^5$, which is just under 0.1 inch.

This may not seem to be much, but if the allowance is not made, there's a fair chance that the plastic will rip something loose, somewhere, someday.

Acrylics have working characteristics similar to those of hard wood or light metal. When cutting, leave the protective paper on both sides. If a sheet must be unprotected, use masking tape at the top and bottom in the region of the cut to protect the polished surface. Use fine-tooth blades specifically made for acrylics or veneer, whether cutting with a jigsaw, sabersaw, or circular saw. This applies to polycarbonates as well. The maximum tooth speed of a 10-inch circular saw, for example, should not exceed 8,000 feet per minute, or some 3,000 r.p.m. However, if you notice any tendency to melting in the kerf, reduce the speed. Hollow-ground blades work well here, as do the more permanent types of plywood blades. The latter do tend to make a slightly rougher kerf, though.

Like glass, acrylic sheet can be scored and broken, but deeper scoring is usually required. Rest the scored sheet over a dowel and snap along the score line. A minimum of 2 inches beyond the score is necessary to control the break. Any narrower trimming should be done with the proper fine-tooth blade. Practice on scrap material before you shoot the whole works!

Drilling should be done at moderate speeds to prevent melting the material and ruining the work. It may be helpful to modify the drill points by grinding to zero rake angle and a 55° to 60° point angle. This allows the drill to enter freely and to scrape the material away rather than cut into it and perhaps chip it.

Tool marks along the edges must be removed for the sake of appearance and maximum strength. The exposed edges of a full-width cover should be polished. Inset edges can be sanded smooth, leaving a frosted finish, but in either case edges must be smooth and true.

Do not countersink screws into the surface of either of these plastics. Stresses set up by the beveled head can lead to crazing, cracking, and failure. Instead, use either oval-head screws with finishing washers, which spread the stresses much better; pan-head screws with flat washers, which is technically very good practice but not as pretty; or you can use strips of flat stainless steel that cover whole lengths of seams, fastened either with pan-head screws if they are thin or, if they are thick, with oval-head screws, suitably countersunk and bedded. Figure 11-5 shows the end result. If you use strips, be sure to leave waterways at the corners as shown in the drawing.

Glazing edge to edge atop the frame allows water to run off, away from the wooden frame and joints. The next most satisfactory approach is to set and bed a transparent panel into a wood frame, again as in Figure 11-5. The preferred method is to let the plastic panel in flush with the surrounding frame. Setting a panel in below the top of the frame will require waterways for drainage. Deep wells invite deep problems; keep things flush.

The transparent sheet has to be bedded in place, as with any other piece of material. The bedding compounds for acrylic and polycarbonate sheet are not quite the same as those for wood on wood. Although silicones have relatively poor adhesive qualities, they will seal the edges and the screw holes in well-secured plastic sheets. Silicone sealer is available clear and colored. Don't be tempted to use other bedding compounds with these plastics. Both acrylics and polycarbonates are sensitive to all sorts of solvents and chemical constituents that may be in the sealant.

Figure 11-5. *Details of constructing a plastic-topped hatch cover. The curved form is not recommended here; the plastic is too thin.*

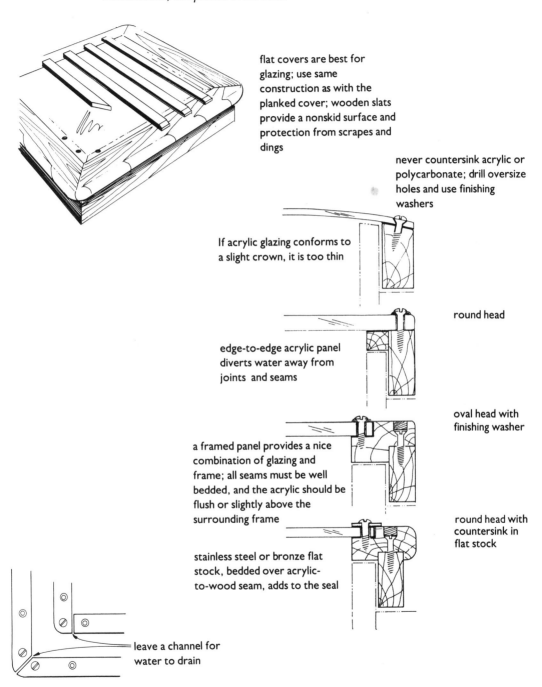

flat covers are best for glazing; use same construction as with the planked cover; wooden slats provide a nonskid surface and protection from scrapes and dings

never countersink acrylic or polycarbonate; drill oversize holes and use finishing washers

If acrylic glazing conforms to a slight crown, it is too thin

round head

edge-to-edge acrylic panel diverts water away from joints and seams

oval head with finishing washer

a framed panel provides a nice combination of glazing and frame; all seams must be well bedded, and the acrylic should be flush or slightly above the surrounding frame

round head with countersink in flat stock

stainless steel or bronze flat stock, bedded over acrylic-to-wood seam, adds to the seal

leave a channel for water to drain

Figure 11-6. *A skylight. The massive ridgepole is three times the width of the frame. Skylight coaming can be joined for removal by releasing dogs around. The higher the seam, the less deckwash will enter.*

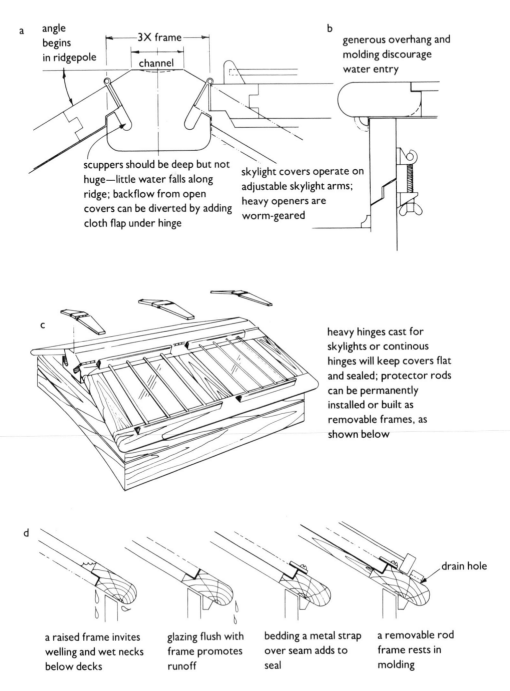

a

angle begins in ridgepole

—3X frame—

channel

scuppers should be deep but not huge—little water falls along ridge; backflow from open covers can be diverted by adding cloth flap under hinge

skylight covers operate on adjustable skylight arms; heavy openers are worm-geared

b

generous overhang and molding discourage water entry

c

heavy hinges cast for skylights or continous hinges will keep covers flat and sealed; protector rods can be permanently installed or built as removable frames, as shown below

d

drain hole

a raised frame invites welling and wet necks below decks

glazing flush with frame promotes runoff

bedding a metal strap over seam adds to seal

a removable rod frame rests in molding

SKYLIGHTS

I like skylights. The pattern they cast below decks exudes friendly warmth. (I wonder whether I might someday counter every design precept and install a skylight on a dory!) On the right boat, in the right location, this addition is sure to please. A large skylight isn't a prerequisite—small skylights add character, too.

Skylights are attractive both from above and below. Below decks they let in light, add architectural interest, and increase visual space. On the deck of the right boat they add charm.

But—there is always a but, isn't there?—whether removable for use as a mini cargo hatch, permanently enclosed but with hinged openings, or functioning as a permanently closed source of light, every skylight has an inherent leak potential. Over time, however, a practical design philosophy has been developed for skylights; it would be well to follow it.

The center beam, or *ridgepole*, is the skylight's backbone for structural integrity. Often it has a shallow channel along the top to collect water and send it off to the ends (Figure 11-6a). Liberal scuppers collect water from beneath the continuous or strap hinges and divert it away to the ends of the skylight, keeping it from the backs of necks below decks. A generous overhang at the sides, transparent panels flush with the frame—all well bedded in silicone sealant—and skirts at strategic locations should keep you dry below while enjoying your boat's new look. Figure 11-6 is an overall sketch of a typical skylight with details of construction.

Waterways in the ridgepole need not be excessively large, since the ridge, no matter how wide, will collect only a minor amount of rainfall, dew, or a sweeping sea. Over the major portion of the exposed area, water will run off if not interrupted by an outer molding or frame. Anything added on top of the frame, such as a molding, should have copious drain holes to promote good runoff.

When replacing an existing hatch cover with a skylight, renew the coamings to match the design of the new part. If you think you may want full hatch access again at a later date, make the skylight in two sections, joining the top and bottom parts with dogs spaced around the perimeter of the middle seam, cinching it down against any water that might try to get in (Figure 11-6b). Alternatively, you might use exterior hinges that would either unhook for removal or simply swing the top structure away (Figure 11-6c). The joint should have liberal overlap. Also, the higher the seam is off the deck, the less wash is likely to get inside. Skylight covers open and close on adjustable arms; one version of these is available from high-quality hardware suppliers such as The Bronze Star, Buck-Algonquin, and others.

If the skylight is large, a worm-gear arrangement might be necessary. This could turn out to be convenient, because a worm-gear closure cannot be opened from the outside. This more elaborate mechanism can eliminate the need to dog the panels closed, except perhaps in extremely heavy weather.

Wooden slats may not be quite enough protection for your skylight. Reserve them for hatch covers; they are fully adequate to preserve the surfaces from errant feet. The panel protectors shown in the drawing are composed of stainless steel rod and wooden bars. These are quite easy to make yourself. If you opt for all-metal construction, have a stainless steel specialist weld them up. The steel bars are meant for heavy-duty loads—they do very well against objects falling from above.

May they never have to prove their worth aboard your ship!

Glossary of Woodworking Terms

Annual growth rings. The growth pattern in springwood (fibrous, faster-growing wood) and summerwood (denser, harder wood), which terminates at the end of each growing season.

APA. American Plywood Association.

Back saw. A small handsaw with a reinforced spine that provides rigidity. Also known as a *miter saw*.

Bandsaw. A stationary saw with a continuous cutting blade that rides over a drive wheel and a tension wheel. It cuts thick stock and can scroll, resaw, or cut off, depending on the blade used.

Batten. (1) A cleat fastened across a series of boards. (2) A thin strip of wood used in lofting curves. (3) A strip of wood or plastic used to maintain sail shape.

Bench grinder. A device with interchangeable motor-driven wheels used to sharpen, hone, clean, and polish cutting tools and other metal.

Bevel. (1) Any edge angle, other than 90°, that slopes away from a major surface plane. (2) An adjustable square used to capture an angle for measurement or to mark the captured angle on a workpiece.

Bezel. A finishing ring for a port or other circular hole.

Bit. A tool that when rotating makes holes or shapes edges. A *combination-bit* will drill pilot and shank holes and countersink for a screw, all in one operation. A *cove* is a convex bit that cuts concave edges or grooves. A *dovetail bit* makes interlocked joints. A *fluting bit* makes ornamental grooves with single, double, or multiple ends. A *router* is any one of a number of bits used in high-speed cut-

ting. A *veining bit* has a rounded end for decorative routing and scrolling.

Blind spline. A spline inset in a blind dado that stops short of exposing either the dadoed groove or the spline that fits between the two joined pieces.

Brace. (1) The structural member that fortifies the primary member, usually oblique to the structure. (2) A driver for an auger bit, formed in the shape of a crank that rotates the bit (as in brace and bit).

Brad point. A twist drill having a center spur that guides the bit in an advancing pilot hole.

Break. Working an edge to remove a sharp corner.

Bullnose. (1) To mill an edge to a half-round shape. (2) An edge made in this way.

Bung. A wooden plug, usually finished flush with the surface, that conceals a screw or nail head.

Butt joint. A joint formed so the sides or ends of two square edges meet.

Button. A wooden plug, usually ornamental, that conceals a screw head or a hole and stands proud of the surface.

Cantilever. To fasten or support a plank by exerting a downward force only at the captured end.

Carriage. The supports under stairs, sloped to the run and rise.

Caulking iron. A wedge used to drive in packing or other waterproofing material to seal seams.

Ceiling. Slats covering frames and beams longitudinally.

Chamfer. A bevel or slant along the edge of a board.

Chuck. A split sleeve tightened around a tool shank by a ring or collet such as a drill chuck. A Jacob's chuck is a tape designed to hold the drill chuck more firmly on the spindle.

Compound Cut. A cut made by setting two angles, neither at right angles to the workpiece.

Counterbore. (1) A deep depression that recesses the head of a fastener well below the fastened surface; it also can receive a bung or button to cover the fastener head. (2) A depression made in this way.

Countersink. (1) A shallow depression that sets the head of a fastener flush with or below the surface of the piece being fastened. (2) A depression made in this way.

Coving. A concave molding at the intersection of vertical and horizontal surfaces.

Cross-cut. A cut made across the wood grain.

Cross-lap joint. Two members, each notched to half depth, that receive each other in such a way that both the top and bottom surfaces are flush.

Crotch, or **Crook.** The grain formed where tree limbs branch off.

Crown. (1) The height measured from the uppermost point of an arc to the drop at the sides. (2) The uppermost point of the arc.

Cutter. A router bit.

Dado. (1) To set into a groove or to cut a rectangular groove. (2) A groove made by dadoing. (3) A tool for dadoing.

Dovetail. A fan-shaped, interlocking joint. A *dovetail key* is a fancy groove-and-spline configuration allowed to run out at the ends.

Dowel. A cylindrical length of wood with glue slots designed to strengthen wood joints or appendages. A *dowel-pinned* joint

uses dowels to provide the strength between the joined parts.

Dressed. Lumber planed smooth during the finishing process.

Drill press. A drill head and motor mounted on a vertical column that also holds an adjustable worktable. With a drill bit or router bit in the chuck, the drill-press spindle is lowered into the workpiece by a wheel/ratchet track.

Escutcheon. A finished plate that covers a rough hole or area.

Face plate. A lathe attachment that supports a short, wide workpiece.

Fair. To smoothly blend pieces to form a curvature.

Fay. To fit or join mating parts, such as timbers or boards, smoothly and tightly.

Figured. Refers to wood-grain characteristics. *Highly figured* wood is flat-grain cut, tangential to the annual rings, exposing both spring- and summerwood on the broad surface of the board.

File. A hardened steel tool, available in many configurations, with ridges that abrade material from a workpiece.

Finger joint, or **Finger-lap joint.** A joint comprised of evenly spaced notches made to receive the matching, male parts of a mating piece.

Fixture. A device used to support a workpiece during machining.

Flat-sawn. Lumber sawn with the flat grain exposed on the wide surface; i.e., sawn perpendicular to the radius and tangent to the annual rings of a log. Also called *plain-sawn*.

Futtocks. Curved timbers scarfed to form a frame.

Grain. (1) The orientation, concentration, and pattern of the cells in a piece of wood.

(2) The texture, porosity, or figuring of wood. *Flat-grain* lumber is cut tangent to the annual growth rings. *Verticle-grain*, also called *straight, comb, edge,* or *rift* grain, is cut radially to the annual rings.

Groove. A plow cut, similar to a dado but made *with* the grain, often near but not on the edge of the wood.

GRP. Glass Reinforced Plastic (fiberglass).

Half-lap joint. A joint formed so that one member is notched to receive the other member, flush with the top surface.

Handsaw. An open saw (one blade, one handle) with teeth used for *crosscutting* (more points per inch) and *ripping* (fewer points per inch). A *combination saw* (somewhere in between) is used in general woodworking.

Hardwood. Wood from a family of deciduous trees (angiospermous).

Holiday. Areas void of paint or varnish unintentionally skipped during application.

Jig. (1) A device that holds a workpiece in place for machining. (2) A device that defines and limits the movement of a tool or holds parts together for assembly.

Jig saw, or **Scroll saw.** A saw that operates in an up/down motion. Stationary jig saws have both upper and lower chucks to hold a thin blade for fancy scrollwork.

Joinery, or **Joinerwork.** Matching and mating woods to form intricate, tightly joined assemblies.

Jointer/Planer. A rotary cutter having three or more blades that—by adjusting the guide fence and depth of cut on the feed table—plane the squared edges used in joining, rabbeting, or beveling.

Laminate. A glued buildup of thin layers of wood or plastic.

Lap joint. Overlapping boards, each cut to half thickness.

Lathe. A metal or woodworking machine that holds a workpiece at both ends of a horizontal axis for shaping with cutting chisels.

Lathe chisels. Any variety of handheld woodcutting tools with sharp metal blades in long wooden handles.

Let in. (1) A joint that accepts the edge of one board into another. (2) The distance by which the edge enters. (3) To make such a joint.

Lute. To seal or pack a joint or a porous surface.

Margins. Edges or borders beyond the functional areas of large expanses that could be embellished with inlays or decorative millwork.

Millwork. Surfaces shaped or dressed by machine.

Miter joint. A joint formed when two edges meet at any angle other than 90°.

Molding. Decorative lengths of recessed curves or rectangles used to finish an edge or to form a transition between two angled planes.

Mortise. (1) A hole, groove, or slot that accepts a mating part, or *tenon*. (2) To join or fasten securely in this way is to *mortise-and-tenon*. (3) To cut or make a mortise.

Nosing. The tread on a step that projects beyond the face of a riser.

Ogee. A molding or margin with an S-shaped profile.

Packing. Cotton or other material forced into a caulking groove to make a joint watertight.

Parting tool. A V-shaped lathe chisel used for cutting, grooving, or separating wood while turning.

Pay. To coat with a waterproof solution.

Pilot hole. A prebored hole drilled on center to guide a bit that is larger than the hole through the same centerline. It is also used to prevent splitting when driving nails.

Pipe clamp, or **Bar clamp.**   A clamp in which the end of one of the jaws is attached to the head of standard metal pipe or bar stock, and the other cam-cleated or slipped into various slots. Pressure is applied by turning an acme-threaded swivel at the head end.

Plain-sawing.   Cutting one sheet after the other straight through the log. Also, *flat-cut* or *plain-sliced*.

Plane.   (1) A tool used to surface and edge wood. A *bench plane* planes with large soles and usually wide blades. A *block plane* is a small plane for truing end grain; the blades have keen, upward-facing bevels. A *bullnose plane* is a concave cutter for rounding edges. A *jointer plane* is a long-sole plane used mainly for truing edges. A *rabbet plane* is an edge plane for producing an edge shelf or a rabbet. (2) Surfacing or edging wood.

Quarter-round.   A convex molding whose cross section has a 90° arc.

Quarter-sawn.   Board resawn from quartered logs so the annual growth rings are nearly at right angles to the wide face. Also, *vertical grain*.

Rabbet.   (1) A channel, groove, or recess cut from the face of a part intended to receive another member, usually on the edge of the wood. (2) To cut a rabbet, to unite edges, to make a rabbet joint.

Radial-arm saw.   A motor and circular-saw blade that moves along an overhead track, drawing the saw across the workpiece. The blade may be rotated and locked in place for ripping.

Rail.   (1) The horizontal member above or below a louver panel. (2) The horizontal member(s) of a door. (3) A retaining fence.

Rasp.   A hardened steel tool with sharp tooth-like edges for cutting away the workpiece.

Rays.   Storage cells in living trees that provide nutrients. They are oriented horizontally and radiate from the center of the tree, crossing its growth rings radially.

Resaw.   To rip with the grain parallel to the wide side.

Ribbon-cut or **Plain-cut.**   Wood cut on the quarter-sawn section so that alternating light and dark, or other opposing patterns, are formed.

Rift-cut or **Rift-sawn.**   Wood, including veneer, cut at 45° to the growth rings.

Rip.   To saw in the direction of the grain, normally lengthwise and through the narrow side.

Rise.   The total height spanned by a ladder.

Riser.   The vertical member between steps or between rungs on a ladder.

Rotary-cut.   Veneer sliced away from a cylindrical log with a knife blade forced against a revolving core that has been centered on a lathe.

Router.   An ultra-high-speed motor with a spindle and collet for inserting a variety of bits to make a variety of cuts, from dadoing and milling to lettering and decorative designs.

Run.   The horizontal distance occupied by a ladder.

Sabersaw.   A portable jig saw equipped with accessories to allow cutting circles, guiding a cut along an edge, or doing scrollwork.

Scantlings.   The dimensions of the wooden members used in construction.

Scarf.   A lap joint formed so the length is much greater than the width; used mainly in joining long members.

Scribing, or **Spiling.** Transferring lines from one member to another or to a pattern using dividers or a circle compass.

Skew. A wood-turning chisel with an angled edge.

Softwood. Wood from a family of ever-green (coniferous) trees. With a few exceptions, softwoods are in the deciduous family.

Spline. (1) A thin piece of wood inserted in a glue joint. (2) A batten for bending into a fair arc or curve. *See also* **Blind spline**.

Spring clamp. To apply moderate tension to hold parts between spring-tension fingers while gluing.

Square. A guide for drawing angles. A *bevel square* is an adjustable, variable-angle square with a locking nut. A carpenter's square *is a long square with a fixed 90° angle. A combination square* has an adjustable head to guide outside/inside angles, depth gauging, leveling, and 45° miter. A *try square* is a small 90° square.

Stand proud. To extend beyond or stand out.

Stiles. In louvered panels, the vertical members into which the louvers are inserted or to which they are attached.

Stopwater. A transverse softwood plug inserted in a joint to prevent leaks.

String. A series of steps. *Open-string* steps are cantilevered beyond the carriage. The ends of *closed-string* steps are captured in the carriage.

Stringers. Fore-and-aft main structural members.

Table saw. A machined worktable, including guide slots, rip fence track, etc., sur-rounding a circular-saw blade. It is used to make precise cuts of small or large pieces, which are then fed into the blade for cutting off, mitering, ripping, and milling.

Template. A cutout pattern that serves as a guide in laying out or making a design or assembly.

Tenon. A tongue-like projection that is inserted into a mortise to make a mortise-and-tenon joint. *See also* **Mortise**. A *shouldered tenon* results when the thickness of a piece of wood is reduced to form a projection that extends some distance in from the end or edge.

Texture. The density (or lack thereof) of the cellular structure of wood.

Thermoplastic. Glues with properties that soften when heated and reharden when cooled.

Thermosetting. Glues that will not soften when heated.

Tongue-and-groove joint. A joint formed with a mating male tongue and female groove, usually but not always on long edges of boards.

Tread. The horizontal member of a step or rung.

Treenails ("Trunnels"). Wooden pegs used in place of nails in the construction of wooden ships.

Truing. (1) The act of making true, as in square, flat, concentric, or balanced. (2) To restore to the original shape.

Twist drill. A drill bit comprising a cylindrical shank with a helical flute to carry away the cut material. The end is sharpened conically, forming cutting edges.

Veneer. Thinly sliced sheets of specialty woods that are applied to the surface of common structural woods.

Vertical grain. *See* **Quarter-sawn**.

Web clamp, or **Band clamp.** Fabric strips with cam cleats that evenly hold the clamped assembly, such as chair legs, while being glued.

Whet. To make very sharp or keen. A *whetstone* is a fine stone used for whetting.

Wood-boring drill bit, or **Spade drill.** A flattened piece of steel with sharp, beveled edges flanking a brad point, which is aligned with the round shank that fits a high-speed drill chuck.

Wood chisel. A steel chisel with a flat blade with one side beveled and honed for surface penetration or carving.

Wood-turning chisel. *See* **Lathe chisel.**

Bibliography

Davidson, Glenn D. *Tool Grinding and Sharpening Handbook*. New York: Sterling Publishing Co. Inc., 1985.

Hartshorn, S. R., ed. *Structural Adhesives: Chemistry and Technology*. Topics in Applied Chemistry. Edited by Alan R. Katritzky and Gebran J. Sabongl. New York and London: Plenum Press, 1986.

Ogberg, Erik, et al. *Machinery's Handbook*. 23d ed. Edited by Henry H. Ryffel. New York: Industrial Press, Inc., 1988.

Vaitses, Allan. *The Fiberglass Boat Repair Manual*. Camden: International Marine Publishing Company, 1988.

Wangaard, Fredrick F. *The Mechanical Properties of Wood*. New York: John Wiley & Sons, Inc., 1950.

Wittman, Rebecca J., *Brightwork*. Camden: International Marine Publishing, 1990.

The WoodBook. Tacoma: Wood Products Publications, 1978.

Index